IN
THE
CLEARING

Center Point
Large Print

Also by Robert Dugoni and available from
Center Point Large Print:

The Tracy Crosswhite Series
  My Sister's Grave
  Her Final Breath

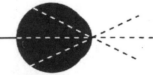

IN
THE
CLEARING

ROBERT DUGONI

CENTER POINT LARGE PRINT
THORNDIKE, MAINE

This Center Point Large Print edition
is published in the year 2017 by arrangement with
Amazon Publishing, www.apub.com.

The text of this Large Print edition is unabridged.
In other aspects, this book may vary
from the original edition.
Printed in the United States of America
on permanent paper.
Set in 16-point Times New Roman type.

ISBN: 978-1-68324-230-7

Library of Congress Cataloging-in-Publication Data

Names: Dugoni, Robert, author.
Title: In the clearing / Robert Dugoni.
Description: Center Point Large Print edition. | Thorndike, Maine :
Center Point Large Print, 2017.
Identifiers: LCCN 2016044597 | ISBN 9781683242307
    (hardcover)
Subjects: LCSH: Cold cases (Criminal investigation)—Fiction. | Women
detectives—Fiction. | Large type books. | GSAFD: Suspense fiction.
Classification: LCC PS3604.U385 I5 2017 | DDC 813/.6—dc23
LC record available at https://lccn.loc.gov/2016044597

For Joe. Time to fly, son. Time to soar.

IN
THE
CLEARING

PROLOGUE

Friday, November 5, 1976
Klickitat County, Washington

Buzz Almond informed dispatch he was rolling, punched the accelerator, and smiled at the roar of the 245-horsepower V-8 engine, the g-forces nudging him back against his seat. Word in the office was that the politicians would be phasing out the gas-guzzling dinosaurs and downsizing to more fuel-efficient vehicles. Maybe so, but for now Buzz had one of the big boys, a Chevy Caprice hardtop, and he intended to keep it until they pried his fingers from the steering wheel.

The shot of adrenaline made him sit up, his brain synapses firing and sending out electrical impulses. Fully operational. In the Marine Corps, they'd called it "combat ready." He saw no reason to change now that he was a Klickitat County deputy sheriff.

Can I get an oorah?

Buzz slowed, lowered the driver's-side window, and adjusted the spotlight, searching for the cross street. Most of the streets around here were marked, but not all; some were nothing more than narrow, unpaved paths. With no street lamps, and with a dense cloud layer shrouding the area, it was dark as ink. You could drive right past a road without ever seeing it.

The light hit upon a cluster of battered mailboxes atop wooden posts. Buzz inched the beam up a metal pole until he saw a reflective green street sign: "Clear Creek Rd." That was it. He made the turn. The car bounced and pitched in the ruts and potholes. The residents groomed some roads in spring and summer. Not this one.

He continued a quarter mile through heavy scrub oak, pine, and aspen. At a bend to the left, a light shimmered in the tree branches. Buzz drove toward it, onto a gravel drive leading to a double-wide. Before he'd parked, a man pushed out the front door and descended three wooden stairs, crossing a dirt yard cluttered with unstacked firewood, scrap metal, and an empty clothesline.

Buzz checked the name he'd jotted on his pocket notepad and got out. The air, smelling of pine, was heavy with the weight of impending snow. First of the season. His girls would be excited.

The ground, starting to freeze from the quick drop in temperature after a week of punishing rains, crunched beneath his boots. "Are you Mr. Kanasket?" Buzz asked.

"Earl," the man said, extending a rough, dry hand. From Earl Kanasket's dark skin and black hair, which he wore pulled back in a ponytail,

Buzz surmised he was a member of the Klickitat tribe. Most had moved northeast to the Yakama Reservation decades earlier, but not all. Earl wore a heavy canvas jacket, jeans, and thick-soled boots. His face was pocked with dark moles and had the weathered look of someone who worked outdoors. Buzz figured him to be early forties.

"You called about your daughter?" Buzz asked.

"Kimi walks home after work. She calls from the diner before she leaves. She's never late."

"The Columbia Diner?" Buzz asked, taking notes. He'd passed the one-room log cabin less than a mile back on State Route 141.

A woman hurried out the door, wrapping a long coat around herself. A young man followed, likely a grown son, given the strong resemblance.

"This is my wife, Nettie, and our son, Élan," Earl said.

The hem of Nettie's nightgown extended from beneath her coat. She wore slippers. Élan stood barefoot in jeans and a white T-shirt. Buzz felt cold just looking at him.

"What time does Kimi usually get home?"

"Eleven. Never late."

"And she called tonight?"

"Every night. She calls every night she works," Earl said, starting to sound impatient.

"What did she say?" Buzz asked, trying to remain calm but getting a sense this was not just a girl late for her curfew.

11

"She said she was on her way home."

Nettie put a hand on her husband's forearm to calm him. "This is not like Kimi," she said to Buzz. "She wouldn't upset us. She's a good girl. She's going to the University of Washington next year. If she said she was coming home, she would be home."

Élan turned his head and folded his arms across his chest, which Buzz thought an odd response.

"So she's in high school?"

"She's a senior at Stoneridge High," Nettie said.

"Could she have gone to a friend's house?"

"No," Earl said.

"And she's never done this before? Never been late?"

"Never," Earl and Nettie said in unison.

"Okay," Buzz said. "Is there anything going on at home or at school that could have caused her to break her routine?"

"Like what?" Earl said, now sounding angry.

Buzz kept calm. "Recent disagreements. Teenage-girl drama at school?" Buzz had no real point of reference—his daughters were four and two—though he recalled that his own sisters and their friends had become royal pains in the butt when they hit puberty.

"She broke up with her boyfriend," Élan said, stopping the conversation cold.

Buzz looked to the young man. When he didn't elaborate, he redirected his attention to Nettie and

Earl. From the blank expressions on their faces, Buzz could tell this was either news to them or something they didn't think worth mentioning.

"When did that happen?" he asked Élan.

"Couple days ago."

Now we're getting somewhere, Buzz thought. "Who's her boyfriend?"

"Tommy Moore," Élan said.

"You know him?"

"Went to school with him, but he wasn't her boyfriend then. I introduced them after."

"When was that?"

"Two years ago."

"They've been dating for two years?"

"No," Nettie said, emphatic.

"No, I was in high school two years ago," Élan said.

"Élan didn't graduate," Nettie said.

Buzz got a strong sense that Earl and Nettie had not approved of their daughter's relationship. "How long did Kimi and Tommy Moore date?" Buzz asked.

Nettie gave a dismissive wave. "It wasn't serious. I told you, Kimi is going to college."

Buzz looked to Élan. "Six months," he said. "They started dating end of last year."

Buzz put a star next to the name "Tommy Moore" in his notepad. "Do you know where he lives?"

Élan gestured toward the trees. "Husum."

Buzz would call it in and get an address. "What does he do?"

"He's a mechanic. And he boxes. He's a Golden Gloves champ."

"Why'd they break up?"

Élan shook his head and hunched his shoulders against the cold. "Don't know."

"Did your sister ever tell you they were having problems?"

"We don't talk."

That caused Buzz to make another mental note. "You and your sister don't talk?"

"No. Tommy said things weren't all that great. Kimi can be a bitch."

"Élan," Earl said, clearly upset.

"Hang on," Buzz said. "Did Tommy say why things weren't great?"

"Just that Kimi got kind of full of herself."

Earl intervened. "It wasn't serious."

Élan rolled his eyes and turned away.

Before Buzz could ask another question, Earl and Nettie looked past him, and he turned and saw a procession of headlights through the trees.

"Could this be her?" he asked.

"No. These are people I called to come and help."

Three vehicles came around the bend into the dirt yard. They parked beside Buzz's patrol car. Men and women emerged, doors slamming shut. The women went to Nettie, consoling her. The

14

men looked to Earl, who turned to his son. "Go with them."

Buzz raised a hand. "Hang on, Earl. Who are all these people?"

"Friends," Earl said. "They're going to look for Kimi."

"Okay," Buzz said, "but I want everyone to just hold on a second."

"Something has happened to her," Earl said. "Go," he said to Élan.

Élan grabbed a pair of boots from the steps and followed the men to their cars, which quickly departed.

"Why do you think something could have happened to her?" Buzz asked.

"Because of the protests."

"The protests at the football games?"

The *Stoneridge Sentinel* and the more widely circulated *Oregonian* had covered the Yakama tribes' protests against Stoneridge High School's use of the name "Red Raiders" and its mascot— a white student wearing war paint and a feathered headdress, riding onto the field on a painted horse and burying a spear in the turf.

"Has somebody threatened you?" Buzz asked. "Or her?"

"It has been a source of unrest in the community. Kimi is my daughter. As an elder, I am a symbol of the protest."

Buzz rubbed at the stubble of his chin. "I'm

going to need a recent photograph and a physical description of Kimi, as well as a list of her closest friends."

Earl nodded to the women, who went quickly into the double-wide. "My wife will provide you names and start calling Kimi's friends."

"You know the path your daughter walks home?" Buzz asked.

"Yes."

"Let's go back over it before the snow starts falling."

They hurried to his patrol car and slid inside. Sensing Earl's unease and thinking of his own children, Buzz said, "We're going to find your daughter, Mr. Kanasket."

Earl didn't respond; he just stared out the windshield, into the darkness.

CHAPTER 1

Thursday, October 27, 2016
Seattle, Washington

Tracy Crosswhite had just emptied the bullets that remained in her Glock .40's magazine, six shots at fifteen yards in less than ten seconds, when her cell phone buzzed. She holstered her weapon, slid off her ear protection, and checked caller ID. Her three students stared slack-jawed at the target. Each shot had been a center-mass hit within the target's smallest-diameter circle.

"I have to take this," she said, stepping away and speaking into the phone. "Tell me you're calling because you miss me."

"You must be a magnet for murders," her sergeant, Billy Williams, said.

Lately it'd felt that way. Seemed every time Tracy and her partner, Kinsington Rowe, were the homicide team on call, someone got killed.

Billy explained that dispatch had received a 911 call about a shooting at a home in Greenwood at 5:39 that evening. Tracy checked her watch. Twenty-one minutes earlier. She'd house hunted in Greenwood, a middle-class neighborhood in north-central Seattle with a decidedly suburban feel.

"Single-family residence. One fatality," Billy said.

"Domestic dispute?"

"Looks that way. The medical examiner and CSI are en route."

"You reach Kins?"

"Not yet. But Faz and Del are both on their way."

Vic Fazzio and Delmo Castigliano were the other two members of the Violent Crimes Section's "A Team." In this instance, they were also the next-up team for a homicide, which meant they'd be assisting with the legwork, if there was any. Most domestic disputes were grounders—easy plays. The wife killed the husband, or the husband killed the wife.

Tracy cut short the shooting lesson and jumped in the cab of her 1973 Ford F-150. The commute north on I-5 was even heavier than usual for a Thursday evening. It took her almost forty-five minutes to travel the roughly fifteen miles from the combat range.

When she approached the address, the emergency lights of multiple patrol units from the North Precinct lit up a single-story clapboard house. Two vans were parked at the curb—the medical examiner's and the CSI's—along with an ambulance. A large press contingent with their own trucks and vans had also descended; shootings in predominantly white middle-class neighborhoods always made the news. Thankfully, no helicopter hovered overhead, likely because a heavy cloud layer hinting at snow would have prevented much in the way of aerial footage. The cold temperatures hadn't deterred the neighbors, however. They'd waded onto the sidewalk and into the street, mingling with the press behind black-and-yellow crime scene tape.

Tracy didn't see Kins's BMW yet, though he lived in Seattle, several miles closer to Greenwood than the combat range.

"Hail, hail, the gang's all here," Tracy said as she lowered her window and showed her badge to an officer on traffic control.

"Welcome to the party," he said, letting her through.

She parked beside the CSI van. Chatter spilled from the police radios. She couldn't count the number of uniformed and plainclothes officers on the lawn, mingling with investigators in black cargo pants and shirts with "CSI" across the back. The medical examiner was still inside with the body. Nobody could do anything until the ME finished.

Tracy greeted a female uniformed officer holding a clipboard with a scene log.

"This zoo belong to you, Tracy?" the officer asked.

Tracy had trained many of the female officers to shoot, but she didn't recognize this one. Then again, she'd recently captured a serial killer known as "the Cowboy," receiving the Seattle Police Department's Medal of Valor for the second time in her career and making her a bit of a celebrity, especially to the younger officers.

"That's what they're telling me." She scribbled her name and time of arrival on the log. "Are you the responding officer?"

The officer looked to a fire-engine-red front door. "No. He's inside with your sergeant."

Tracy considered the house. It appeared well kept, recently painted, and likely north of $350,000 in a seller's market. The lawn smelled like newly laid sod, and the glow from landscape and porch lights revealed recently spread beauty bark in flower beds with hearty rosebushes and well-established rhododendrons. *Divorce,* Tracy thought. *They were fixing up the property to sell. The dead body inside won't help the asking price.*

She ascended three steps and ducked under red crime scene tape stretched taut across the entry. Inside, Billy Williams talked with a uniformed officer in a simple but well-maintained front room. A conical crystal sculpture lay on the dark bamboo flooring that flowed between two square pillars meant to differentiate the living room from the dining area and open kitchen. The walls looked freshly painted, the color choices—soft blues and hunter greens—something out of a home-improvement magazine.

Paramedics were attending to a brunette woman seated on a dark-blue leather couch. She was grimacing and pointing to her ribs. She also had a bandage wrapped around her head, and the left side of her face appeared swollen, with a small cut near the corner of her mouth. Tracy estimated her to be midforties to early fifties. Beside her sat a young man in the awkward throes of puberty— hair unkempt, lanky arms protruding from a size-too-small T-shirt, and pipe-cleaner-thin legs poking out from baggy cargo shorts. He had his head down, staring at the floor, but Tracy could see the left side of his face was a splotchy red. Both the woman and the young man were barefoot.

"That's Angela Collins and her son, Connor," Billy said, keeping his voice low. Billy resembled the actor Samuel L. Jackson, right down to the soul patch just beneath his lower lip and the knit driving caps he favored, this one plaid. "Her estranged husband is in a bedroom down the hall with a bullet in his back."

Tracy looked down a narrow hall to a room at the end where several members of the medical examiner's office milled about. A pair of black dress shoes and suit pants were visible to midthigh. The rest of the body was hidden behind the door frame and wall.

Tracy tilted her head toward Angela Collins. "What's she saying?"

21

"She said she shot him," Billy said, giving a nod to the officer.

Tracy turned to the officer. "She confessed?"

"To me and my partner," the officer said. "Then she asked for the words and sat down. Her lawyer is apparently on the way."

"She called her lawyer?" Tracy asked.

"Apparently," the officer said. "I heard her talking to the paramedics. She said her husband hit her with that thing." He pointed to the sculpture on the floor.

"But did she specifically say she shot him?"

"Absolutely. To me and my partner."

"And you read her Miranda rights to her?"

"She signed the card."

"Where's the gun?" Tracy asked.

The officer pointed down the hall. "On the bed. A .38 Colt Defender."

"You didn't secure it?"

"No need. She was just sitting right there, waiting for us with the door open."

"What's the kid saying?" Tracy asked.

"Not a word."

Kins ducked under the tape, slightly out of breath. "Hey."

"Where were you?" Billy asked, eyeing Kins's suit and dress shirt, absent a tie.

"Sorry. Didn't hear my phone. What do we got?"

"Looks like a grounder," Tracy said.

"That'd be nice," Kins said.

Billy explained the situation to Kins. Then he said, "I'll have Faz and Del start with the neighbors, find out if anyone saw or heard anything tonight or in the past. And let's make sure we fingerprint that thing." He pointed to the sculpture.

"Detectives?" The female police officer who'd greeted Tracy on the sidewalk spoke from behind the red tape. "There's a man at the curb, says he's the woman's lawyer. He's asking to speak to her."

"I'll handle it," Tracy said. She ducked under the tape and stepped back onto the porch but stopped when she saw Atticus Berkshire, counselor at law, standing at the curb. "Damn."

Many of the cops and prosecutors in King County had had the unpleasant experience of encountering Atticus Berkshire. Those who hadn't certainly knew of him. A notorious defense attorney, when Berkshire wasn't fighting to get his clients off criminal charges, he was suing the police department for violations of those clients' civil rights, or for police brutality. He'd hit the city for several large and well-publicized verdicts. Urban myth among SPD was that Berkshire's mother had named him after the lawyer in *To Kill a Mockingbird*, thereby condemning him to become a criminal defense lawyer the same way parents condemned

23

their sons named Storm to become weathermen.

"Detective Crosswhite," Berkshire said before Tracy had made it halfway down the sidewalk. "I want to speak to my daughter."

That bit of information gave Tracy pause. Recovering, she said, "That's not going to happen for a while, Counselor. You know that."

"I've instructed her not to say a word."

Tracy raised her hands, palms up. "For the most part, she's listening."

"What do you mean, 'for the most part'?"

"She said she shot him. Then she asked for her Miranda rights."

"That's not admissible."

"We'll let the judge decide that." Tracy couldn't see how a judge would exclude the statement, since Angela Collins had said it while still under stress from a startling event, making it an "excited utterance," but she'd let the lawyers fight that battle.

"What about Connor?" Berkshire said.

"The boy? He's not saying anything either."

"I meant, may I see him?"

"Not until after we speak to him," Tracy said.

In court, Berkshire was easy to dislike, with his expensive Italian suits, tasseled loafers, and obnoxious demeanor. He wore down prosecutors and judges with tactics that straddled the line between unethical and dirtbag, but he was even more infamous for his bombastic rants against injustice and prejudice. They worked more often than they should have, but Berkshire had the benefit of preaching his nonsense to liberal Seattleites. Tonight, however, there was a thin glimmer of vulnerability to him—dressed in jeans, his hair not perfectly coiffed, his daughter and grandson part of a crime scene. Tracy almost felt sympathy for him.

"I've instructed him not to speak with you either," he said.

And then it was gone. "Then it will be a short conversation."

Berkshire grimaced, a facial expression not ordinarily in his trial lawyer's repertoire. "What would you do if it was your daughter and grandson?"

"What would you do if it was your investigation, and you were a homicide detective?"

Berkshire nodded.

"I assume your daughter and son-in-law are divorced?" she said.

"In the process."

"And it's gotten ugly?"

"I won't answer that."

"It's going to be a long night. You might want to wait at home."

"I'll wait right here."

Tracy left him on the sidewalk. A senior prosecutor from the county's Most Dangerous Offender Project would be coming, since MDOP responded to every homicide scene in King County. He or she could deal with Berkshire.

Inside, Kins was walking back from the bedroom. "You talk to the lawyer?"

"Atticus Berkshire," she said.

"Shit."

"It gets worse. Angela Collins is his daughter."

"No," Billy said.

"I think our grounder just took a bad hop," Kins said.

CHAPTER 2

It had been a long night and a longer morning. Tracy and Kins had worked late with King County Prosecutor Rick Cerrabone to prepare the certification for determination of probable cause, setting out the known evidence showing that Angela Collins had shot her husband and should be detained in jail pending the filing of formal criminal charges.

Tracy flashed her shield to the court corrections officers and stepped around the metal detector inside the Third Avenue entrance to the King County Courthouse. She found Kins and Cerrabone huddled outside the district court. Cerrabone was the MDOP prosecutor who'd come out to the scene the night before, and he and Tracy and Kins had worked multiple homicides together.

Tracy was delayed because she'd been researching the King County Superior Court's civil files. She handed Cerrabone a legal pleading. He put on reading glasses as Tracy gave them both the highlights. "Angela Collins filed for divorce about three months ago," she said. "And from all appearances, it's been nasty from the start. She alleged cruelty, emotional and physical abuse, and adultery."

"Sounds like her civil attorney is taking lessons from her father," Kins said.

Washington was a "no-fault divorce" state. There was no need for either side to assign blame. The idea was that making such allegations was inflammatory and usually intended to embarrass, or to try to gain the moral high ground when it came to divvying up the estate or child custody.

"Mediation failed. They were scheduled to go to trial next month," Tracy said. "The index fills three computer screens. It looks like they're fighting over every asset. The attorney's fees will wipe out most of the estate."

"Not anymore," Kins said.

Cerrabone flipped the pleading back to the first page. "Berkshire will allege self-defense. That's going to complicate things." Once a defendant made a self-defense claim, the prosecutor bore the burden to prove the killing had *not* been in self-defense, not the other way around.

"But if it was self-defense," Kins said, "why isn't she talking to us and telling us what happened?"

"Probably because she grew up watching *Hill Street Blues* and because the first words her father taught her were 'Anything you say can and will be used against you in a court of law,' " Tracy said. "Or she's covering for the kid."

They'd discussed the possibility that Connor Collins had shot his father and that Angela

Collins's quick confession had been motivated by a desire to protect her son—something they'd have to investigate going forward.

"Battered wife syndrome still plays well in Seattle," Cerrabone said. Early afternoon, he already had a five-o'clock shadow, which accentuated his hangdog appearance—pronounced bags beneath his eyes and cheeks that sagged, though Cerrabone wasn't heavy. Faz had pegged Cerrabone as a "dead ringer for Joe Torre," the one-time New York Yankees manager.

Tracy knew Cerrabone well enough to know he would want to slow down the train and give her and Kins time to gather the evidence and sort it out before formally charging either Angela Collins or Connor Collins; he was fine with whatever played out. King County prosecutors didn't like to bring charges and ask questions later, and they really despised having to dismiss charges due to a lack of corroborating evidence.

Cerrabone folded his glasses and returned them to the breast pocket of his charcoal-gray suit. "Let's go see what Berkshire has in store for us."

Tracy followed Kins and Cerrabone into the cramped courtroom. Spectators and media filled the usually empty benches in the gallery. More people stood at the back of the room.

Atticus Berkshire sat in the first bench. Any trace of the sympathetic father and grandfather had vanished. Berkshire's silver curls were swept back from his forehead, just touching the collar of his blue pin-striped suit jacket. He was busy typing on an iPad, head down. An oscillating fan on the corner of the clerk's oak counter swung from side to side. With each sweep, papers weighted down by her nameplate fluttered like the wings of a bird. There were no counsel tables—attorneys and their clients stood at the counter during what were typically brief hearings.

At 2:30 p.m. Judge Mira Mairs entered from the right, strode between two burly corrections officers, and quickly took her seat. An American flag and the green flag of the state of Washington hung limply behind her. Ordinarily, Mairs would have been considered a good draw for the prosecution, but Mairs had forged a career prosecuting domestic violence cases against husbands and boyfriends, and Tracy feared she could be overly sympathetic to Angela Collins's anticipated self-defense argument. Mairs instructed the clerk to call the case first, no doubt so she could get back to the normal afternoon routine.

Angela Collins entered in white prison scrubs with the words "Ultra Security Inmate" stenciled on the back, her hands cuffed to a belly chain. After a visit to the hospital to treat the bump on her head with three stitches and to x-ray her jaw and ribs—both were negative—Collins had spent the night in jail. The cut near the corner of her mouth had scabbed over and looked to be turning a dark blue.

Cerrabone stated his appearance. Mairs looked to Berkshire, who was whispering to his daughter. "Counselor, are you joining us this morning?"

Berkshire straightened. "Indeed, Your Honor. Atticus Berkshire for the defendant, Angela Margaret Collins."

Mairs picked up the certification and folded her hair behind her ear. It flowed gently to her shoulders, as black as her judicial robe.

"Your Honor," Berkshire started. "If I may—"

Mairs raised a hand but did not look up, turning over the pages and setting them on her desk as she read through the document. When she'd finished, she gathered the pages and tapped them on her desk to even them. "I've read the certification. Anything else to add?"

"Yes, Your Honor," Berkshire said.

"From the State," Mairs interrupted. "Anything else to add from the State?"

"Yes, Your Honor," Cerrabone said. "It has come to the State's attention that in addition to what is set forth in the certification, the defendant and the deceased were involved in a contentious civil divorce that was set to go to trial next month after a failed mediation."

Cerrabone could have elaborated, but Tracy knew he preferred not to try his cases in the press. Berkshire had no such qualms.

"A civil divorce my client initiated after years of mental and physical cruelty," Berkshire said, becoming animated. "The shooting took place in Mrs. Collins's residence after the deceased had moved out and had no legal right to be there. In fact, she had obtained a restraining order."

"There you have it," Kins whispered to Tracy. "Self-defense. He was attacking with his back to her."

"Save your arguments, Counselor," Mairs said. "I find that there's probable cause to detain the defendant. Do you wish to be heard on bail or defer to the arraignment?"

"The defense wishes to be heard," Berkshire said.

"The State objects to bail," Cerrabone said. "This is a murder case."

"This is a self-defense case," Berkshire said.

Mairs lifted a palm as if to say "Have at it" and sat back in her chair.

"As the State well knows," Berkshire said, "every person in the state of Washington is entitled to bail. Mrs. Collins has not been convicted of any crime, let alone been charged. She is innocent until proven guilty, and that presumption of innocence applies here. The only issues here are Mrs. Collins's ties to the community, whether she is a flight risk, and her criminal history, with which I will start. The defendant has never had so much as a parking ticket. She has been an upstanding member of the community. She has a seventeen-year-old son who lives with her, as well as parents who live in the area. She is far from a flight risk. We would ask that the court release Mrs. Collins on personal recognizance."

Mairs looked to Cerrabone.

"Your Honor," he said, "Mrs. Collins purchased a handgun while the couple was in the midst of a contentious divorce that was approaching trial. She admitted in a 911 call that she shot her husband. She also admitted that she called her attorney. When officers arrived at the home, she again admitted to shooting her husband, and she asked to be read her Miranda rights. All of this is evidence of someone operating with all of her faculties, and possibly evidence of premedi- tation. As for self-defense . . . she shot Timothy Collins in the back."

"She bought the gun because of a long history of physical and verbal abuse by her former husband," Berkshire said, not waiting to be asked to respond, "including the night of the shooting. And she asked for her Miranda rights at her attorney's instruction."

Mairs sat forward. She'd clearly made up her mind, and she was ready to get on with it. "I don't believe the defendant is a flight risk, nor do I believe she is a danger to the community. I am going to order that she surrender her passport and any weapons she possesses. The defendant will be placed on home confinement with an ankle monitor. Bail will be set at two million dollars."

"May I be heard on the amount of bail?" Berkshire said.

"No."

"Your Honor—"

"It's a murder case, Counselor. Bail will remain at two million dollars. Madame Clerk, call the next case."

Berkshire took another moment to speak softly to his daughter before she departed. Angela Collins would be taken back to jail, processed, fitted with an ankle monitor, and released, assuming she could come up with a couple hundred thousand dollars and a bail bondsman willing to cover the difference. That likely meant signing over a deed of trust on the house to the bail bondsman, or borrowing from her father.

Tracy and Kins followed Cerrabone out of the courtroom and into the hall. "I have another hearing. I'll call you later," Cerrabone said.

As the prosecutor departed, Tracy made her way outside the courthouse with Kins. On a Friday afternoon, Third Avenue was already congested. The commute home was likely going to be a bitch. She and Dan O'Leary, the man she'd been dating a year, had no chance of easily getting out of Seattle on their drive south to Stoneridge, a small town on the Columbia River.

"I'm sorry to be bailing on you," Tracy said to

Kins as they walked up the hill to the Justice Center. She and Dan were attending a funeral— for the father of Jenny Almond. Jenny had been the only other woman in Tracy's Academy class.

"Don't sweat it," Kins said. "Faz says you promised him a lunch if he helped out. You should have just bought him a car. It would have been cheaper."

CHAPTER 3

By the time Tracy and Dan rolled their suitcases into the lobby of the Inn at Stoneridge, the sun had already set. The restaurant and garden patio had closed, and rather than the "awe-inspiring images of the mighty Columbia carving its path through canyon walls," as the inn's website proclaimed, the river looked like the world's largest blacktop highway.

At least the room was as romantic as advertised. The soft light of the bedside lamp colored the cedarwood walls gold, and soft jazz played from the nightstand stereo. Dan pulled back the curtain covering a sliding glass door. "Can't see the mountain," he said. It was too dark and overcast to see the snowcapped peak of Mount Adams to the north.

"I'm sorry we didn't make our dinner reservation," Tracy said. Dan had gone to considerable effort to get them a table at the inn's four-star restaurant. They'd had to cancel when it became apparent they wouldn't get there in time. Instead, they stopped and ate fast food.

"But consider the carbo-loading we did for our morning run," he said, smiling but not able to completely mask his disappointment.

"We're running in the morning?" she said.

"We are now."

"Ugh. I'm going to take a shower," Tracy said. "Care to join me?"

Dan had picked up the remote control. He gave her a sheepish smile. "I'm really beat," he said. "I know you are too. I vote we veg—watch some TV, and crash. That okay?"

She knew he was tired; Los Angeles lawyers were wearing him out in a contentious personal injury lawsuit, but she was concerned Dan was becoming frustrated at their inability to find quality time together. They'd grown up childhood friends but had lost touch until Tracy returned to their hometown of Cedar Grove for answers about her little sister's disappearance twenty years before. Hunters had found Sarah's remains buried in a shallow grave, and Tracy wanted a new trial for the man accused of killing her, because she'd believed he was innocent. She'd hired Dan, the best attorney in town, and they developed a romantic relationship. But Tracy lived in Seattle, two hours away, and no sooner had she returned home when she became embroiled in the hunt for the Cowboy.

She wrapped her arms around Dan's neck. "Are you upset?"

He set down the remote. "If I was upset, I'd be upset at you, which I'm not. I'm disappointed at the situation—that we didn't get to enjoy the evening we'd planned."

"We can still have part of the weekend we had in mind," she said.

"Sort of a 'you wash my back and I'll wash yours'?" he said.

She smiled. "That assumes you're taking me up on my offer, and one of us is turning around in the shower."

They didn't make it to the shower, and Dan didn't seem too disappointed he had to postpone watching ESPN. They made love on the bed until, exhausted, they fell asleep wrapped in the Egyptian cotton sheets.

CHAPTER 4

Buzz Almond's funeral included all the pomp and circumstance befitting a man who'd served more than half his life as the sheriff. An honor guard of Marines and Klickitat County deputies stood stone-faced in crisp dress uniforms, white-gloved hands gripping the handles of a flag-draped casket. Jenny Almond, who'd succeeded her father as sheriff, stood with her two older sisters, their mother pinched tight between them, arms interlocked. Three spouses and seven grandchildren took their places behind the women.

Tracy had colleagues whose spouses worried each time they left the house, but in the end, it wasn't bullets or bad guys that killed the large majority of cops. It was the same insidious diseases that befell all humanity. For Theodore Michael "Buzz" Almond Jr., it had been colon cancer. He was sixty-seven.

The procession stopped at the foot of brick steps leading to the entrance of Saint Peter's Catholic Church. A priest and two altar boys, their robes rippling in the breeze, descended the steps and greeted the family. Tracy knew they would remember little of this day, as she remembered little of her father's funeral. She took Dan's hand as the members of the honor guard lifted the casket onto their shoulders and two bagpipers blew the mournful wail of the Highland pipes that had carried her father and now would carry Buzz Almond home.

They held the public reception at the Stoneridge High School gymnasium, the only building in town large enough to accommodate the crowd who'd come to pay their respects. A private reception followed at the family home, and Jenny had invited Tracy and Dan. As she and Dan drove there, they passed orchards of fruit trees and rolling fields. The only disruption to the open space was a construction site for an impressive athletic complex rising above a manicured football field. A billboard-size sign staked in the lawn identified the contractor as Reynolds Construction.

State Route 141 wound farther into the foothills, and after another five minutes they left the pavement altogether for a dirt-and-gravel road that led to an expanse of lawn and a scene out of a Norman Rockwell painting. Young boys in khakis and barefoot girls in Sunday dresses ran around cradling a football and swinging on a rope swing in the yard of a two-story white clapboard farmhouse partially shaded by the limbs of cottonwood and birch trees. The home had a pitched roof, black shutters, and a wraparound porch with ornate pillars and a spindle railing, where several adults stood watching the children.

Dan parked the Tahoe alongside half a dozen other vehicles, and Jenny descended the porch steps to greet them.

"You found it," she said.

"It's beautiful," Tracy said.

"Come on inside."

Jenny led Tracy and Dan through a blur of introductions, mostly for Dan's benefit; Tracy had met the family at Jenny's wedding and had visited after the birth of each of her two children. She and Dan again offered their condolences to Jenny's mother, who sat in a chair in the living room holding Jenny's little girl, Sarah, named in honor of Tracy's sister.

"Look who's here, Sarah," Jenny said.

Tracy hadn't seen the little girl recently. Her golden curls extended to her shoulders, and she had a gap between her two front baby teeth. Tracy held out her arms, but Sarah buried her chin in her grandmother's shoulder, sneaking cautious glances.

"Are you going to be shy now?" Jenny said, lifting her. "Go see your auntie Tracy. Go on."

Tracy smiled and held out her arms again. "Can I have a hug?"

Sarah looked to Jenny, who nodded. Then the little girl leaned out, and Tracy pulled her close, taking in the beautiful scent of childhood.

Sarah held up three stubby fingers. "I'm free," she said.

"I know."

Jenny's husband, Neil, emerged from the kitchen holding two beers. "Dan, the men are about to take on that horde of boys and girls out there in a game of flag football. I don't suppose we could interest you in helping us out. I have a cooler of cold beers if that helps influence your decision."

Dan took the beer. "Just point me in the right direction."

"Don't hurt yourself," Tracy said.

"Momma, can you watch Sarah a while longer?" Jenny said. "I want to talk to Tracy for a minute."

"Of course I can," Anne Almond said. "Come give Gramma some lovin', honey."

Tracy handed Sarah back to her grandmother and followed Jenny. The house was dark hardwood floors, antique light fixtures, and modest but well-cared-for furniture. Framed family portraits and photographs adorned the walls and the fireplace mantel. Jenny led Tracy to a study at the back of the house. A bay window looked out over the lawn, where the flag football game was getting under way.

"This house is incredible," Tracy said.

"The dollar goes a lot further here than in Seattle, especially back in the seventies. Plus, my parents got some help from my mom's parents,"

Jenny said. "They bought the house and the apple orchard, then sold most of the orchard to the neighbor. It was a great place to grow up, but now we're worried my mom's going to be lonely out here by herself."

"She won't move?" Tracy's mother had been unwilling to leave their huge home in Cedar Grove after her husband's death.

"Right now the home gives her comfort. We've lined up a ten-day cruise up the Rhine River with her sister. We'll talk about it more when she gets back. Until then, we'll all take turns looking in on her."

"She's lucky to have so much family." Tracy still felt guilt for leaving her mother in Cedar Grove when she moved to Seattle, though she knew she had to go, for her own mental well-being. "Sarah's getting so big."

"We survived the terrible twos, barely." Jenny smiled. "You did so much for me, Tracy. If it weren't for you, I'd probably still be working at Costco, I never would have met Neil, and I never would have had Trey or Sarah."

When Tracy and Jenny met at the Academy, Jenny had been barely twenty, an eager young woman who wanted to follow in her father's footsteps but who had little chance of graduating. Homesick and overwhelmed by the workload, Jenny had been living in a depressing motel room. Tracy insisted Jenny move into Tracy's two-bedroom apartment and join Tracy's study group and training team. Jenny's scores improved dramatically, and Tracy taught her to shoot well enough to pass her qualifying exam.

"You would have found your way. You *have* found your way."

Jenny leaned against the desk, clearly emotionally spent after a long couple of days. "I'm going to miss my dad. Maria and Sophia lost their father too, but I also lost a mentor and a friend. The first few days in the office without him were tough."

"You'll do fine, Jenny."

"Dan seems nice. Do you think he might be the one?"

Tracy shrugged. "I'd like to think so," she said, "but it's been a crazy year. At least he hasn't dumped me."

"Are you kidding? He's in love with you. He came to a funeral for a friend of yours he's never met. That's love."

"I hope so," she said.

Jenny walked behind the desk. "So, I have an ulterior motive for bringing you back here. There's something I was hoping to discuss with you. The timing could be better, I know, but I thought I should do it now or I might not ever get around to it." She pulled out a six-inch-thick brown legal file from the desk drawer and set it on top.

"What is it?" Tracy asked.

"It's a cold case," Jenny said before catching herself. "Well, not exactly. It's complicated. It's the first case my father ever investigated as a deputy sheriff. Nineteen seventy-six. I wasn't born yet, but most people who grew up here are familiar with Kimi Kanasket."

"Who is she?" Tracy said.

"Local high school girl who disappeared walking home one night. My dad got the call."

Saturday, November 6, 1976

Buzz Almond and Earl Kanasket had retraced on foot Kimi's usual walk home from the diner. It hadn't been easy. Buzz couldn't remember a night that dark. And then it had started to snow—big heavy flakes that clung to the tree limbs and covered the ground. Even with flashlights, they'd found no visible signs of Kimi—no footprints, no discarded bag, no article of clothing. And as each minute passed without any sign of the young woman, Buzz regretted having told Earl they'd find her.

After an hour he dropped Earl back at the double-wide, which remained teeming with people wanting to help. Phone calls to Kimi's friends had been equally unfruitful. Buzz drove to Husum, a small compound of homes and industrial buildings situated on both sides of a bend in the White Salmon River, to talk to Tommy Moore, Kimi's ex-boyfriend. Moore's roommate, William Cox, answered the door in shorts and a T-shirt. Despite the late hour, he did not appear to have been sleeping. Cox said Moore had come home around midnight but left when he found out that Élan Kanasket and a group of men, some armed, had come looking for him. Cox said he didn't know where Moore went but that he had been on a date earlier that evening. If Kimi Kanasket had recently broken up with Tommy Moore, it didn't sound as though Moore was too upset about it.

Just after four, with the first light of day still several hours off and the snow continuing to fall, Buzz returned to the sheriff's office in Goldendale to fill out the necessary missing-person paperwork and to bring his sergeant up to speed so he could apprise the day shift of the situation. When he'd finished, Buzz reluctantly drove home to relieve Anne, who, despite being very pregnant, was still working the morning shift at the hospital. They needed the money with the new baby coming.

The call came as Buzz was cleaning up after lunch and starting the process of bundling Maria and Sophia in their winter gear. He'd promised to take them out in the snow, which had accumulated enough to make a decent snowman. That was going to have to wait—much to his daughters' disappointment. Buzz buckled his girls into the backseat of his Suburban and drove them a stone's throw down the road to Margaret O'Malley's home. O'Malley had retired after thirty-five years teaching first grade and couldn't get enough of Buzz's girls.

"What about the snowman, Daddy?" Sophia asked.

"We'll make one later, honey," Buzz said, though the knot in his stomach was telling him that was another promise he'd likely not be able to keep.

"Come on, girls," Margaret O'Malley said, ushering them inside. "I need a couple of helpers to make chocolate chip cookies."

That did the trick. Snowman forgotten.

After dropping the girls at Mrs. O'Malley's, Buzz drove quickly into Stoneridge. It looked like a ghost town. No one walked the sidewalks, and the parking spots in front of the stores were nearly empty of cars. The Stoneridge Café was closed. So was the pizza-and-beer pub, the flower store, the barbershop, and the hardware store. Almost all had homemade signs in the windows that said things like "Go, Red Raiders!" and "State Bound!" Buzz had read something in the local paper about the high school football team playing in its first-ever state championship, and he grew worried the drugstore might also be closed, but it remained open. He hurried inside and bought a Kodak Instamatic and four rolls of film before driving out of town on State Route 141.

He turned left on Northwestern Lake Road and went down the hill, slowing to a stop atop the narrow concrete bridge spanning the White Salmon River. Search and Rescue vehicles filled Northwest Park's dirt-and-gravel parking area, along with two fire trucks, a Klickitat County Sheriff's Office vehicle, and a blue-and-white Stoneridge Police car. Men wearing waders and rubber boots with their winter clothing worked along the river's edge.

Buzz parked beside the two fire trucks. It had stopped snowing, but several inches covered the ground and the picnic tables and benches, and had flocked the trees along the riverbank as well as the larger boulders protruding from the gray waters. Buzz put on his aviators to deflect the bright stream of sunlight that had burst through the cloud layer. Deputy Andrew Johns stood talking with a Stoneridge Police officer Buzz didn't recognize, their breath white ribbons. Buzz had become familiar with most, though not all, of the other deputies, but he wasn't as familiar with the Stoneridge officers—of which there were four.

"Heard this was your call, Buzz." Johns clapped his gloved hands then tucked them under his armpits. "Damn, it got cold fast."

"What's Search and Rescue said?" Buzz asked.

Johns pointed to two men dressed in fishing gear standing near one of the picnic tables. "Those two guys were fishing the banks. Thought they saw something in the water hung up in the branches of that fallen tree. Worked their way downstream for a closer look, but whatever it is, it's submerged by the current. They think it's a body."

Buzz's stomach dropped. "Do you know them?"

Johns shook his head. "Two guys from Portland."

"You get a statement?"

"Just gave it to you. Search and Rescue's stringing a cable across the river to give themselves something to hook on to. River's not flowing that strong, but the rocks are slippery. They might know more by now."

Search and Rescue had cleared off a picnic table to stage its equipment. Two of its men, in rubber waders and boots, were tightening a bolt that would lock a cable they'd looped around the trunk of a fir tree. The cable extended across the river, where two of their colleagues were securing the cable in a similar fashion.

"All right?" one of the men shouted across the river.

"We're good," his colleague shouted back.

The two men on Buzz's side of the river cranked a hand winch and began to cinch the cable until it was suspended like a tightrope a foot above the gray water. The men would clip on to it as they entered the water and made their way across to the sunken tree.

"You guys know anything more?" Buzz asked someone on the Search and Rescue team preparing to enter the current. Not in uniform and not familiar with the men—he hadn't yet worked a case with Search and Rescue—he showed them his badge. "I got the call last night about a missing girl."

He hoped they didn't hear the quiver in his voice or would at least attribute it to the biting cold; hoped they'd tell him it wasn't a body, just a backpack or piece of clothing from a summer rafting trip that had remained submerged; hoped he wouldn't have to make the drive out to Earl and Nettie Kanasket's double-wide and tell them he'd found their daughter, wishing again that he'd never promised them anything.

"Definitely a body," the first responder said.

The shouts and squeals of children drew Tracy's attention to the bay window. Dan cradled the football, dodging a pack of kids in hot pursuit. It didn't resemble any football game Tracy had ever witnessed, but they all looked and sounded like they were having a good time.

"If this is too close to home, Tracy, you can just tell me to stop."

Tracy shook her head. "It's fine," she said. Like

Kimi, Sarah had been about to start college when she disappeared. Tracy had become a homicide detective out of a strong desire to determine what had happened to her sister, and to help other young women like her.

"The pathologist who did the autopsy and the prosecutor concluded it was a suicide," Jenny said. "They said Kimi Kanasket jumped from a bridge into the White Salmon River and drowned. The rapids knocked her around pretty good on the rocks. She had broken bones, and bruises on her arms and chest. She might have flowed all the way to the Columbia, but her clothing got hung up on the branch of a submerged tree. The current wedged her body beneath it."

"And the theory was she did it because of the ex-boyfriend?"

"Tommy Moore. He'd come into the diner that night with another girl."

"What did he have to say about it?"

"According to my dad's report, Moore confirmed that he took another girl into the diner where Kimi worked, but he said he quickly left, took the girl home, and went to his apartment."

"His date confirm that?"

"Pretty much. Her statement's in the file too. She said Moore got upset because Kimi 'dissed him,' and he drove her home."

"Dissed him how?"

"Apparently, she acted like she didn't care."

"Anyone vouch for whether Moore went to his apartment?"

"My dad took a drive out there. Moore's roommate said he'd come home but that he took off again when the brother's posse showed up armed and asking questions."

"Roommate know where Moore went?"

"No."

Tracy flipped through the file. "You think there's more to it?"

"I think my father believed there was more to it."

"Where'd you find this file?" Tracy asked.

"Right here, in my father's desk."

"Where are the closed files usually kept?"

"A file this old would have been moved to the off-site storage unit. But this was never a cold case."

"What do you mean?"

"After I found it, I checked our computer records at the office. There is no record that a Kimi Kanasket file was ever sent to storage. The records at the office indicate it was destroyed."

"Destroyed when?"

"No date provided."

"By who?"

"Doesn't say."

"What's the policy on destroying old files?"

"Now? Now we keep closed homicide files for as long as eighty years, or until the detective who worked the case says it can be destroyed."

SPD had a similar policy. "Did you check with the detective who worked this case to see if he authorized it?"

"He's long gone. He died in the nineties."

Tracy pointed to the file on the desk. "So then, either that file is the official file or a personal file your father kept."

"That was my conclusion. And if it's the official file, then my father either checked it out and indicated it had been destroyed, or the last person who looked for it concluded it had been destroyed because it was missing."

"Either way, your father took it."

"There are some notes in the file indicating he was looking into things from time to time. I think this case weighed on him."

Tracy flipped deeper into the file contents, the pages two-hole-punched and held by a clasp at the top. "Witness statements, the coroner's report, photographs, sketches." She let the contents fall back to the first page. "Looks like a complete file."

"Appears to be."

"You get a chance to look at it?"

"Some."

"What do you think?"

"I was born shortly after Kimi disappeared," Jenny said. "We didn't live in Stoneridge then. We moved there when my dad became sheriff. I don't recall my father ever really talking about it. Yet, I *knew* about Kimi Kanasket. Everyone did. I can remember people saying things like 'Don't walk the road alone late at night. You'll end up like Kimi Kanasket.' "

"You want me to take a look?"

"Forensics are better now, and it just feels like the cancer robbed my dad of the chance to finish this. I feel like I owe it to him to at least take a closer look, but I'm his daughter. I'm not sure I can be objective. I'm also an elected official, and I may have to reopen the file. If that's the case, I'd like an independent assessment to justify my decision. If there's nothing to it, so be it. If there is . . ." Jenny shrugged.

Another squeal, but this one sounded more urgent. When they looked out the window, they saw Trey on the ground crying, Neil trying to console him.

"Is he hurt?"

"That's his 'We lost' cry," Jenny said. "He's competitive, like his father."

"And his mother," Tracy said.

Jenny smiled. "I get it from *my* father."

"So do I," Tracy said, picking up the file.

CHAPTER 5

Emily Rodriguez, fifty-seven, lived one house to the north of Tim and Angela Collins's home. The first thing Kins noticed when he and Faz entered her home was the large picture window that faced Greenwood Avenue.

"Thank you for speaking to us again," Kins said. Faz and Del had interviewed the woman the night before.

Rodriguez looked uncomfortable. "It's so sad," she said. "So sad."

"Did you know the family?"

"Not really. I'd wave in passing, say hello, that sort of thing."

Kins nodded, letting the woman catch her breath. "Ever hear any arguing, yelling, anything to indicate they were having problems?"

"No."

"Any neighbors ever indicate they'd heard there were problems in the home?"

"I don't talk much with my neighbors. I'm not unfriendly or anything, I just don't know them very well. A lot of people I knew have moved. But I never heard anything."

"How long have you lived here?"

"Me? Thirty years."

"Do you know when the Collinses moved in?"

55

"About five years ago, I'd say."

"What about the son? Did you ever speak with him?"

Rodriguez shook her head. "Again, maybe in passing, but nothing I can recall. I'd see him getting on and off the bus in the morning." She pointed out the window. "He waited right there at that bus stop."

Kins stepped to the window. "I noticed in your witness statement you said you thought you heard a car backfire and looked out the window. I'm assuming it was this window?"

"That's right. It was a bang, the way an engine will sometimes do that."

"And you said that when you looked out the window, you saw a city bus?"

Rodriguez joined Kins and Faz at the window. "At that bus stop. Route Five."

Kins smiled. "You're familiar with it."

"I rode that bus downtown and back for more than twenty years."

"What did you do?"

"I was a paralegal at a law firm."

"Do you recall what time it was when you heard the bang?"

"I didn't look at my watch or anything," she said.

In her witness statement, Rodriguez didn't provide an exact time, but Kins hoped he could narrow it down using the city bus schedule, which he'd checked on the Metro Transit website that morning. "According to the schedule, that bus makes a stop at that location at 5:18 and then again at 5:34." Angela Collins had called 911 at 5:39, so he guessed Rodriguez heard the shot at 5:34.

"That's right. I would catch the 4:35 at Third and Pine downtown, and it would drop me here at 5:18."

"Do you know if the bus you saw was the 5:18 or the 5:34?"

"I'm not sure. This was pretty upsetting." Rodriguez massaged her temple.

"Take your time," Kins said.

She closed her eyes, grimacing. Kins looked to Faz, who frowned and shrugged. He'd gotten the same answer.

"I'm sorry," Rodriguez said. "I don't . . ." She opened her eyes.

"What were you doing before you heard the noise?" Kins said, trying to ground Rodriguez in a task that might refresh her recollection.

"I was . . ." She looked to the window, then turned to a flat-screen in the corner of the room. "I was watching TV."

"Do you recall what you were watching?"

"KIRO 7," she said.

"Local news."

"That's right." Kins could almost see the wheels starting to spin in her head. "I watch it from five to five thirty, then switch to *World News Tonight* on ABC. I was watching a story about housing prices rising on the Eastside. The noise startled me, and I went to the window to see what it was."

"So that was during the local news, right?" Kins said. "Does that help you with respect to when you heard the shot?"

Rodriguez paused. "It does. It had to be the 5:18 bus." She nodded. "It had to be. Didn't it?"

Yes, it did, Kins thought.

And that raised a whole different set of questions.

The call came in to the Justice Center as Kins and Faz were leaving Emily Rodriguez's home, and the operator diverted it to Kins's cell. When Kins disconnected and told Faz that Atticus Berkshire wanted to bring Angela Collins in to give a statement, Faz summed up his disbelief.

"Right, and I'm going on a diet."

But an hour later, Berkshire did indeed come in with Collins.

They were all seated at a round table in the soft interrogation room, Faz overwhelming his plastic chair, forearms folded across his chest and resting on his stomach. Angela Collins sat beside her father. She'd dressed in yoga pants and a loose-fitting sweatshirt. The bruising on the side of her face had become a mottled purple, yellow, and black.

"As I indicated, Detectives," Berkshire said, "Angela is prepared to tell you what happened that night. You may ask her questions, but I may instruct her not to answer a question if I believe the question is inappropriate, and I may terminate this interview at any time." He, too, was dressed casually, in a checked button-down, glasses perched on the bridge of his nose. "Are those ground rules acceptable?"

Kins was in no real position to negotiate, but he also wasn't about to accept Berkshire's terms on video. He was still trying to figure out why Berkshire would allow his daughter to give a statement. He and Kins had speculated that whatever Angela Collins had to say, it would have been carefully rehearsed, and intended to further her anticipated self-defense argument.

"You're willing to talk to us today with your lawyer present?" Kins asked Angela Collins.

She nodded.

"You have to answer audibly," Berkshire said.

"Yes," she said, touching her lip as if it hurt to talk.

"And you understand that this conversation is being videotaped and recorded?" Kins asked.

"Yes."

"And, again, you agree to us recording what is said?"

"Yes."

Kins was being cautious, even more surprised

59

Berkshire would allow them to record the interview.

"All right," Kins said. "Whenever you're ready."

Angela Collins took a deep breath, grimaced, and exhaled. "Tim came to the house to pick up Connor. He was upset."

"Tim was upset, or Connor was upset?" Kins was pretty sure she meant Tim, but he wanted to get her in the routine of answering his questions and prevent her from providing a soliloquy.

"Tim was upset, but Connor was also upset."

"Why was Connor upset?"

"He didn't like going to his father's apartment."

"Why not?"

"Tim was hard on Connor. He was always on him about something."

Kins made a mental note to pursue that line of inquiry. Could the kid have snapped from persistent abuse? "What was your husband upset about when he came to the house?"

"He was upset that my attorney had asked for an increase in support." She slurred the last word and again paused to touch her lip. "He said he didn't have any more money to give me. He said I was already taking more than seventy percent of what he was clearing after taxes. He accused me of hoarding money."

"According to the terms of a negotiated restraining order, your husband wasn't supposed to go into the house," Kins said, expecting Berkshire to object that Angela was there only to provide a statement. Berkshire, however, had his head down, taking notes on a pad.

"That's right."

"You let him in anyway?"

"No." She shook her head. "Connor opened the door, and Tim forced his way in."

"Did Tim hit Connor?"

"Yes, but not then."

"What happened next?"

"Tim became verbally abusive. He said I was spending money on worthless things. That's when he picked up the sculpture and began shaking it. He said it was a waste of money. I told him to put it down."

"Where was Connor when this was going on?"

"I'd sent him to his room at the back of the house and told him to shut the door."

"Then what?"

"The argument escalated. Tim got more and more worked up. I told him I was calling 911. That's when he hit me with the sculpture."

She said it matter-of-factly, like someone reciting lines but showing no real emotion. "Where did he hit you?"

Angela Collins touched the wound on the left side of her head.

"How many times did he hit you with the sculpture?"

"Just once. That's all it took to knock me down."

"Then what happened?"

"He kicked me in the stomach and started yelling at me."

"How many times did he kick you?"

"I don't know."

"Then what?"

"He dropped the sculpture and shouted for Connor that they were leaving, but Connor wouldn't come out of his room. He'd locked himself in. Tim went back there and started pounding on the door, telling Connor if he didn't open it, he'd break it down."

Kins was wondering how Collins could recollect such details if she'd been hit in the head hard enough to cause a wound that would require three stitches. "And Connor opened the door?" he asked.

Angela Collins nodded. "Tim told him to get his stuff, that they were leaving, but by now Connor didn't want to go with him. He told him no, and that's when Tim hit him."

"You saw it?"

"No, but I heard it. Tim has hit Connor before. He slapped him hard across the face. It sounded like a bullwhip."

Angela Collins started to shake, and Atticus Berkshire placed a comforting hand on her back. Kins slid a box of tissues closer, taking note of the lack of tears. Angela blew her nose, then sipped from a glass of water before continuing. "I'd gotten to my feet, and I got the gun from the box in the closet."

"You got the gun first, then went down the hall?"

"That's right. I just wanted to scare him, to make him leave us alone, but when I went down the hall I saw Tim grab Connor."

"Grabbed him where?"

"He grabbed Connor by the shirt."

"Where was your son in the room?"

"He'd retreated to the corner. His face was red where Tim had hit him. Connor resisted when Tim tried to get him to go with him."

"How did he resist?"

"I don't know. He just did. And that's when Tim raised his hand again . . . and I pulled the trigger and shot him."

Again, Kins noted the absence of tears. He'd had friends go through some brutal divorces, but he couldn't imagine any of them having so little feeling for an ex-spouse that they couldn't muster any tears—especially one they'd shot. He tried not to look at Berkshire as he asked his next question, certain it would draw an objection. "Your husband had his back to you?"

"Yes," she said.

Berkshire never looked up.

"How far were you from him?"

"Just a few feet."

"He didn't turn around, didn't hear you?"

"She can't speculate about what he heard," Berkshire said, still without raising his head. He flipped his notepad to a clean page and resumed scribbling.

"He gave no indication he heard you?" Kins asked.

"I don't think he expected that I would get up," Collins said. "I don't think he expected me to be there."

"He didn't expect you to be behind him?"

"No."

"You don't recall him turning his head, shoulders, nothing?" According to the ME's initial report, the trajectory of the bullet wound was consistent for someone with his back to the gun.

"No."

"Did you say anything to him to try to get him to stop before shooting him?"

She shook her head. "I was afraid he'd attack me and take the gun. That's what they taught us in the class, that if you take the gun out you have to be prepared to use it, because if they get it they'll use it on you."

"So you intended to shoot him?"

This time Berkshire intervened. "That's not what she said."

"I don't know what I intended. It all happened so fast, and I was afraid for me and for Connor."

"What happened next?" Kins asked.

"I told Connor to wait in the living room, and I called my father. And he told me—"

"Don't discuss what I told you," Berkshire said, still scribbling.

"You called your father before you called 911?"

Angela Collins looked to her father. Berkshire raised his head and nodded. "Yes," she said.

"Why?"

She shrugged. "I don't know."

"What did you do with the gun?"

"I dropped it on the bed."

"Did Connor touch it?"

"I don't think so."

"Has Connor ever touched that gun?"

"I don't know."

"You keep it locked in a box in the closet?"

"Yes."

"He didn't take shooting lessons with you?"

"No."

"Did you do anything between the time you shot your husband and when you called your father?" This was the answer Kins was most anxious to hear, how Angela would account for the nearly twenty-one minutes between the time she fired the gun and the time she called 911.

Collins shook her head. "No. I just dropped the gun on the bed. I had to find my cell phone. I couldn't recall what I'd done with it. I was pretty shaken up. So was Connor."

"How much time passed between when you shot your husband and when you called your father?"

"If you know," Berkshire said, perhaps picking up that Kins had information they did not.

"I don't know."

"How much time passed before you called 911?"

"I don't know."

"An hour?" Kins said, baiting her.

"Oh, no. It was minutes. I called within minutes."

"By minutes, you mean one or two minutes?" he asked, trying to lock her in.

"One or two. No more than five."

"So definitely within five," he said, certain Berkshire would jump in and object, and again surprised when he didn't.

"Definitely," she said.

"And other than dropping the gun on the bed and getting your cell phone, you don't recall doing anything else."

"No."

"Did you touch Tim's body?"

"No."

"Did Connor?"

"I don't believe so. No. No, he wouldn't have."

"The sculpture remained on the floor where your husband dropped it—is that right?"

"Yes."

"Did you or Connor touch it?"

"No. We left it there."

Kins went back over some of the details of Collins's story to be certain he'd pinned her down. After forty-five minutes, Atticus Berkshire said Angela was still emotionally distraught and tired, and put an end to the proceedings. Kins thanked them for coming in and walked them back to the elevators.

After Collins and Berkshire had departed, Kins found Faz in the bull pen. "What do you think?" Kins asked.

"I think Tracy was right," Faz said rocking in his chair. "I think Berkshire coached her on what to say and how to say it."

"But he didn't know about the neighbor and the bus."

"What time did she call her father?" Faz asked.

"At 5:39."

"And we know she called 911 after she called her father. So what was she doing for twenty-one minutes after she shot him?"

"According to her, not a damn thing." Kins smiled.

"She's locked in now. You pinned her good," Faz said.

"Yeah, but it still doesn't answer the bigger question," Kins said.

"Why the hell would Berkshire allow her to give a statement in the first place?"

"Exactly."

• • •

After Berkshire and Collins had departed, Kins and Faz turned their attention to the restraining order, specifically to Angela Collins's signed affidavit that the restraining order was necessary because Tim had come to the house one evening and become violent. In her statement she said Tim shoved her into the door frame, then pushed her over a table, necessitating a trip to the emergency room. The ER doctor's report confirmed bruised ribs, and bruising along Collins's upper arms. Nothing else in the file showed that Tim had a violent temper or a propensity for violence, though they were admittedly just getting started.

"According to court documents, the matter was resolved when he agreed not to set foot in the house on days he was to pick up Connor," Kins said. "He was supposed to wait in the car."

"She didn't press charges?" Faz asked. "If she really was an abused spouse, why wouldn't she press charges?"

"Maybe she figured the restraining order was enough."

"Not if you believe what's in the divorce papers," Faz said. "Read that, and she was married to Attila the Hun."

Kins flipped to CSI's preliminary report, which had been sent over while they'd been interviewing Angela Collins. The report included dozens of photographs, as well as the latent print examiner's findings. The examiner identified positive finger-print hits for Angela, Connor, and Tim Collins throughout the house, which was to be expected. They'd found additional prints as well, but so far none of those generated hits when run through AFIS, the Automated Fingerprint Identification System, which kept a record of the prints of people who had been convicted of crimes, served in the military, or entered specific professions.

Kins sat forward when he read the next sentence. "Did you see this?" he said to Faz. "The examiner found both Angela's and Connor's fingerprints on the Colt Defender."

"So the kid did touch the gun," Faz said.

"Apparently." Kins continued reading, stopped, and reread the same sentence a second and then a third time. "They didn't find any prints on the sculpture."

"What?" Faz got up from his desk and walked across the bull pen to Kins's cubicle.

Kins pointed to his computer screen and read the sentence aloud. "Negative for *any* prints."

"How can that be?" Faz said. "That don't make no sense."

Kins continued reading. "But they *did* find Connor's fingerprints on his father's shoe. Why would the kid's prints be on one of the shoes?"

"Maybe he tried to move him?"

Kins shook his head. "ME's report says there was no indication the body was moved. Lividity is consistent with a body that had been lying in one spot." Kins rocked in his chair. "The only way that sculpture could be clean is if someone wiped it clean, right?"

"Or no one touched it in the first place," Faz said.

"Then how'd it get on the floor?"

"Got knocked over during the argument."

"Why would she say he used it to hit her?"

"She needed to explain the cut on her head."

"How else would she have gotten it?"

"Don't know."

"Well, at least we know somebody was doing something during those twenty-one minutes," Kins said.

"You think she's covering for the son," Faz said.

"Very well could be."

CHAPTER 6

Back in the car on their drive home from the Almonds' house, just past Kelso, Dan reached for the radio and turned down the Seahawks game, drawing Tracy's attention. She'd been staring out the window, watching the acres of farmland pass along I-5, the daylight fading quickly, as it did in the fall.

"I thought you were enjoying the game," Tracy said.

Dan angled toward her, his left arm on the steering wheel. "Enjoying? The Forty-Niners are kicking our butts. I'm not enjoying it."

"Oh," Tracy said.

"You've been awfully quiet. I don't think you've said more than two sentences the past half hour, and you've obviously tuned out the entire third quarter, or you'd have known we're down by twenty points."

She smiled. "Okay. Guilty."

"Does it have anything to do with that file back there?" Dan gave a small nod toward the backseat.

"You noticed that, did you?"

"You're not the only one with detective skills. So, what is it?"

"An old case Jenny found in her father's desk."

Dan reached into a bag of wasabi-flavored

71

almonds. He was on a quest to lose five to ten pounds and didn't go anywhere without some form of nut to snack on. "A cold case?"

"Not exactly. In 1976 a seventeen-year-old Native American girl went missing on her way home from work. Two fishermen found her body in the White Salmon River the next afternoon, caught on the limbs of a submerged tree. The autopsy and the prosecuting attorney concluded she jumped into the river and drowned."

Dan popped more nuts in his mouth. "Jumped? As in, on purpose?"

"The official conclusion was that she was upset over a recent breakup with her boyfriend. Unfortunately, it happens too often in high school. One minute they're in love; the next minute they hate each other. Jenny thinks her father believed there was something more to it. She asked me to have a look."

"Can you do that? It's a different county."

"We can. It usually happens if a body is found in one county but it's suspected the murder took place somewhere else—things like that. But the sheriff of a county can always ask for assistance. Jenny wants a fresh take, in case she has to reopen the investigation."

"How do you think Nolasco is going to react?" Dan asked, referring to Tracy's captain and longtime nemesis.

"Johnny Boy's been on his best behavior since

he got his hand slapped by OPA," she said. The Office of Professional Accountability was reviewing a decade-old homicide investigation by Nolasco and his then partner, Floyd Hattie. Tracy had found the file for the case while hunting the Cowboy, and her review of it revealed certain improprieties that called into question Nolasco's methods. OPA had broadened its inquiry to Nolasco's and Hattie's other cases, and word was, it was finding more misconduct. Only the support of the union had kept Nolasco at his desk.

"You think maybe it could be too close to home?" Dan said, concern creeping into his tone.

"They're always going to be too close to home," she said. "A disproportionate number of victims who get abducted, abused, and murdered are young women. I can't change that."

"No, but you don't have to volunteer either."

"I know, and when Jenny started telling me about the case, I thought my first reaction would be to say no. But the similarities between Kimi and Sarah are what made me want to take a look. Maybe it's because I know what something like this does to a family."

"Forty years is a long time," Dan said. "Is there any family left still alive?"

"The mother passed away. The father would be is in his mid- to late eighties. Jenny thinks he lives on the Yakama Reservation. The girl also had a brother."

"What if they don't want to talk about it?"

Tracy hadn't thought about that. "I don't know," she said. "I guess I'll cross that bridge if I ever get to it. I might not find anything that warrants reopening the investigation anyway."

After saying good-bye to Dan, who had an early flight to Los Angeles the next day and still needed to get back and prepare for a week of depositions, Tracy shut the door to her West Seattle house and took care of Roger, her black tabby. Roger let her know loudly that he was not happy about being abandoned for two days, never mind that he had an automatic feeder, plenty of water, the full run of the house, and a teenage neighbor who came in to check on him each day.

As Roger devoured his canned food, Tracy poured herself a glass of wine and took it into the dining room, eager to review Buzz Almond's file. She turned on her iPad, found a country music station, which she liked to listen to when working, and let Keith Urban fill the silence.

The first thing that struck her about the file was its thickness—hefty for an investigation that had quickly concluded that the victim committed suicide. What created much of the bulk were four gold-and-white Kodak envelopes, the kind she used to pick up at the Kodak counter in Kaufman's Mercantile Store in Cedar Grove. She opened the first packet and thumbed the pictures but quickly set them aside. She never started a review with photographs, since she had no idea what they were meant to depict. She unfolded the two brass prongs holding the file folder together and carefully slid the contents free.

She flipped to the first entry, which turned out to be a yellowed newspaper article folded in half to fit the length of the file. It had been cut from the *Stoneridge Sentinel*, the date handwritten above the headline: *Sunday, November 7, 1976.*

Stoneridge Red Raiders
Reach Pinnacle, Win State Title

Tracy quickly skimmed the article. The Red Raiders had defeated Archbishop Murphy 28–24, capping an undefeated season for Coach Ron Reynolds and capturing the school's first state championship in any sport. A parade was to be held in Stoneridge that Monday afternoon to celebrate the accomplishment.

Accompanying the article was the type of iconic photograph found framed in high school trophy cases everywhere. Young men, looking exhausted but jubilant, beamed at the camera, their uniforms grass- and dirt-stained, their hair matted with perspiration, their faces smeared with black eye grease and bits of dirt. They held aloft a shimmering golden football mounted atop a wooden base.

Tracy moved to a second article, hand-dated

Monday, November 8, 1976, this one commemorating the parade in the team's honor. In the accompanying photograph, three boys wearing letterman jackets sat atop the backseat of a convertible, fingers raised. A sizable and animated crowd of fans waving Stoneridge High pennants and pom-poms lined the sidewalks, streamers and confetti fluttering all around them. Like the previous picture, it was a moment forever frozen in the small town's history, and that was likely the reason Buzz Almond had included the articles in the file. Trying to get witnesses to remember an event months or even just weeks earlier could be difficult, but the fact that Kimi Kanasket had disappeared the weekend of what was apparently the most celebrated sporting event in Stoneridge's history gave Buzz Almond, and now Tracy, a point of reference to ground witnesses' recollections. It was like asking people who lived through the sixties "Where were you when Kennedy was shot?" It was also an indication that Buzz Almond had deduced that the investigation could take years.

Tracy set the second story aside and reviewed an article on Kimi Kanasket's death.

Local Girl's Body Pulled
from White Salmon River

This article was given far fewer inches of print—just half a column and a few inches long, with Kimi's senior photo halfway through. It said that as a junior at Stoneridge High the previous year, Kimi had competed in the state track championship in the hundred-yard dash and the high hurdles, finishing second and third, respectively. She was survived by a mother and father, Earl and Nettie Kanasket, and an older brother, Élan. There was no mention of suicide. There was no mention of an investigation. There weren't even any follow-up articles.

Having grown up in a small town in the mid-1970s, Tracy knew people didn't air their dirty laundry or others'. If Kimi Kanasket had killed herself, Tracy doubted anyone would have been eager to publicize it or to read about it. A stigma was firmly affixed to suicide and, unfairly, to the family. When Tracy's father shot himself two years after Sarah's death, he destroyed not only his own legacy, but also the family's. People talked—never in front of Tracy or her mother, but they talked. It was one of the reasons Tracy wanted her mother to move with her to Seattle.

Tracy next found a wallet-size photo of the young woman stapled to a missing-persons report. Kimi had lustrous black hair that flowed well past her shoulders. Visible just beneath her right earlobe was an intricate feathered dream-catcher. Tracy suspected that Kimi's youthful facial features would have become more angular with age, making Kimi a stunningly attractive woman. But Kimi Kanasket, like Sarah, wouldn't get that chance. She would be forever young.

Buzz Almond's responding officer's report was next. The onionskin paper and uneven type indicated that it was his original report and not a copy. It looked thorough—nearly seven pages—and documented everything, starting with Almond's receiving the call from dispatch and his conversations with the Kanasket family at their home.

A separate report documented Buzz Almond's conversation with Tommy Moore the following Monday, the day of the parade.

～

Monday, November 8, 1976

Buzz Almond left his house before the sun had risen, though it was officially his day off. He avoided downtown Stoneridge. With the parade preparations under way, most of the streets had been cleared of snow, but portions were blocked off with sawhorse barricades and orange cones. People would be up early, despite the chilly temperatures, to set up folding chairs for the best seats. The superintendent had canceled school, and the mayor had proclaimed the day Red Raider Day. Many of the local businesses were shutting their doors between 11:00 a.m. and 1:00 p.m. so everyone could take part in a celebration that would wind its way through downtown and end with speeches and a potluck in the school gymnasium.

Not being from Stoneridge, Buzz thought the hoopla was more than a little over-the-top, but he'd read about such things—high school football games in small towns in Texas that drew 20,000 spectators, and standing-room-only crowds for basketball games in Indiana. He got a sense that the victory wasn't just about sports, but rather a validation of a way of life, proving that the small-town kids could compete just as well with the big-city boys, which somehow equated to small-town living being equal to, if not better than, urban living.

Lost in the euphoria was the fact that a young woman's body had been pulled from the river. Buzz was starting to sense that maybe the town didn't think of Kimi as one of their own, and he wondered if that was because of the increased tension caused by the protests outside the football games. For white residents, the name "Red Raiders" was synonymous with high school football, and both were sacrosanct. The suggestion that the name was offensive didn't sit well. If anything, the locals countered, the name and the mascot were flattering to Native Americans; their football boys were fierce warriors ready to do battle.

Buzz was up early to get his own choice seat, though not along the parade route. He intended to wait outside Tommy Moore's apartment. Moore had not returned over the weekend; Buzz had periodically checked while on patrol, and he'd asked other deputies to do the same on their day and swing shifts. No one had seen Moore's white Ford truck. But Buzz figured come Monday, Moore had to go to work or risk getting fired.

So Buzz returned to Husum. The main intersection for the unincorporated town consisted of a gas station, industrial buildings, and a few warehouses. Just north of a grocery store, he turned into a dirt-and-gravel parking lot littered with trucks, tractors, and harvesting machinery in various stages of disrepair. All had been dusted with an inch or two of snow. He drove along the side of the well-worn stucco building for M&N Mechanics to the back of the lot. His hunch had been accurate. Moore's white Ford sat parked near the long staircase leading up to the second-floor apartment.

Buzz killed the lights, pulled in behind the truck bed, and shut off the engine. He sat a moment, watching the windows of the apartment for any sign of life. Seeing none, he stepped out into the chilled air and quietly shut the door. The yard held the distinct odor of petroleum. The snow crunched beneath his boots as he walked alongside Moore's truck, where he noticed the front fender and hood had been smashed in. He bent to take a closer look. The damage was significant, indicating a high rate of speed, and the lack of any rust or flaking paint was a sign that it had been recently inflicted. Upon closer inspection, he noticed that someone had banged out the buckled fender to keep it from rubbing on the oversize tire, which had deep treads and grooves, likely for off-road activities.

Buzz returned to his vehicle, grabbed his Instamatic camera, and took a few photographs of the damage. Then he pocketed the camera and stepped carefully to the wood stairs. Ice beneath the thin layer of snow made them slick. He held on to the railing and climbed deliberately. At the landing he peered inside a window but didn't see any light or any movement. He knocked on the door and stepped to the side. He heard the sounds of someone startled awake, indecipherable voices followed by footfalls.

"Who is it?"

"Klickitat County Sheriff's Office. Open the door, please."

Silence ensued, followed by more muffled voices.

Buzz knocked again. "Open the door, please."

After a few seconds, the door pulled open, revealing a well-built Native American man wearing nothing but boxer shorts. Buzz had already met the roommate, William Cox. This was Tommy Moore. Moore had black hair that touched his shoulders and a body adorned with tattoos, the largest an American eagle—wings spread, talons extended—across most of his chest. He looked up at Buzz with sleepy blue eyes that, with his bronzed skin, reminded Buzz of the kids with surfboards he and Anne had watched on Waikiki Beach on their honeymoon. Those were eyes that could break a girl's heart. Maybe Kimi Kanasket's.

"Tommy Moore?"

"Yeah," he said with a hint of defiance.

"Where've you been the last couple days?"

"Visiting my mother."

"Good for you. A son should visit his mother. Where does she live?"

"On the rez in Yakima."

"We've been looking for you, Tommy."

"Yeah, I heard." Moore looked back inside the apartment where his roommate stood in a T-shirt and sleeping pants.

"Need to talk to you about Kimi Kanasket."

"Heard that too."

Buzz could feel the heat seeping out the open door, along with a dank odor that reminded him of the smell of wet wood. "We can do it standing out here in the cold, but I'm a lot better dressed for it than you."

Moore stepped back and allowed Buzz to enter. He'd been inside the apartment on Friday night. It was what he'd expected to find for two young men. The furniture was mismatched essentials—a couch, a chair, and a television. Nearby was a square table with two folding chairs beneath a chandelier made from deer antlers. The walls were unadorned by pictures or photographs, and the ceiling was stained where the roof had leaked. A garbage pail overflowed with fast-food bags. Cigarette butts and two spent joints filled an ashtray on the coffee table, the odor of tobacco and weed strong.

Moore moved toward the ashtray.

"Leave it," Buzz said. He wasn't interested in busting them for pot, and the cigarette odor didn't bother him. He'd been a pack-a-day smoker in the Marines, but when Anne said she wouldn't marry a smoker, he quit cold turkey.

"You have any weapons in here?" Buzz asked.

"Couple hunting rifles, a few knives," Moore said.

"Where are those?"

"In the closet in my bedroom."

"Can I shower?" the roommate asked. "I have to go to work."

"Go ahead," Buzz said. The young man glanced at Moore before leaving the room. Buzz reached into the breast pocket of his jacket and removed a spiral notepad and pen.

"I got to get to work too," Moore said.

"Good thing you have a short commute."

Moore sat on the couch.

"What happened to your truck?"

"Hit a tree on the rez."

"When was that?"

"The weekend."

"This past weekend?"

"Yeah."

"Looks pretty bad."

"I banged it out and got it running. I don't have the money at the moment to fix it right."

Buzz leaned forward in the chair so he could take notes. "You and Kimi dated?"

"Yeah."

"How long?"

"A while."

"How long is a while?"

"Since summer."

"So, three to four months."

"Sounds right."

"You broke up when?"

Moore dropped his focus. Then he said, "Maybe a week ago."

"Why'd you break up?"

"Just did."

"Did you end it, or did she?"

"It was mutual."

"Why'd you want to end it?"

Moore shrugged. "No point."

"No point what?"

"No point in dating anymore."

"Why not?"

"She's always busy. Cross-country, track, studying. She was leaving for college anyway."

"Why'd she want to break up with you?"

"Same reasons."

"Were you frustrated?"

Moore just shrugged. "Like I said, it was mutual."

Buzz wasn't detecting an attitude as much as ambivalence, which seemed especially odd given that Kimi had just been pulled from the river. "When'd you last see her?"

"Friday night."

"Where?"

"The diner."

"You went there?"

Moore nodded. Buzz played a hunch based on what the roommate had told him and what he knew about the nature of young men and young women. "You bring anyone with you?"

"Yeah."

"Who?"

"Cheryl Neal."

"Who's Cheryl Neal?"

"Just a girl."

"Of all the places to eat, you bring her to the diner where your ex-girlfriend works?"

"I like their chicken-fried steak."

"Yeah? Is that what you had to eat?"

"No."

"Why not?"

"We didn't stay long."

"Hmm," Buzz said as if taking time to consider something. "You drove fifteen minutes to a diner where you knew you would run into your ex, and you didn't stay to eat?"

"No."

"Why not?"

"I decided I wasn't hungry."

"What about your date?"

"She wasn't hungry neither."

"So what did you do?"

"Drove her home and came back here."

"What time did you get here?"

"I don't know. Midnight maybe."

"Was your roommate home?"

"He told you he was."

Buzz sat back and considered Moore. The young man was well trained in the art of the boxer's stare, not about to be intimidated. "Did you bring Cheryl Neal to the diner to make Kimi feel bad about breaking up with you, Tommy?"

"I said it was mutual."

"Yeah, I know what you said. But when it's mutual, a guy doesn't bring a new girl to a place he knows he'll run into his old girlfriend unless he has a reason."

"I told you, I like the chicken-fried steak."

"Really? You weren't trying to make Kimi jealous?"

"No reason to. Plenty of other girls out there."

"Why would Kimi's brother and friends come looking for you?"

"I don't know. You'd have to ask them."

"I'm asking you. I went to the house. When they learned Kimi was missing, her brother came here. Why would he do that if the two of you had broken up?"

Moore shrugged one shoulder. "Ask Élan."

"You two friends?"

"Not really."

"Enemies?"

"No."

"How'd you hear we pulled Kimi out of the river?"

"Read about it in the paper."

"How'd that make you feel?"

Moore lost focus again, a blank stare. Buzz was content to wait him out. After a few moments, Moore reengaged. "Sucks," he said.

⌒

Tracy poured out the remainder of her wine in the kitchen sink and switched to chamomile tea. Tommy Moore was, at the very least, a liar and an ass. Was he also a murderer?

Roger lay sprawled across the dining room table, snoring. Tracy picked up the first packet of photographs and went quickly through them, finding three photographs of damage to a white Ford truck. As Buzz Almond had described in his report, the front right side looked like the vehicle had impacted something at a high rate of speed— maybe the tree Tommy Moore said he hit. It also looked like someone with experience at bodywork had done initial repairs to get the truck functional again.

Tracy set the photographs aside. Buzz Almond had done exactly what Tracy would have done after speaking with Tommy Moore. His next report documented his trip to the home of Cheryl Neal, who lived in Stoneridge with her parents and two brothers. Since school had been canceled that day for the parade, the Neals were at home. Tracy could only imagine how thrilled the girl's parents must have been to have a sheriff's deputy knocking on the door that early in the morning.

Cheryl Neal confirmed Moore took her to see *The Rocky Horror Picture Show*, then to the Columbia Diner. She said she knew Moore had been dating Kimi Kanasket but said Moore told her they'd broken up. Neal said she and Kimi were "not friends," denied they were "enemies," but admitted she knew Kimi worked at the diner. Tracy suspected Moore had asked Neal out precisely because she and Kimi were "not friends," and that Neal enjoyed the idea of Moore taking her to the diner where Kimi worked. The plan had apparently backfired, however. Buzz Almond's report noted that Neal told him Moore abruptly left the diner "pissed off" about something and drove her home at roughly eleven. She couldn't vouch for where Moore had gone after that.

But he would have had plenty of time to go back to the diner, or to park along State Route 141, and wait for Kimi. If they'd dated for months, he would have known her routine.

Tracy flipped to the autopsy report, which she noted had been filled out by the Klickitat County Prosecuting Attorney's Office. At present, only six counties in the state of Washington had dedicated medical examiners, sixteen had coroners, and the remaining smaller counties had an individual designated as the prosecuting attorney/coroner. Those counties usually contracted autopsies to a local pathologist because they didn't have their own dedicated facilities or staff. Tracy doubted it had been different in 1976. For those reasons, without even reading the report, she was already suspect of the findings.

The coroner's report appeared to be a copy, which made sense; the prosecuting attorney's office would have maintained the original. Tracy deduced from the poor quality of the copy that the original had been typed on onionskin paper, or something equivalent, and had been generated from microfiche. The type was so small it was hard on the eyes, especially late at night after a long weekend, but Tracy pushed on.

The external examination indicated that photographs had been taken for identification purposes and to document the condition of the body. Tracy found them in Buzz Almond's file, and they weren't pretty. She skimmed the general examination report just enough to get the basics— female, five foot seven, 125 pounds, black hair and eyes. The pathologist noted contusions, abrasions, scrapes, and cuts of various lengths and severity over much of the body, including the forearms, legs, and face. Kimi's right tibia was fractured, and her chest showed signs of blunt-force trauma. She also had bruising over much of her back and upper right shoulder. The pathologist concluded that the external injuries were "consistent with the expected impact of the body being thrown up against and dragged over boulders and rocks and submerged debris in a rushing current." The coroner also noted the aspiration of fluid into Kimi's air passages, including her lungs, which he concluded was consistent with someone being suddenly immersed in cold water. "The deceased inhaled water due to the reflex from stimulation of the skin." Kimi had also vomited and aspirated some gastric contents, also consistent with someone who "inhaled water," which he said "causes coughing and drives large volumes of air out of the lungs, leading to a disturbance of the breathing and vomiting."

Tracy flipped another page, but the report abruptly ended with the pathologist's signature just beneath his opinion.

"This woman came to her death as a result

of multiple traumas to the head, chest, and extremities."

Donald W. Frick, MD

She flipped through the remainder of the file, which included photocopies of two invoices from a company called Columbia Windshield and Glass, one stamped "Paid" in faded red ink for $68, and a second receipt for $659 from Columbia Auto Repair. Neither receipt noted what the payment was for, the name of the owner, the type of vehicle, or the license plate number. She reconsidered the photographs of Moore's truck. The windshield had a crack.

"No doubt now," she said. Roger lifted his head from the table. "Tommy Moore was suspect number one."

Running out of steam, she shut the file. "Come on, Roger, bedtime."

Roger stood and stretched. Tracy carried him to the bedroom, her mind still going over the file. Putting aside for a second the indisputable fact that a deputy sheriff was conducting an unauthorized investigation, and abiding by the adage that nothing in an investigative file was irrelevant, Tracy had to assume Buzz Almond had included everything for a reason, but she was a long way from knowing those reasons.

CHAPTER 7

Wednesday, November 10, 1976

Buzz Almond hugged and kissed his wife, Anne, at the front door. "Love you," he said.

"Love you," she said.

"Take care of my girls."

"Take care of my Buzz."

It was their routine, and Buzz knew it eased Anne's concern to hear the words. She worried each day he left for work. And with two little girls at home and a third child on the way—maybe that boy Buzz silently hoped for—Anne had every right to worry. Her parents were well-off and would take care of her and the kids if anything ever happened to him, but they both knew money was a poor substitute for a husband and a father. He hated knowing she worried like she did, and he hated leaving his girls alone at night.

Anne slid her arms around his waist just above the cumbersome belt that held his revolver, nightstick, flashlight, radio, and handcuffs. "You haven't been yourself the past few days. Is it that Indian girl?"

"Kimi Kanasket," he said.

"Such a tragedy," Anne said. "What's bothering you?"

"I don't know," he said, though he did. "Just the thought of it, I guess. A girl that young, bright future ahead of her."

"Do they know what happened yet?"

"They're waiting on the autopsy."

Anne snuggled as close as she could get with the belt between them. Her hair smelled of coconut—some new shampoo—and when he lowered his nose and nuzzled her neck, Buzz detected the familiar odor of caramel. Neither of them knew why. They'd done a smell test of Anne's creams and perfumes, and none of those had been the source. It was her natural scent, they assumed, and it was a surefire way to get Buzz's motor going. "You are as sweet as candy," he told her.

"Well, maybe when I get home this afternoon and you get off-shift, we can find a way to take your mind off of work and onto something more pleasant."

He smiled. "I'd like that. You have a magic spell to make Sophia and Maria sit still for half an hour, do you?"

"Not half an hour, but I might have a spell or two to last fifteen minutes."

He pulled back and feigned indignation. "Has it come to that already? A quarter of an hour?"

"It's not the number of minutes that counts, it's the quality. And you, Buzz Almond, make every minute special."

"Try explaining that to the guys at the station."

"I hope you don't," she said. "I'd be too embarrassed to look them in the eye again."

"You? I'd be the one they started calling Quick Draw."

She laughed and slapped his chest. "You just come home to me, Buzz."

"How could I not, with those thoughts on my mind?" He kissed her again and left her in the doorway looking prettier than the day he'd married her.

Later, on patrol, his thoughts vacillated between the anticipated rendezvous with Anne, and Earl Kanasket. He couldn't imagine the man's grief, couldn't imagine losing one of his daughters. He'd heard people say that a parent never recovers from the loss of a child, but it had been one of those sayings that had little meaning without context. Buzz had seen enough young people die during two tours in Vietnam; it was something he'd never gotten used to, and he hoped he never did. But he hadn't been a father then. He didn't know what it was like to truly love a child of your own flesh and blood. He'd never seen a parent's anguish, not until that horrible moment when he'd driven to Earl and Nettie Kanasket's home and delivered the news that their daughter was dead. Earl had been stoic, like a boxer who'd taken a solid right to the head, still on his feet but uncertain of his surroundings or circumstances. Nettie had simply melted, her legs giving way, collapsing to the floor.

Buzz wished he hadn't made that promise about finding Kimi and bringing her home. It haunted him.

His sergeant had told Buzz to give his reports to Jerry Ostertag, the detective assigned to the case, and put it behind him; his job was done. Buzz was to move on to the next call. But the more he told himself that's what he'd do, the more uncertain he felt about the way he'd left things. He couldn't put his finger on it, but something just wasn't sitting right with him. The night he'd arrived at their home, Nettie Kanasket had said Kimi would never cause them any problems, and all indications were she hadn't. Left unsaid was that it had been Élan who'd given them trouble, like setting their daughter up with Tommy Moore.

Kimi was a good student and a responsible daughter. According to the article in the *Sentinel* she'd earned a partial scholarship to UW, where she would run track. She was athletic, bright, beautiful, and, by all accounts, well-adjusted. Would she really throw herself in the river over a boy? Over Tommy Moore? Buzz supposed it possible, but he didn't think so. For one, he wasn't convinced the breakup had been mutual, as Moore insisted. People who said such things were usually protecting their egos. He thought it much more likely Moore had been the dumpee rather than the dumper.

And he couldn't ignore the damage to Moore's truck.

Buzz came out of his reverie when he drove past the Columbia Diner. He checked his rearview mirror, determined it was safe to make a U-turn, and drove back to the diner's gravel parking lot. He sat a minute, debating with himself, then shut off the engine and got out. The temperature had warmed a few degrees, though it remained cold enough to see his breath.

Buzz walked up the wooden stairs and stepped inside to the smell of deep-fried food. The whole place couldn't have been more than eight hundred square feet, with just five booths and half a dozen barstools at the Formica counter, where a lone man sat working at a piece of fried chicken with a fork and knife, and nursing a mug of coffee.

A waitress greeted Buzz from behind the counter. "Just seat yourself," she said, despite the sign that instructed customers to wait to be seated. "Be with you in a minute."

Buzz took a booth near the picture window with a view of the parking lot and the road. The waitress approached with a pot of coffee, turned over his mug, and filled it. "Get you a menu?"

"Just a cup of coffee," he said.

"You're new," she said, looking at his uniform.

"I am. Just a few months."

"Welcome." She was an attractive middle-aged woman, tall and thin, with hair pure silver and cut short as a man's, revealing hoop earrings.

Blue shadow brought out the blue of her eyes. "Where're you from?"

"Most recently? Vietnam."

"Sorry to hear that. Army?"

"Marines, by way of Orange County in Southern California."

"Orange County? Disneyland's down there, isn't it?"

"Not far. Anaheim."

"Took the kids one summer. Hotter than blazes. And the smog? I don't know how people can breathe that all day, especially kids."

"Those are two of the reasons we didn't go back."

"How many you got?"

"Two girls. One on the way."

"Good for you. Got some apple pie to go with that coffee."

"Homemade?"

"Don't insult me. I wouldn't serve it if it wasn't." She stuck out a hand. "I'm Lorraine." Her name was also on the copper name tag pinned to her uniform.

Buzz looked at the four pies in the glass case near the cash register. "I'd love a piece of apple pie, Lorraine."

Lorraine departed and returned with a thick slice and a fork. She stood waiting for Buzz to take a bite. His taste buds exploded when the apples and cinnamon hit his tongue. "Wow," he said. "I'll deny ever saying it, but this is better than my mother's."

Lorraine gave him a smile, but it had a sad quality to it. The entire diner, nearly empty, had a sad quality to it. Buzz saw no reason to hide his intent for coming in. "I was the officer who responded to the call when Kimi Kanasket went missing."

Lorraine grimaced as if stabbed in the chest, but what she said surprised Buzz. "Then you know it doesn't make any sense."

"What doesn't make any sense?"

"That Kimi would do such a thing."

"How'd she seem to you that night?"

Lorraine sat across from him, her knees angled so they were in the aisle. "She seemed fine. She seemed just fine."

"I heard her boyfriend came in."

"Tommy Moore," she said, nearly spitting his name. "Jackass brought a girl in here with him."

"What was Kimi's reaction?"

"Honestly? She seemed fine with it. I asked her if she was okay, and she said she was. She said she'd ended it. She was going to UW next year anyway. Besides, her parents didn't like Tommy." It confirmed Buzz's suspicion that Kimi had broken up with Moore.

"She ever say why not?"

"Dead-end kid going nowhere fast; they wanted better for Kimi."

"Heard her brother introduced them."

"Élan? I don't know about that."

"What's his story?"

Lorraine rolled her eyes. "Another dead-end kid. Dropped out of high school. Lives at home. Not sure he does much of anything except cause his parents grief."

"Kimi ever talk about her relationship with him?"

"Not really, but I didn't get the impression they were close."

"So Kimi didn't seem sad or angry about Tommy coming in with another girl?"

"Nope. She waited on the table, cheerful as ever. Maybe a little more cheerful. She was no dummy. She knew what Tommy was doing, and that irritated him. He got up and left without even ordering."

"Did he say anything?"

"Nope, just grabbed his date by the hand and bolted. Drove off in a huff. Back tires spitting up gravel."

"Kimi finish her shift?"

"Yep." Lorraine pointed to a phone mounted on the wall near the cash register. "She used that phone to call home and let them know she was on her way. Did it every night she worked." Lorraine picked up the napkin from beneath the table setting and blotted the tears pooling in the corners of her eyes.

"So, no indication she was upset or depressed?"

"She hugged me and said she'd see me Saturday night." She took a moment to compose herself before continuing. "I told her not to bother, not with the football game that night, not with the whole town clearing out. This place was going to be a graveyard anyway."

"She wasn't going to the big game?"

Lorraine shook her head. "No. Some of the Indians were planning a big protest about the 'Red Raiders' name."

"I heard about that."

"Kimi's father is one of the tribal elders. He didn't want Kimi too involved, since she goes to school there, which made it hard enough."

"Kimi ever indicate she received any threats or harassment because of the protests?"

"Nothing serious. She said some of the students would make an occasional derogatory comment, but she just ignored them. She was more mature than most kids her age. Kimi had her own way of protesting. When she ran cross-country and track, she covered the word 'Red' on her tank top."

"Hmm," Buzz said, thinking that pretty smart. "Let me ask you straight up, Lorraine—"

"Do I believe Kimi jumped in the river because of Tommy Moore?" She shook her head and dabbed again at her tears. "I know that's what they're saying, but I'm having a hard time believing it. She was always so levelheaded, and like I said,

Tommy coming in didn't seem to bother her none. Maybe it did. Maybe she just hid it so I wouldn't see it."

"Tommy ever pick her up after a shift and drive her home?"

"Couple times, yeah."

Buzz looked at his watch. "Thanks, Lorraine. I appreciate the conversation—and the pie. I better get going. Could I box up the rest of this so I can eat it later?"

"You'd have hurt my feelings if you hadn't asked." She stood and started for the counter, then turned back. "You don't think Kimi did it, do you? You don't think she jumped in the river?"

"I wouldn't know," Buzz said, not wanting word to get back to the detective, Jerry Ostertag, that he was conducting an investigation. "I just make the reports."

"So is anyone going to pursue this?"

"I'll let the detectives know," he said.

"Seems like somebody should."

Buzz Almond placed the Styrofoam pie box on the passenger seat. Lorraine had slid in a fresh slice of pie to go with the one he'd partially eaten. "For your wife and girls to share," she'd said.

Buzz backed from the parking lot onto 141, drove around a bend in the road, and slowed when he saw a turnout he'd missed the night he and Earl Kanasket walked the road. He pulled in and got out, keeping to the shoulder. A few steps in, he noticed an undefined dirt path partially covered by foliage, ferns, and thimbleberry and blackberry vines. He pushed the brush aside and saw where tire tracks had left the road. Some of the foliage also looked to have been freshly broken, the stems still green. He started down the path, following the ruts in the road, the frozen ground crunching beneath the soles of his boots.

A few feet in, he stopped and crouched for a closer look. The tire tread looked to have been made by oversize truck tires, the kind he associated with off-road vehicles, the kind he'd noted on Tommy Moore's truck. He also noticed something else: impressions where it looked like the heel of a shoe had struck the ground.

He stood and continued, walking along the side of the tire tracks so he didn't step on them or the shoe impressions. The shrubs and branches clawed at him, snagging the fabric of his uniform as the path narrowed and wound its way east a couple hundred yards before widening again and angling up a rise. Buzz climbed the hill, feeling the exertion in his thighs and calves and hearing his labored breathing. He continued to notice broken tree limbs and branches scattered on the ground, and shrubbery that looked to have been trampled and crushed. By the time he crested the hill, each breath marked the air in white bursts, and he needed a moment to catch his wind. In the Marines he'd have charged up and down hills like this a hundred times and not broken a sweat. Now he was huffing and puffing . . . and lasting fifteen minutes in the bedroom.

He found himself looking down on an oval-shaped clearing, an amphitheater of green and brown. It looked like something man-made, but he was certain it was natural. For one, no stumps littered the sight to indicate that it had been logged. And two, who would have bothered?

The tire treads stopped at the top of the hill, with nothing on the downhill side until the flat area at the bottom, where the ground looked like it had been torn up good. Buzz's heart started to pound with a rush of adrenaline, which had nothing to do with the exertion from climbing the hill. He turned and hurried back down the way he'd come, using his forearms to push the foliage aside where the path narrowed.

When he reached his patrol unit, he opened the passenger-side door and hit the button on the glove box. It sprang open, ejecting the Instamatic camera and the extra rolls of film.

CHAPTER 8

Tracy made two detours on her way to the Justice Center on Monday morning. First, she drove to the King County Medical Examiner's Office on Jefferson Street, in an area of Seattle referred to as Pill Hill because of the abundant number of hospitals and doctor's offices, and the blood bank. She met Kelly Rosa in the building lobby. Rosa had been the forensic anthropologist in charge of exhuming Sarah's body from its shallow hillside grave and performing an analysis of the remains. She and Tracy had known one another for several years and had become close working cases together.

"Is that it?" Rosa asked, meeting Tracy in the lobby.

Tracy handed Rosa an envelope containing a copy of the coroner's report on Kimi Kanasket, which included the photographs.

Rosa opened the package and slid out the report, holding it at arm's length. "Lord, is this some kind of eye exam? What year is this?"

"1976."

"You said it was old. Klickitat County? No medical examiner. It was likely farmed out to a local pathologist."

"That's what I figured."

Rosa took out the photographs, considering them a moment before sliding them back into the envelope. "It's going to be a while," she said. "I'm testifying in that Carnation matter, and we're pretty backed up here."

Everyone in Seattle knew what Rosa meant by "the Carnation matter." After years of legal delays, a woman and her boyfriend were on trial for the brutal murder of the woman's entire family on Christmas Eve. And while Rosa worked for the King County medical examiner, she was also available to all thirty-nine counties in Washington State.

"I understand," Tracy said. "I don't need it tomorrow."

"You said she was swept away in a river?"

"That's the scenario."

"I know a guy," Rosa said. "Worked with him once on another case where a body was found in a river. Let me take a look, and then I'll decide if we should bring him in or not."

"Sounds good," Tracy said.

"He's not bad to look at either," she said, smiling. Then the smile faded. "Maybe one of these days we'll work an easy one together."

"You wouldn't be involved if it was an easy one."

From the medical examiner's office, Tracy made her second detour, to the King County Courthouse on Third Avenue. The sheriff's

105

office was located in room W-116. Kaylee Wright, a senior crime-scene analyst—known in the profession as a "sign-cutter" or "man-tracker"— was at her desk, which was rare. Ordinarily, Wright spent much of her time out looking for bodies in remote locations, or teaching classes around the world on the science behind sign-cutting and its relevance in modern forensics. Tracy didn't have to be con-vinced. She'd witnessed Wright's work firsthand. Wright could tell not only the types of shoes the victim and perpetrators were wearing, but where each had stepped and who'd stepped there first. She could even tell from analyzing blades of grass if the person had been standing or sitting or lying on the ground.

At five eleven, Wright was one of the few women in law enforcement taller than Tracy, and she maintained the build that had made her a college volleyball player. When she and Tracy worked cases together, like the shooting of a Russian drug dealer in Laurelhurst several years back, they were referred to as "Salt and Pepper" because of Tracy's light complexion and blonde hair and Wright's darker complexion and black hair.

Tracy handed her the envelope. "These are the originals. The negatives are in the front of each pack."

"I'll keep them safe," Wright said, opening

one of the envelopes and flipping through a few of the photos. "1976. I was two then."

"So was I," Tracy said.

"They look like good shots, given what the photographer was working with back then. I'm guessing from the quality and the date stamp that whoever took these used an Instamatic of some sort. You sure you don't want to give me a hint about what I'm looking at?"

Tracy wanted Kelly Rosa's and Kaylee Wright's analyses to be completely independent and not influenced by anything Tracy told them, though admittedly she didn't know much at this point.

"I'm not certain what's depicted or why," Tracy said. "I'm hoping you can tell me."

Wright slid the pack of photographs back into the envelope. "All right. I like a challenge. How soon do you need it? I'm leaving for a conference in Germany tomorrow."

"Must be rough," Tracy said. "Berlin?"

"Hamburg. It's not as glamorous as it sounds—meetings and panels every day. I intend to sample several German beers."

"Barry going with you?"

"Did I mention there will be German beer?"

"So it's working out?"

"We'll find out. They say it's a good test if you can stand each other while traveling in a foreign country. How are you and Dan getting along?"

"So far, so good." Tracy checked her watch. "I better get in. Kins and I pulled that murder in Greenwood, and he carried the burden while I was away this weekend. Enjoy Germany. Hoist a beer or two for me."

The city had recently begun calling the Justice Center building "Police Headquarters." "Justice Center" apparently now referred to the adjacent building on Fifth Avenue that housed King County's municipal court. To Tracy and the veterans, though, the SPD building would always be the Justice Center. Whatever the name, one thing that hadn't changed was the volume of Vic Fazzio's gravelly voice and New Jersey accent when Tracy stepped off the elevator onto the seventh floor. She heard Faz well before she entered the A Team's square-shaped bull pen.

"You got a hot date, Sparrow?" Faz was saying. He liked to use the nickname bestowed on Kins when he'd worked undercover narcotics and he had grown out his hair and a wispy goatee like the Johnny Depp character in the *Pirates of the Caribbean* movies.

"You're wearing enough aftershave, you could become an honorary Italian," Del said.

"I'd have to put on a hundred pounds to join 'your' club," Kins said.

"Like I'd be in a club that would have Fazzio," Del said.

Faz and Del looked to have been plucked straight from central casting as bodyguards in a mafia movie like *The Godfather*. At the moment, they sat at their cubicles but with their chairs swiveled to face Kins, who was at his desk across the center workstation.

"Hey, Professor, check out our boy Joe Friday," Faz said when Tracy entered the bull pen, referring to the suit-wearing detective from the TV series *Dragnet*.

Kins stood up from his chair holding his coffee mug. "If I had known wearing a suit was going to make the news, I would have dressed like a bum like you two." Kins nodded to Tracy to follow him. "Brother of Tim Collins called. Wants to talk. I got a lot to fill you in on."

Tracy turned to follow.

"Hey, Professor," Faz called out. "I got a gas mask you could borrow for the elevator ride."

Kins brought Tracy up to date on what had transpired over the weekend, including Angela Collins and Atticus Berkshire coming in and giving a statement. Tracy was as surprised as Kins that Berkshire had allowed it.

"There must be a reason," she said. "Berkshire doesn't do anything unless it helps his client or stirs the pot."

Mark Collins lived in an upper-class section of Madrona, a neighborhood fifteen minutes east of downtown Seattle that extended from the top of the hill to the shores of Lake Washington. Collins's stately Georgian-style red brick home was likely worth a couple million dollars in the current hot market. He answered the door in khakis and a button-down. He looked like his younger brother, though taller and thinner, and while his brother was blond, Mark had red hair.

"Thanks for coming," he said, sounding and looking grim. He led them into a den with an impressive flat-screen TV that nearly took up an entire wall. "Can I offer you anything to drink? Coffee? Water?"

"We're good," Kins said. "Our condolences to you and your family."

Kins and Faz had spoken to the other members of Tim Collins's family the night he was shot and the following day, but Mark had been traveling. Kins got the impression that, as the oldest, Mark was the patriarch, and the others were waiting for his guidance.

Mark Collins nodded. "I heard her father is arguing self-defense."

"That appears likely," Kins said.

Collins shook his head. "If anyone needed some self-defense, it was Timmy."

Other members of the family had made similar statements. "How so?" Kins asked. He'd made the contact. Tracy sat taking notes.

"Angela is incredibly manipulative when she

wants something. Over the years she wore Timmy down. She wore us all down."

"How'd she do that?"

"She picked fights with each of us until none of us could stand being around her. One time, she'd start something with me; at another, it'd be my sister or my wife or my brother-in-law. Pretty soon, Timmy would say he couldn't come for Sunday dinners because Angela didn't feel comfortable. What we didn't realize is she had done the same thing with all his friends. It was her way of isolating him."

"For what purpose?"

"To manipulate him, get him to do what she wanted. Tim became very codependent."

"Can you give me an example?"

Collins didn't hesitate. He'd either thought about this, or he'd told others what he was about to tell them. "Tim made a good living, Detectives. He was an engineer at Boeing, but he nearly had to file for bankruptcy because of Angela's spending. Either he bought her a new car or a boat, or the house she wanted, or the vacation they couldn't afford, or she'd divorce him. Tim wouldn't say no."

"But she filed for divorce anyway?" Tracy said.

"And we were happy she did. We'd been working on Tim to leave her for years, but he wouldn't because of Connor. Have you met him?"

"Briefly," Kins said.

"So you know the kid is a bit fragile. Anyway, we finally got Tim to understand that the relationship wasn't healthy. But he made the mistake of telling Angela he intended to file for divorce, and the next afternoon she served him with papers, including all the bullshit allegations."

"Do you think she'd already consulted a lawyer, or was this done totally in reaction to your brother telling her he wanted a divorce?" Tracy asked.

"Definitely the latter. She was angry, and when Angela gets angry, she gets vindictive. Once Tim wanted a divorce and she realized she couldn't use him anymore, she was hell-bent on destroying him."

Mark picked up a sheet of paper from the coffee table and handed it to Kins. "Those are people who can confirm what I'm telling you—relatives and friends of Timmy's."

Kins took a moment to scan the multiple names and phone numbers before handing it to Tracy. "Did your brother ever mention any physical altercations with Angela?" he asked.

"Complete bullshit," Mark said, anger creeping into his tone. "Total, complete bullshit. Timmy never laid a hand on her and never would. He also never cheated on her. I told his attorney to ask for names. Of course Angela couldn't produce any. The first time she accused him of abuse was after they'd separated. Timmy went to the house to pick up Connor, and Angela confronted him, angry that he wasn't giving her enough money, even though he was complying with the court order. Tim tried to get out the door, and Angela blocked his path. He nudged her as he stepped past. Next thing he knows, the police are at his apartment and take him away in handcuffs. Angela claimed he shoved her into the door and over a table." Collins leaned forward as if to make a point. "And here's the scariest part about Angela—she went to the hospital to be treated for bruises."

Kins glanced at Tracy to gauge her reaction, but she remained poker-faced. "How do you think she got the injuries?" he asked.

Collins shook his head again. "Self-inflicted. I know it sounds crazy, but she had to have done it to herself."

"Why?"

"To set Timmy up. She staged the whole thing. I had to get Timmy a criminal defense lawyer. When the attorney started pressing for additional facts, Angela didn't pursue it. She couldn't."

"Why not?"

"Because she had no facts. It didn't happen the way she said. Besides, she needed Tim to continue working so she could get the spousal support. It was just her way of letting Tim know she still had control over him, and that she would do anything to destroy him if he crossed her."

"You say she isolated your brother from you and the rest of the family."

"That's right."

"So you didn't spend much time around them."

Mark Collins cleared his throat. "No. But I know my brother, and I know he wouldn't hit her or cheat on her. When she filed the divorce papers, he was really upset about the allegations. He was trying to keep things civil for Connor, but that wasn't going to happen."

"Connor signed an affidavit that his father pushed his mother."

Mark shrugged. "Did he? I'd bet that was Angela who signed Connor's name. She's done things like that before. She'd get Connor's cell phone and send Tim these horrible e-mails and texts, to make it look like they were coming from Connor. And even if Connor did sign the affidavit, what else could he do? He had to live with her, and he's afraid of her. Angela has isolated him also. Have you met him? The kid is seventeen, and I swear he can't boil water, never goes out with friends, never had a job or made his own money, and doesn't have a girlfriend. He's totally dependent on her."

"What does he do?"

"Far as anyone knows, goes to school and goes home to his room to play video games."

"What do you think happened to your brother?" Kins asked. "Why was he at the house that night?"

"He went to pick up Connor. He had him for the weekend starting Thursday night. I don't know why he went inside. But I'll bet Angela had something to do with it."

"What was his relationship like with his son after his son's affidavit?"

"Tim knew Connor loved him, and he knew what Angela was capable of. If anything, the affidavit only confirmed that he had to find a way to protect Connor from her." Collins picked up a multipage document from the table and handed it to Tracy and Kins. "Timmy was in the process of redoing his will to leave everything in a trust for Connor, and he named me as the trustee. It wasn't a fortune, not the way Angela spent money, but it wasn't inconsiderable when you factor in Timmy's share of the Greenwood house, a rental unit he bought before they married, and his Boeing 401k and life insurance, as well as what he stood to inherit."

"You think she killed your brother for the money?"

"Since the divorce isn't final and the new will isn't executed, she gets everything as the surviving widow and has full control over his assets. How crazy is that? They were separated. They were getting divorced, she professed all kinds of vile things about Tim, but now she gets *all* the money as his widow? Why is there no law against that?"

"I don't know," Kins said.

"I have Tim's iPad. I went to the apartment and took it. I don't care if I wasn't supposed to. Timmy had an appointment scheduled with his attorney for the Saturday after Angela shot him. I'm betting that meeting was to finalize his new will and the trust, and that's why Angela shot him on Thursday night."

"How would she have known your brother was redoing his will?" Tracy asked.

"Or about the appointment?" Kins said.

"Connor," Mark Collins said softly. He motioned to the papers on the coffee table. "I found much of this right out in the open on my brother's desk."

"You're saying Connor saw it and told his mother?"

"No," Mark said. "Knowing Angela, she probably had Connor deliberately snooping for her."

"Mr. Collins," Tracy said, "what if I told you I have a suspicion that Angela confessed because she's protecting Connor, that I think it might have been Connor who shot your brother?"

"Is there any evidence of that?"

"Nothing specific."

Mark Collins seemed to give it some consideration. "Angela convincing Connor to commit the crime—yeah, I can see that," he said. "But confessing? No. I've never known Angela to do anything that didn't immediately benefit her. So if that turns out to be the case, you can be damn sure there was something in it for her."

Kins looked to Tracy. She shook her head to indicate that she had no further questions. They stood. "Thank you, Mr. Collins," Kins said. "We'll keep you advised on our investigation."

"Why isn't she in jail?" Collins asked. "Why isn't she in jail if she admitted she shot him?"

"The judge didn't deem her a flight risk," Kins said, "and she has no prior criminal record. She's out on bail. That doesn't mean she's out of the woods. It's not uncommon for the prosecutor to wait until all the evidence is gathered to charge someone."

"But you indicated she came in and reconfirmed what happened."

"She did," Kins said. "But we have reason to doubt she's telling us the truth."

Collins exhaled, clearly exasperated. "It wouldn't be the first time she's lied. Far from it."

"Sometimes these things take time, Mr. Collins," Tracy said, "but in the end, the system usually delivers justice."

Mark Collins looked somber. "Maybe so, Detectives, but the judicial system doesn't ordinarily deal with the likes of Angela."

CHAPTER 9

Kins dropped Tracy back at the Justice Center, telling her he had an appointment to talk with his son Eric's high school counselor. Tracy set her purse in her cubicle, scanned the documents Mark Collins had provided, then e-mailed them to Cerrabone with a note for him to call her.

She'd no sooner hit "Send" when Faz materialized. "You have lunch plans?" he asked.

"No," she said, sensing that he was interested in cashing in on his free lunch. "What did you have in mind, Faz?"

"I took the liberty of booking us a reservation at Tulio," he said. "Best clams in the city."

"Very considerate of you. My Visa card thanks you. It has cobwebs on it, but I can use the air miles."

"Wait till you get the bill," Del said, pushing back his chair. "You'll have enough miles for a trip to Europe."

Tulio was within walking distance, north on Fifth Avenue. The nice weather was holding, midfifties with clear skies. As they walked, Tracy filled Faz in on the interview with Mark Collins.

"So what did you think?" Faz asked.

"I think he sounded like someone trying to

protect his brother. I've never bought the 'she threw herself down a staircase' theory."

Faz held the door for her, and they stepped inside. The dining area consisted of half a dozen tables draped with white cloths, and booths along the walls. The kitchen was at the back, and diners could watch the two chefs at work.

"I can taste the clams already," Faz said.

"While you salivate, I'm going to wash my hands." Tracy spotted the sign for the restrooms and started for the back of the restaurant.

Halfway there, she thought she heard a familiar voice and glanced to her left, into the dining area. Kins sat in a booth near a window, leaning forward, engaged in conversation. Opposite him sat Amanda Santos, the FBI profiler who'd worked the Cowboy investigation, and a dead ringer for Halle Berry.

Del was waiting when Tracy and Faz returned. "All right, Fazio, get it over with. Tell me how the clams were the best you've ever had."

"Garlic and onions, a little salt and pepper." Faz kissed his fingers and let them bloom. "Magnifico."

It was a worthy performance. Maybe Faz could have been in the movies. He didn't have the clams. They didn't eat at Tulio. Tracy had done a one-eighty when she'd spotted Kins and returned quickly to the front of the restaurant. She'd had no idea what excuse she'd use to convince Faz they had to leave, so she was glad when she didn't need one.

"I saw him," Faz had said, already opening the door for her and stepping outside. "I figured something was up. I've heard him on the phone a couple times keeping his voice low. Then the suit. Who wears a suit anymore if you don't have to?"

"I knew things weren't great at home," Tracy said, now wondering if Santos was the reason she'd beaten Kins to the Collins crime scene. "But he said he and Shannah were working things through."

"Hey, we don't know he's done anything."

"No," she said. "But he lied and said he was meeting his son's high school counselor."

"Not our place to judge," Faz said. "Nobody knows what goes on between a man and a woman in the privacy of their own home."

"Agreed, but I'm not his wife. I'm his partner."

When Tracy made Homicide, her first partner quit, not willing to work with a woman. The second asked to be reassigned when his wife complained. Kins had readily accepted her, and for the eight years they had worked together, they'd agreed to a policy of total honesty.

Back at her desk, still upset, Tracy busied herself going through the Collins file and trying to catch up on all the reports. The neighbors said they all knew the couple had separated, though they didn't know the reason. No one had ever heard or seen anything to confirm Angela Collins's accusation of physical or emotional cruelty.

Nearly two hours later, Tracy turned from her computer when Kins returned. She watched him hang his coat on a hanger and hook it to the top of his cubicle.

"How was the meeting?" she asked, drawing a glance from Faz.

Kins shrugged. "You know, same BS. Took a bit long, but Eric's doing better. He's got his algebra grade back up to a B."

"That's got to be a relief."

"Yeah. Yeah, it is. You got that list of names from the brother? I'll start making calls."

Tracy handed Kins the list without further comment, and he went to work. So did Tracy. She made good progress talking to Tim Collins's friends and other relatives. Each confirmed, to varying degrees, what Mark Collins had told them—that Angela isolated Tim, seemed to pick unnecessary fights, and could be particularly "difficult" when she didn't get her way. That, however, was a double-edged sword, since it also confirmed the couple's relationship could be volatile.

The emergency room doctor had also returned Kins's call, and Kins relayed the substance of their conversation. The doctor didn't specifically remember Angela Collins, but he'd pulled her chart, which confirmed that Angela had minor bruising along the right side of her torso and near her ribs. Angela had told the doctor that her estranged husband had shoved her into the door frame and she fell over a table, but X-rays didn't reveal any fractures. He'd sent her home and told her to take an anti-inflammatory for the pain. He said he'd never questioned whether or not Angela was telling the truth about how she'd been injured, or if her injuries were consistent with her explanation.

Early evening, Kins grabbed his suit coat, draping it over his shoulder. "I'm going to hit it. Will has a soccer game."

"You don't want to miss that," Tracy said.

"Shannah will have my head."

"Before you go, there's something I need to talk with you about," Tracy said. "My friend, Jenny Almond—"

"The one who became sheriff?"

"Right. She's asked me to take a look at a 1976 case her father worked."

"Cold case?"

"Not exactly. The facts are complicated. I don't want to keep you from the soccer game. Just wanted you to know I'm going to ask Nolasco to let me work it, and I wanted to make sure you're all right with it."

"You want my help?"

She shook her head. "Nolasco would never allow both of us to work it. He may not even allow me to."

"He's been pretty quiet around here with OPA on his ass," Kins said. "You want to do it, go for it. Collins isn't going anywhere fast, and Faz is itching to stay involved."

"I just didn't want you to think I was doing something behind your back."

"No worries," Kins said, departing.

"Subtle," Tracy said to herself. "Real subtle."

She checked the time on her computer. She'd put off talking to Nolasco about Kimi Kanasket until the end of the shift, because a day not dealing with Nolasco was always better than a day dealing with him. Time, however, had run out. She walked along the outer glass wall to Nolasco's office, thinking, again, that the man would have a killer view of downtown Seattle and Elliott Bay if he ever opened his blinds. He didn't.

Nolasco sat at his desk, head down. Tracy knocked on the open door. "Captain?"

Nolasco looked annoyed. He always looked annoyed. "Yeah."

"Got a minute?"

Nolasco very deliberately set down paperwork on one of many piles on his desk and motioned to one of two empty chairs. Tracy entered and sat. She could see files on the carpet behind Nolasco's desk and pieced it together. Nolasco had his old case files pulled and was going through them, likely preparing for OPA's inquiry of possible improprieties in those investigations, an inquiry he no doubt blamed on Tracy. They said timing in life was everything, and Tracy couldn't have picked a worse time to want something.

"What is it?" Nolasco asked.

"Wanted to run a case by you."

"Angela Collins?"

"No. A cold case down in Klickitat County."

His eyebrows knitted together. "What's that got to do with us?"

She explained the circumstances, leaving out Jenny Almond's name, with whom Nolasco also had a history from their days at the police academy.

"We got somewhere in the neighborhood of two hundred fifty open and unsolved cases in the cold unit," he said. "You couldn't pick one of those?"

"The sheriff wants an outside inquiry to avoid any appearance of impropriety, and because there's some indication that if things aren't as they seem, it could implicate members of the community, including law enforcement."

"Any potential DNA for analysis?" Nolasco asked, focusing on the single most important factor in deciding whether to reopen an old case. Advances in DNA analysis and other technology made it now possible to solve cold cases detectives never could have solved with technology available at the time of the crime. But in the case of Kimi Kanasket, there was no DNA.

Tracy didn't lie. "No."

"And your witness pool has aged forty years. How many are even still alive?"

"I'm working on that."

"What about Angela Collins?"

"Faz and Del are looking for something to do," she said. "That kid pled in the drive-by they were working. Faz testified at the sentencing today."

"Faz and Del have their own files."

"Faz is looking to work a homicide."

Nolasco sat back. "What about Kins?"

"I'd work this one alone. Kins is taking the lead on Collins."

Nolasco rocked backward in his chair. "If I say no, then what? You going to take it to Clarridge?"

Sandy Clarridge had been police chief both times that Tracy received the department's Medal of Valor. In both instances she'd made Clarridge look good at a time when he and the department had been under scrutiny. She didn't want to play that card. It would only make her life with Nolasco more miserable.

"I think the upside could look good for the

department," she said, subtly answering Nolasco's question without directly challenging his authority or bruising his already fragile ego.

"Sounds like a hobby to me," he said. "You want to use some of your personal days, go ahead. Otherwise, we got enough here to keep us all busy."

What Nolasco failed to consider was all the overtime Tracy had accumulated working the Cowboy investigation. She'd built up a boatload of personal days that she'd lose if she didn't use them by the end of the year. With Dan in Los Angeles and Kins on a path to becoming a full-blown member of the idiot club, Tracy was happy to use those personal days to get out of the office.

She grabbed her coat and purse and started from her cubicle, intending to call Jenny on the drive home, but stopped when her desk phone rang. The small window on the console indicated an inside line. She hoped it wasn't Nolasco calling to rescind his backhanded consent, just screwing with her, which used to be his full-time hobby.

"Detective Crosswhite," the duty officer at the desk in the building lobby said. "I got somebody here says he needs to speak to you or Detective Rowe."

"I don't have anybody scheduled to meet with

me. I'm not sure about Kins. He's gone for the day."

"He doesn't have an appointment, but he says it's urgent."

"Who is it? What's his name?"

"Connor Collins."

CHAPTER 10

The officer behind the bulletproof partition nodded in the direction of Connor Collins. The young man stood in the lobby looking very much like a high school kid on his way home from school, a ball cap propped backward on his head, backpack dangling from his shoulder, skateboard tucked under his arm.

"I have something to tell you," he said as Tracy approached.

Tracy raised a hand, stopping him. "I can't speak to you. You're represented by an attorney."

She'd contemplated not even coming down the elevator, telling the officer to send Connor away. She'd tried calling Cerrabone, but he wasn't picking up his office phone, and his cell phone went straight to voice mail. The receptionist said he'd left for the day. She'd also tried Kins, but he also didn't answer. She immediately wondered if he was with Santos.

Connor shifted on the balls of his feet. "I don't have an attorney. I never did. My grandfather just said that."

"It doesn't matter," she said. "You're seventeen."

"I turned eighteen yesterday." He reached for his back pocket. "You can check my driver's license. So I'm an adult, right? I can decide for myself. I wanted to talk to you about what happened that night, when my dad came to the house."

Connor was holding out his license like an underage kid with a fake ID hoping to buy beer. He wore blue jeans and a black hooded sweatshirt with a gothic design—wings of some sort. Tracy studied his pupils and the whites of his eyes. He didn't appear to be under the influence of any drug. She didn't smell pot, just the faint scent of teenage body odor.

"Let's go upstairs. I don't want you to say anything to me until I say you can speak. Understood?"

Connor nodded.

They rode the elevator in silence to the seventh floor. Tracy deposited Connor in one of the hard interrogation rooms, then went into the adjacent room and turned on the video recorder. She returned to her cubicle and tried Cerrabone and Kins again, without success. She walked to the back of the floor, where the administrative staff sat, and found Ron Mayweather, the A Team's "fifth wheel," still at his desk. The fifth wheel was a detective assigned to assist one of the Violent Crimes Section's four units.

"You have time to sit in on an interview with me?" she asked. "Something unexpected in the Collins case."

"Yeah, no problem," Mayweather said, rising from his chair.

When they entered the interrogation room, Connor sat up straight. He'd propped his skateboard against the wall and put his backpack on the floor beside it. He didn't stand when Tracy introduced Mayweather, nor did he offer his hand. He just gave a nearly imperceptible nod and a soft "Hey."

Tracy and Mayweather took the two seats across the small metal table. "I'm videotaping and recording everything being said," Tracy said. "You understand that?"

Connor nodded.

"You have to answer out loud," Tracy said.

"Oh. Yes," he said.

"You can sit back. Relax."

Connor sat back. After getting him to state his name, address, and date of birth, Tracy introduced herself and Ron Mayweather, gave the date and time, and briefly summarized the situation. Then she said, "Let's back up and start over, Connor. You came to the police department this afternoon, correct?"

"Yes."

"How did you get here?"

"I took the bus and rode my skateboard."

"No one came with you?"

"No."

"You said you do not have an attorney representing you?"

"No. I mean, right. I said that. I don't."

"Your grandfather, Atticus Berkshire, is not your attorney?"

"No. He's not my attorney. He's my mom's attorney."

"Does he know you're here?"

"No."

"Does your mom know you're here?"

"No."

"Why didn't you tell them you were coming here?"

"They would have tried to stop me. But I'm eighteen. I'm an adult. So I can do this."

He dug a hand into the front pocket of his jeans. "Here's my license again. In case you don't believe me. My birthday was yesterday."

"Happy birthday," Mayweather said.

Connor glanced at Mayweather, looking uncertain.

"You've handed me your driver's license." Tracy took a moment to consider it before handing it to Mayweather. "It confirms that you turned eighteen yesterday. And you're here of your own volition? No one forced you or coerced you to come here?"

"I came because I wanted to."

"Okay. When we met in the lobby, you said you had something you wanted to tell me. Is that correct?"

"Yes."

Tracy looked to Mayweather, who nodded his

131

consent. "Okay, Connor. What do you want to tell me?"

Connor sat up and glanced at the camera again. "Okay. Well, what I wanted to tell you was that my mother . . . she didn't shoot my father."

"She didn't?"

"No," he said, shaking his head. "I did."

"Stop talking."

Tracy played the video. Rick Cerrabone stood with one hand covering his mouth. Kins sat near the one-way glass, largely ignoring the video and watching Connor Collins, who remained in the hard interrogation room.

After Connor's confession, Tracy and Mayweather had stepped out of the room to discuss the situation. Both agreed that Tracy had followed established protocol but that Connor's confession now mandated that he be read his Miranda rights. After Tracy did so, Connor described again how his father had come to pick him up and forced his way into the house. He confirmed that his father and mother had quarreled, and further confirmed Angela Collins's statement that his father had picked up the sculpture and used it to hit his mother, knocking her to the ground. He said his father then kicked her in the stomach.

From that point, however, his and his mother's stories diverged. Whereas Angela Collins said she sent her son out of the room, Connor said he intervened and his father slapped him hard across the face. Connor said the distraction, however, had allowed his mother enough time to get to her feet and run down the hall, locking herself in the bedroom. His father followed her and was threatening to kick in the door, and that's when Connor remembered the gun in the closet. He said he got the gun and went down the hall, but by then his father was in the room with his mother, threatening to hit her. Connor pulled the trigger, shooting his father in the back.

"What did you do with the gun after you shot your father?" Tracy asked.

"I put it on the bed," Connor replied.

"Then what did you do?"

"Nothing. My mother was pretty hysterical. She said we needed to call my grandfather. She told me to go into the living room and sit on the couch."

"Did you do that?"

"Yes."

"Did you touch your father?"

"Touch him? No."

"Did you touch the sculpture?"

"No."

"How long was it from the time you shot your father until the time your mother called your grandfather?"

"I don't know."

"Who called 911?"

"She did."

Tracy shut off the video, and the room was silent for several moments.

"I thought he was going to tell me what Angela told you and Faz," she said to Kins. "I figured he'd back up her story and say it was self-defense."

Cerrabone lowered his hand. "Where's Mayweather now?"

"Typing out a statement for Connor to sign," Tracy said. She turned to Kins. "This could explain the twenty-one-minute gap between when the neighbor heard the shots and when Angela Collins called 911. She was cleaning up after the kid's mess."

"Or the kid's lying, and they were covering up her mess," Kins said, standing from his chair and turning away from the window. "The brother said Angela's a master manipulator and that she's been working the kid for years. She could have put him up to it."

"Up to what?" Tracy said.

"Taking the blame."

"For murdering his own father?" Tracy shook her head, not buying it. "What kind of person would do that? What kind of mother would do that?"

"A very, very sick one," Kins said.

"They each have a motive to lie," Cerrabone said. "That's the problem. Both their fingerprints are on the gun. They're also the same height, so the trajectory of the bullet won't tell us anything. They each have a story that fits with the evidence."

"Not all the evidence," Kins said. "There's still the problem of the lack of fingerprints on the sculpture, and the kid's prints on his father's shoe, which doesn't fit with either story." He looked to Cerrabone. "Can we charge them both and see if one of them blinks?"

"Not with what we currently have. Not without risking having the charges against both of them dismissed." Cerrabone massaged the back of his neck, a habit when he got frustrated. "Besides, Berkshire would see through it and use one against the other to raise reasonable doubt as to both. This seems calculated to me."

"Could be the reason Berkshire let Angela tell us her story," Kins said. "So we'd have two competing stories and not be able to prove which one is the truth."

Tracy pressed her temples, feeling the beginning twinge of a headache. "Berkshire's a scumbag, but that's his daughter and his grandson."

"I know, but if it's the only way to get his daughter off . . ." Kins said, letting the thought linger.

Cerrabone leaned against the edge of the table. "This was already going to be a difficult case with the domestic violence allegation. Now . . ."

He let out a breath and shook his head. "I'm not sure where it leaves us."

"This is why we should have GSR kits at every homicide," Kins said, referring to gunshot-residue kits. Detectives could use them to take swabs of a person's hand to detect primer and gunpowder residue. SPD didn't use the kits because they weren't conclusive. They could prove only that a person had been near a discharged weapon, not that he necessarily fired it.

"But we don't," Cerrabone said. "And it's too late now."

"He's declined an attorney," Kins said. "Why not go back in and confront him with the discrepancies in the evidence."

"If we do and this is a ruse, we'd be educating him and his mother and Berkshire," Tracy said. "That just gives them time to come up with something to explain the discrepancies. I say we keep that to ourselves for now."

"Couple other problems," Cerrabone said. "One, he might technically be an adult, but he looks fourteen. Berkshire, or whoever they get to defend him, will say he was scared and intimidated, and a jury will buy it. Two, unless they both recant and tell the same story, we have reasonable doubt up the wazoo, whoever we charge. Berkshire would, without a doubt, refuse to waive a speedy trial, and we could lose any chance of ever convicting either of them. I'm going to talk this over with Dunleavy," he said, referring to the King County prosecutor, Kevin Dunleavy. "I'm going to recommend that we let them both go for now. Meanwhile, we'll continue to work this and see if something shakes free. It always does."

"Yeah, but in the interim, this isn't going to play well in the media, especially if the brother raises hell," Kins said.

"So talk to him," Cerrabone said. "Explain the situation. Tell him we're not giving up, but we need time to work the evidence."

Tracy and Kins looked through the one-way glass. Connor Collins sat with his legs extended, head tilted back. Their would-be grounder had not just taken a bad hop; it had become a fly ball into the sun, against a bright-blue sky, and neither Tracy nor Kins were wearing sunglasses.

CHAPTER 11

The following morning, Tracy and Kins called Cerrabone, who'd spent a late night talking with Dunleavy. He had agreed with Cerrabone's assessment not to charge either Angela or Connor Collins, but to wait until they'd developed more evidence.

"And nothing yet from Berkshire?" Kins asked, still puzzled by Berkshire's silence.

"Not a word," Cerrabone said.

They all had expected the Berkshire they knew to be raising holy hell that they'd taken a statement from Connor without an attorney present. "Could be further evidence he's orchestrating all of this," Kins said.

"You get a hold of Mark Collins?" Cerrabone asked.

"Faz and I are heading out that way now," Kins said.

With a seeming stall in the Collins case and Kins and Faz working the evidence, Tracy turned her attention to Kimi Kanasket. She ran the names Earl and Élan Kanasket through Accurint, a database that provided access to public records, which meant it provided last known addresses. Going back forty years, Tracy suspected she was testing the limits of the system, but she was relieved to find a matching address in Yakima for both men. A quick Google search confirmed the address was on the Yakama Reservation. On a hunch, she also ran Tommy Moore's name through the same database and determined that Moore also lived on the reservation.

Next, she ran all three men through a Triple I criminal background check. Moore had been arrested in 1978, 1979, and 1981, each time for drunk and disorderly conduct. On one of those occasions, he'd also been charged with assault and battery. In 1981 he'd been charged with breaking and entering, and in 1982 he'd spent time in jail for possession of a controlled substance. After that, his record was clear. The lack of any further arrests was ordinarily a strong indication the criminal had died, but the recent utility records said otherwise. Tracy wondered if Moore was one of the lucky few who had managed to somehow turn his life around.

Neither Élan nor Earl Kanasket had criminal records.

Tracy also ran the men's names through the Department of Licensing database and obtained current and available prior driver's licenses. DOL's policy was to purge older license photos, but Tracy had found she could often go back three to four license cycles—ten to twelve years. She needed the current photos for herself. She would need the older photos if she tried to refresh someone's recollection about any of the three men. It helped to have a photo as close in appearance to the time of the event being discussed, like Kimi Kanasket's senior photo. That thought made her scribble a note to also go to the Stoneridge Library to browse through high school yearbooks and old newspapers from that period to get a pulse of the school Kimi attended and of Stoneridge during that time.

When she'd finished, Tracy called Jenny and told her she would be coming back to Stoneridge.

"Your captain approved you working the case?"

Jenny knew of Tracy's relationship with Nolasco, since she'd been at the Academy when Tracy kneed him in the groin and broke his nose after he'd groped them both during an arrest scenario. "Not exactly. I'm using some personal time."

"I hate to see you do that," Jenny said. "I could make some calls."

"Don't worry about it. I lose the time if I don't use it by the end of the year." She told Jenny what she intended to do and said she'd call her when she'd checked into a hotel.

"No sense doing that," Jenny said, "especially if you're the one footing the bill. You can stay at my mom's. We sent her off on the cruise today with her sister. You'd have the whole house to yourself."

Tracy thought about the beautiful home on the expansive lawn. "You sure it's no trouble?"

"Absolutely. My mother will be thrilled to know someone is staying there. By the way, you were on my list of people to call today. Turns out the forty-year reunion for the class of 1977 is in a few weeks, and they're planning all kinds of events. I'm anticipating there will be a lot of people coming back to town who remember those days."

"Good to know."

"I can help line up interviews if you like."

"Thanks, but I'm not there yet. And I like to surprise people."

Tracy arrived at the Almond farmhouse just before sunset. She parked behind Jenny's black-and-white SUV with the bar of lights across the roof and the six-point gold star emblazoned on the doors. When she stepped from her truck cab, Tracy noticed a drastic change in the temperature from when she'd left her home in West Seattle. Her truck didn't have a temperature gauge, but she guessed from the goose bumps on her arms and the shivers running down her spine that the temperature had dropped close to freezing.

The twilight sky, a deepening blue, made it look as if an artist had brushed uneven strokes of magenta along the contours of the rolling hills surrounding the property. Shadows crept across the lawn and draped the fruit trees in gray light. Tracy turned at the sound of the front door opening, with Jenny momentarily obscured behind the screen. She pushed it open and stepped out, hesitated, and reached back inside. Lights illuminated the porch, stairs, and yard.

"I was just appreciating how peaceful it is out here," Tracy said as Jenny descended the porch steps.

"A lot quieter when you don't have seven kids running around the lawn," Jenny said. "But that's how I remember growing up. Utter chaos, kids running all over the yard screaming. We had a lot of fun when Dad moved us here."

"Thanks again for letting me stay."

"I talked to Mom today. She said to tell you to make yourself at home." Jenny shivered and rubbed her arms. "Come on. I'll show you around and get you set up."

Tracy retrieved her suitcase from the cab and followed Jenny inside.

Jenny picked up several newspapers from an entry table beneath an ornate mirror. "Here are some articles about the reunion weekend."

Tracy flipped open the *Goldendale Enterprise* and found an article on the fortieth-anniversary celebration of the Stoneridge High School state football championship to be held in conjunction with the class of 1977 reunion. A boxed sidebar listed the weekend festivities, including a charity golf tournament and a Saturday morning parade through downtown to honor the members of the football team. The dedication of the school athletic complex to Stoneridge's legendary coach, Ron Reynolds, would take place that night at halftime of the homecoming game against rival Columbia Central.

"I'll show you the rest of the house," Jenny said.

The kitchen had marble countertops and state-of-the-art appliances. Jenny pulled open the refrigerator, which looked a lot like Tracy's, mostly condiments. "Eat whatever you want, but check the expiration dates. Mom never adjusted to Dad's loss of appetite. We've thrown out a lot of perishables and cartons of milk the last six months. I also recalled your not-so-healthy eating habits and took the liberty of bringing over a couple Tupperware containers of leftovers. Nothing fancy. Lasagna and some chicken."

Jenny led Tracy upstairs to the last room at the end of the hall and flipped on the light, revealing a canopy bed, a large dresser, an antique white vanity, and a love seat angled to see out the window. Tracy set her suitcase at the foot of the bed and joined Jenny at the window.

"Beautiful," she said. The window looked out over the property to the rolling hills. The brush strokes of magenta had merged to a single thin line on the horizon as twilight faded and night encroached. "It reminds me of the view out my bedroom window when I was a kid."

"This was my room," Jenny said. "Maria and Sophia shared the other room. It was a bit of a sore spot that I got my own room, but only when they wanted to use it as leverage to bargain with my parents. They were closer in age and liked sharing a room."

"It's perfect. Thank you."

They went back downstairs, to the dining room. "Where will you start?" Jenny asked.

"Earl Kanasket," she said. "I owe him the courtesy."

"You found him?"

"Hopefully. Last known address is on the reservation," Tracy said. "Appears to live with the son, Élan. Records also indicate Tommy Moore lives out there. If so, I'll pay him a visit as well."

"Give yourself a couple hours to get there," Jenny said. "And let me know if you need anything. I can give you a tour of the town and introduce you to the Stoneridge chief of police." Some small towns contracted with the local sheriff's office, but some, like Stoneridge, also kept their own force. "I gave him a courtesy call and let him know you'd be in town. He has no jurisdiction, since Kimi died outside the city limits, but he tends to get his panties in a bunch easily."

Tracy laughed. "I'll keep that in mind."

Jenny looked to the grandfather clock in the front hall. "Speaking of panties in a bunch, I better get home and feed the kids. You need anything, you have my cell." She handed Tracy a set of keys, and Tracy followed her outside. The shadows had reached the porch steps, and it felt as if the temperature had fallen a few more degrees.

Jenny got into her car and lowered the passenger-side window. "Call if you need anything," she said.

Tracy watched the SUV navigate the perimeter of the property, then turn north. As the sound of the car engine faded, Tracy was again struck by the utter quiet. She imagined the sounds of a family sitting down at the table to eat, or to watch *The Wonderful World of Disney* after taking Sunday evening baths, which had been her and Sarah's routine. The thought triggered a memory of her family's unexpected trip to Disneyland, Sarah squealing on the Pirates of the Caribbean, covering her eyes in the Haunted Mansion, and the smile that didn't leave her father's face for three days. Their final night, as they watched the parade on Main Street, Tracy had asked him, "Can we come back, Daddy?"

"I think we've worn the park out, don't you?" he'd said. "But you'll come back someday. You'll come back with your sister and your own kids, and you'll make memories for them."

That had never happened.

A psychopath had stolen that dream from all of them.

A chill ran up and down Tracy's spine, and she quickly retreated inside, where she put on a hooded sweatshirt. She brought the newspapers to the dining room table, sitting beneath a retro oil-lamp chandelier. In addition to the articles on the reunion, the newspapers were filled with small-town news—a report on a swimming pool feasibility study, the gardening tip of the week, and an article encouraging citizens to serve on committees to plan Stoneridge's future. The centerpiece of the front page, however, was the reunion and stadium dedication. In the photograph accompanying the article, a man in khaki pants and a polo shirt stood outside the entrance to the athletic complex Tracy and Dan had seen under construction. The caption identified him as Eric Reynolds, the quarterback of the 1976 championship team and president of Reynolds Construction, which was donating the man-0power, equipment, and concrete to renovate the stadium. The unspoken quid pro quo was apparently the naming rights.

The article continued to an inside page with a collage comparing past and current photographs. In one, a fifty-seven-year-old Eric Reynolds, balding in a horseshoe pattern, stood behind a large man bent over as if to hike him a football. Reynolds looked still capable of stepping onto the field and playing. The photo was juxtaposed next to another taken forty years earlier of the same two men in the same positions but in their high school football uniforms. In that black-and-white photo, Reynolds had long hair and a bright smile. The caption identified the center hiking the football as Hastey Devoe. Time had not been nearly as kind to him as it had been to Reynolds. As a young man, Devoe had been big, but he'd carried his weight well, and his boyish features and wide-eyed stare made him look precocious. In the more recent photo, Devoe's bulk had become slovenly, and his face had the fleshy, sagging features of a man who liked his food and probably his alcohol.

The photographs made Tracy nostalgic. Forty years had passed. Half a lifetime.

Not for Sarah. And not for Kimi Kanasket.

CHAPTER 12

Tracy awoke to the persistent crowing of a distant rooster. Unable to get back to sleep, she slid on her winter running clothes and headed out along the ridgeline. The initial cold hit her like an ice bath, chilling her to the bone, but she started slow, allowing her muscles and joints to loosen up until her core warmed and she could kick up her pace. About forty-five minutes later, after a quick shower and breakfast, she jumped in her truck and set out to find Earl Kanasket and either get his blessing or a kick in the pants—if he was still alive and still living at his last known address.

After a little over an hour and a half driving along US 97, Tracy approached the small city of Toppenish on the two-thousand-square-mile Yakama Reservation. She pulled off the exit and drove through a main street of one- and two-story stone and brick buildings that had the feel of an Old West farming community. Large murals adorned the sides of many of the buildings, the elaborate drawings depicting late eighteenth- and early nineteenth-century living—Native Americans riding bareback on painted horses, farmers plowing fields behind the reins of plow horses, a steam engine billowing smoke into a pale-blue sky.

Tracy's GPS directed her along streets with modest but well-maintained homes to a T inter-section and an expansive field of dark green that stretched seemingly to the horizon. Kale had become the new food fad. The address for Earl Kanasket was the last house on the left, a one-story blue-gray structure with an older-model Chevy truck and a Toyota sedan parked in a carport—a good sign, at least, that *someone* was home. The house listed slightly to the left, as if the attached carport weighed it down.

Tracy parked at the curb and stepped out, approaching a waist-high chain-link fence. She reached for the latch to the gate but hesitated when she noticed two signs, the first warning of a "Guard Dog on Duty" with a picture of a German shepherd. The second sign depicted a hand holding a large-caliber revolver and the words "We Don't Call 911." Tracy took a moment to consider the patch of crabgrass on the opposite side of the fence, but she didn't see any signs of a vicious beast. That didn't stop her from keeping a close watch on the corner of the house as she pushed through the gate and made her way up the concrete walk. She treated strange dogs the way she treated the ocean. She gave each a healthy dose of respect and never turned her back on either. The porch had been modified to accom-modate a wheelchair. She took that as another good sign that Earl Kanasket was living there.

The screen door had been propped against the side of the house, the hinges rusted and broken. Not that it would have done much good—the mesh was shredded. Tracy thought again of the guard dog. She knocked and took one step back and to the side, her hand on the butt of her Glock, not interested in being in the line of fire in case either posted sign was accurate. Inside the house a dog barked, but far from ferocious, it sounded tired and hoarse. The door handle jiggled, and an instant later the door popped open with a shudder. An old man sat in a wheelchair, his weathered face a road map of years. Next to him stood a shaggy-haired dog, its face white, its eyes watery and unfocused. The animal's tongue hung out the side of its mouth, as if the effort to reach the door had exhausted him.

"Good afternoon," Tracy said, employing her most disarming smile. One advantage she had over her male colleagues was that people were less intimidated by a strange woman knocking on their door. "I'm hoping you're Earl Kanasket."

"I am." Earl's voice sounded as hoarse as the dog's bark, but his eyes were clear, and so dark they made Tracy think of a crow's eyes. "And who are you?"

"My name is Tracy Crosswhite. I'm a detective from Seattle."

"Detective?"

"Yes, sir."

"What would a detective from Seattle want down here on the rez?" It was a legitimate question, and Tracy didn't detect any hostility or concern in Earl Kanasket's tone. She figured at eighty-plus years of age, you didn't get worked up about too many things.

"A chance to talk," Tracy said. "About your daughter, Kimi."

"Kimi?" Earl leaned back in his chair as if pushed by a gust of strong wind. "Kimi's been gone forty years."

"I know," Tracy said. "And I know this is probably a shock coming out of the blue like this." She paused. This was where Earl Kanasket would get angry and tell her to leave, or get curious.

"Yeah, you could say it is." His thinning white hair was pulled back in a ponytail that hung down his back. "So what's this about?"

"Well, it's a bit of a story, Mr. Kanasket. I wonder if I could come in and sit down and tell it to you?"

Earl studied her a moment. Then he nodded, just a small dip of his chin. "I think you'd better," he said, tugging on the wheels so his chair rolled backward. The dog also retreated with effort. Tracy shut the door and followed Earl into a tired but clean room just to the right of the entry. The air was stale and held the odor of a recent fire in the hearth. The furnishings were functional—a couch and two chairs for sitting, an oval-shaped throw rug over a hardwood floor for warmth, a flat-screen television for entertainment, and a lamp for light.

As Earl positioned his chair so that his back was to the window facing the field of kale, Tracy stepped to a chair near the fireplace. Rust-colored dog hair on the arms and seat indicated that this was the dog's preferred spot, but for now he remained content to be at his master's side. Tracy sat. She'd given some thought on the drive about how to begin. "I graduated from the police academy with a woman named Jenny Almond. Her father was Buzz Almond, the sheriff of Klickitat County."

"I know that name," Earl said. "But he wasn't sheriff. Not yet, anyway. He was a deputy. He came when Kimi went missing."

According to the Accurint records, the Kanaskets moved to the Yakama Reservation not long after the recovery of Kimi's body from the White Salmon River.

"That's right," she said.

"He said he'd find Kimi. I think he meant it."

"Did he tell you what happened to Kimi?"

Kanasket took his time, seeming to ponder each question, as if age and wisdom had taught him patience before opening his mouth to speak. "They said she threw herself into the river."

"Is that what Buzz Almond told you?"

"I don't remember who said it, just that it was

said. Didn't believe it then. Don't believe it now."

"Well," Tracy said. "I'm not certain Buzz Almond believed it either. He kept a file, Mr. Kanasket." She reached into her briefcase and pulled out the file, then stood and handed it to Earl Kanasket. He took it tentatively, as if uncertain he wanted to hold it, and Tracy didn't blame him for that. The file documented the worst memories of his life, memories she was certain he'd take to his grave.

"It appears Buzz Almond continued to investigate what happened to your daughter, which wouldn't have been the usual way things were done in the sheriff's office. The usual way would have been for him to turn his file over to a detective. So the fact that he kept the file indicates, perhaps, that he didn't agree with the conclusion reached by others."

"What does he have to say about it?"

"He's dead. He died of cancer a few weeks ago. His daughter found the file in his desk at home and asked me to take a look. I came here to let you know, and hopefully to get your approval."

Earl's eyes narrowed, and his gaze bore into Tracy with such intensity she was certain this time that he would ask her to leave. "My approval?"

"Yes, to look further into Buzz Almond's investigation."

Earl turned his head and looked at the only

framed photograph in the room, a picture of Kimi with a woman Tracy assumed to be his wife. After a moment he redirected his attention to Tracy. "Tell me what's in the file."

Tracy retook her seat and explained the contents. She said she was having the coroner's report reviewed in Seattle and had also sent several dozen photographs to be studied by an expert. While she spoke, Earl Kanasket sat motionless, hands resting on the file in his lap. His bony fingers never moved to open it.

"Photographs of what?"

"A path in the woods leading to a clearing."

"I know it."

"You do?"

Earl nodded, though again it was a barely perceptible tilt. "It holds bad spirits."

"Bad spirits?"

"Dead who are not at rest."

When Sarah died and her father took his own life, Tracy lost what remained of her faith, never having been much of a believer in things like heaven or life after death. But she couldn't reconcile the moment in the mine above Cedar Grove when she'd felt Sarah's presence as strongly as if Sarah had been physically present. After that, Tracy didn't dismiss talk of spirits. "Why there?" she asked.

"What do you know of it?"

"Nothing."

Earl shut his eyes and took a deep breath before opening them. "Many years ago they hung an innocent man in the clearing. They said he committed murder, and they brought him to an old oak tree so everyone in the town could witness the hanging. When they asked him for his final words, he said he was innocent, and if they hung him he would rise from his grave and burn the town to the ground. A month after the hanging, a fire burned most of the buildings in downtown Stoneridge, but the cause of the fire was never determined. When they finally opened the man's grave, they found it empty. Shortly after those events, the oak tree died. Since then, nothing grows in the clearing."

The dog sat up and barked, causing Tracy to flinch. Earl Kanasket never moved, never shifted his gaze from her face. Seconds later she heard the sound of heavy boots climbing the front porch and felt the house shudder as the front door popped inward.

"Dad? Whose truck is in the—?"

A man carrying a brown grocery bag stepped into the room. His eyes shifted between Tracy and his father before settling on her. "Who are you?"

Élan bore a passing resemblance to his father. His hair, more gray than black, extended past his shoulders, and he had the same dark eyes, though where his father's eyes engaged, Élan's repelled, in an intense, challenging gaze.

Tracy stood. "My name is Tracy Crosswhite. I'm a detective from Seattle."

"What do you want? Why are you talking to my father?"

"She's here about Kimi," Earl said.

"Kimi?" Élan scoffed. He set the groceries on an end table and walked farther into the room. "Is this some sort of a joke?"

"No," Tracy said. "It's not."

"What could you possibly want to know about Kimi?"

"She doesn't believe Kimi killed herself," Earl said.

Élan glanced at his father, then back to Tracy. "The former sheriff kept a file on your sister's death," she said.

But the more she tried to explain, the more agitated Élan looked, like a man with bugs crawling up his back. He cut her off. "What possible good do you think will come of this, huh? Are you going to bring Kimi back?"

"No," Tracy said. "But if your sister didn't kill herself—"

"What? What are you going to do? Arrest someone? They didn't arrest anyone then, and they haven't arrested anyone in forty years. They . . . didn't . . . care. Kimi was just another dead Indian."

"We have technology now that wasn't available back in 1976—technology that might reveal evidence that your sister's death wasn't a suicide."

"Might?" Élan stepped closer, not enough that Tracy felt threatened, but it was clear he intended to intimidate. "Might? You came out here to tell us you *might* find out something? You mean you don't even know anything yet?"

"I came to get your father's approval and to let him know the sheriff has reopened the file."

"You want his approval? My mother went to her grave grieving Kimi's death. My father has been without his daughter for forty years. And you come here and tell us you might have . . . what? What could you possibly have?"

"The coroner's report. Witness statements. Photographs."

"Photographs of what?"

"The clearing," Earl said.

Again, Élan's glance flickered between his father and Tracy. "The clearing? What does the clearing have to do with anything?"

"The deputy took photographs of it," Tracy said. "I'm having them analyzed."

"Why? Do you think a ghost killed Kimi?" Élan smiled, but it was a dark smile. "Maybe it was Henry Timmerman come back to life to seek his revenge."

Tracy couldn't blame Élan for his skepticism. She'd grown more and more skeptical with each year that she couldn't solve Sarah's death. After twenty years, she'd all but given up hope.

"Your sister never made it home. Don't you want to know why?"

"We know why. She threw herself in the river."

"Do you believe that?"

"What difference does it make whether I believe it or not. That's what they told us."

"What if they're wrong?"

"What if they're not? Are you going to get my father's hopes up like that deputy who told us he was going to find Kimi? He found her all right. He found her in the fucking river. I think you should leave." Élan stepped back and motioned to the door. "I think you should get the hell out."

"Stop," Earl said, his voice soft and calm. Élan lowered his arm and looked away, like a chastened boy not about to challenge his father, but also not about to listen. Earl rolled his wheelchair to Tracy. The dog padded alongside him. Earl reached up and took Tracy's hand. His skin was cool to the touch and so thin it revealed every bone and knuckle. "The deputy was young," he said. "He was starting a career, and he had a family to consider. You are not just starting your career. And you have no family."

"No," Tracy said, not entirely certain what he was getting at and how he would know that she had no family. "I don't."

Earl released her hand and offered back the file. "Finish what Buzz Almond started."

"I'll try." Tracy took the file, glanced at Élan,

and started from the room. Élan eyeballed her as she stepped past him and pulled open the door. She wasn't surprised that he followed her down the porch and out into the yard. She wasn't about to look like she was running from him, so she turned and faced him.

"My father might trust you," he said, "but I don't."

"Why's that? Why wouldn't you trust me?"

"Trust isn't given. It's earned."

"So why not give me a chance to earn yours?"

"Because we've been trusting you for two hundred years and you just keep ripping us off."

It was the type of generic statement Tracy had heard often as a police officer when someone had no specific or rational answer to one of her questions. Instead, they accused her of being a racist. "I'm Norwegian and Swiss," she said. "And a little Irish. What did I rip off from you?"

Élan smiled, but again there was no humor in it. "What? Did my father wow you with that little show back there—the part about you not being young and not having a family? Do you think he's some kind of Indian medicine man?" He glanced at her hand. "You're not wearing a wedding ring. And you aren't exactly young. I wouldn't get too worked up about it if I was you."

"You didn't answer my question. Why wouldn't you want to know? If you're big on injustices, why wouldn't you want to right this one, this one above all others?"

"Because in the end you won't find anything, and even if you did, nothing will come of it. That's the way it's always been." He took a half step toward her. "Don't come back here unless you have something *real* to tell us. Don't come with your 'might haves' or 'maybes.' Don't make promises you can't keep. And don't send an old man to his grave with expectations you aren't prepared to fulfill."

Élan gave her a final withering glare, then turned and went up the steps and back inside, the door slamming shut. Tracy looked to the right, to the plate-glass window facing the field of kale. Earl Kanasket had rolled his wheelchair to the window, but this time he was facing it, watching her.

After driving by the address provided for Tommy Moore and finding the name "Moore" on the mailbox but no one home, Tracy drove into downtown Toppenish and found a restaurant to grab a bite to eat. She ordered a turkey sandwich, sipped on an iced tea, and thought of Buzz Almond and how he must have regretted telling the Kanasket family that he would find Kimi and that she was going to be all right. It was not an infrequent mistake made by young officers with good intentions. Tracy had been in that helpless situation herself, both as an officer and as the relative of a victim of a horrific crime, but she had quickly come to learn the two were not the same.

For a police officer, a violent crime was one case in a career. You did your job and went home. For the family, the crime was a life-altering moment they would never forget. Buzz Almond wouldn't have been human if he hadn't wanted to ease the Kanaskets' worry, but he must have felt incredible guilt when he watched the Search and Rescue team pull Kimi Kanasket's body from the water and realized he wasn't going to be able to deliver on his promise. Tracy wondered if that was why Buzz had maintained an interest in the case. She also wondered why, if he thought Kimi Kanasket hadn't killed herself, he hadn't pursued it further.

Earl Kanasket said Buzz Almond had been starting a new career, with a family to consider. Was he implying that Buzz Almond had reason to be concerned about the well-being of his family, or simply making a statement of the limitations Buzz was operating under? If the latter, Earl Kanasket was correct in his assessment of Tracy. She had no such limitations. If the former, however, Earl Kanasket's comment very well could have been intended as a warning.

CHAPTER 13

Tuesday, November 9, 1976

After filling out his reports for his shift, Buzz went looking for Jerry Ostertag, who was not at his desk.

"He went to take a leak," another detective said.

Buzz jogged down the hall and around the corner, the soles of his shoes slipping on the worn linoleum when he tried to slow. He called out, "Detective Ostertag?"

Ostertag stopped and wheeled at the sound of someone calling his name. Buzz took a quick step toward him. "Sorry to shout at you like that." He extended a hand. "Buzz Almond. Wanted to talk to you a minute about the Kimi Kanasket case."

Ostertag looked twenty pounds overweight—not obese, but like a man who finished his plate and liked a cocktail every night, as well as his sweets. He'd begun the middle-aged man's first concession, wearing the buckle of his belt below his protruding stomach.

"Almond. Right. I thought the name sounded familiar. I got your reports. They were good. Very thorough. Thanks for those." Ostertag worked a toothpick from one side of his mouth to the other and looked at Buzz through silver-framed glasses that resembled the ones Telly Savalas wore on the popular detective show *Kojak*. Buzz wondered if that was why Ostertag also shaved his head.

"Thanks. Listen, I spoke to Lorraine at the Columbia Diner."

"Who?"

"She's the waitress at the diner where Kimi Kanasket worked the night she went missing." Buzz had assumed Ostertag would have spoken to Lorraine, but that had apparently not been the case.

"Right. And you talked to her . . . why?"

"I just stopped in to get a bite to eat, and we got to talking," Buzz said, again conscious not to look as though he was stepping on Ostertag's investigation. "Anyway, she said Kimi wasn't upset about Tommy Moore coming in that night."

"Hang on." Ostertag raised a hand and turned to a man in a suit passing in the opposite direction. "Hey, Carl, we still on for tomorrow?"

Carl turned, talking while he walked backward. "I reserved the court for six thirty. Figured we could grab breakfast after we play."

"Loser buys?"

"Hey, I never pass up a free meal."

"Bring your credit card," Ostertag taunted. "Winning makes me hungry."

Ostertag redirected his attention to Buzz. "Sorry.

I gotta kick his ass in racquetball tomorrow morning. Keeps him in line. So you were saying something about a waitress?"

"Lorraine," Buzz said. "She said Kimi wasn't upset about Tommy Moore breaking up with her. That Kimi even waited on his table that night."

"Remind me again—Moore was the boyfriend, right?"

"Ex-boyfriend," Buzz said, wondering what the hell Ostertag had been doing. "He brought a date with him to the diner to get a rise out of Kimi, but he stormed out when he got no reaction."

"Hang on again. I'm sorry. I was on my way to take a leak. Drank too much damn coffee this morning, and my back teeth are floating. I'm gonna drown if I don't take care of it."

Ostertag crossed the hall and disappeared behind the swinging door to the men's room, leaving Buzz in the hall feeling like an idiot. He took a few steps farther down the linoleum and tried to look like he was doing something. After several minutes, Ostertag propped open the door with his foot while he finished drying his hands with a brown paper towel. He tossed the wad back inside, presumably at a garbage pail. When he stepped into the hall, he seemed surprised Buzz remained waiting for him.

"So after I spoke to the waitress," Buzz said, "I was driving away, and I spotted a turnout, maybe a hundred, hundred and fifty yards past the diner.

I couldn't see it that night when Earl Kanasket and I walked the road because it was too dark, and it had started snowing. Anyway, there's a path there, and I noticed footprints and tire tracks. So I followed them and—"

"And you came to a clearing," Ostertag said, loosening the knot of his gold tie and undoing the top button.

"You know it?"

"Everyone on the force knows it."

"You've been out there?"

"More times than I cared to be when I was on patrol."

"I mean for this investigation."

"This investigation? Why would I be out there for this investigation?"

"The footprints and tire tracks lead to the clearing. I'd say two, maybe three people. Hard to tell."

Ostertag's brow furrowed. "I meant, what does that have to do with Kanasket?"

"Well, I mean that was the direction she would have headed walking home. She'd have walked 141. If something spooked her—"

"Like what?"

"I don't know." Buzz fought against becoming irritated.

Ostertag frowned. "How long you been on the force . . . ?" As his voice trailed off, it was clear he'd forgotten Buzz's name.

"Buzz," he said.

"How long you been on the force, Buzz?"

Buzz was not in the mood to hear sage advice from an overweight desk jockey who probably got a college deferment from the draft while Buzz spent two tours slogging through the jungles of Vietnam commanding his own platoon. "Couple months."

"This your first case? First big case?"

"Yeah, but what does—?"

"Let me give you a piece of advice, help you with your career. Your job is to respond to the calls and get those witness statements. And you did a nice job; I'm going to note that to my sergeant. My job is to follow up and investigate. You do your job and let me do mine, and everything is smooth sailing. Right?" Ostertag smiled. The toothpick flicked to the corner of his mouth.

"I understand," Buzz said, mentally counting to ten. "But I took photographs. I was going to get them developed. I could show you."

Ostertag continued to smile. "You took photographs of footprints and tire tracks?"

"Right."

"Let me tell you about the clearing, Bert."

"Buzz."

"The kids like to go out there on the weekends because it's isolated. They bring a couple six-packs of beer, get drunk, and get in their cars and spin donuts. Other times, it's a guy and his date. He takes her out there to look for ghosts."

"Ghosts?"

"A legend about some guy getting hanged there and coming back and burning down the town. They say his ghost is still out there, that you can hear him moaning when the wind blows. You know, bullshit high school stuff guys tell their dates, hoping to get them scared so they cling close and he gets his hands up her shirt or down her pants, right? You got pictures of footprints and tires tracks that could belong to every kid at Stoneridge High and every car parked in the parking lot."

"I don't think so."

Ostertag scoffed. "You don't think so?"

"The ground froze that night when the temperature dropped. That means whoever was out there Friday night, their footprints and tire tracks froze."

"Froze?"

"In place. They froze in place. Anybody going out there after that wouldn't leave tracks or footprints because the ground would have been too hard. So the tracks had to have been from Friday night. It had rained earlier in the week. The ground would have been soft, which is why the tires chewed up the path."

"How do you know those tire tracks haven't been there a week, or a month, or six months? You see what I'm saying?"

"But it could be something. I mean, shouldn't we follow up on it?"

"We?" Ostertag scratched at the side of his head. "Listen, I'm gonna ease your mind. We got the pathologist's report back this afternoon. If it makes you feel any better, he confirms the kid killed herself. Jumped in the river, got banged around good on the rocks, and drowned."

"Yeah?" Buzz asked. "How could he know that?"

"Water in the lungs, for one. She was alive when she hit the water. Hundred percent certain."

"What I mean is, Lorraine said Kimi wasn't upset when she left. So how could he know she *jumped* in?"

"That's what they say about suicides, right? You can't tell because the person is calmest right before they do it. They got their mind made up. It's a relief. Everybody says, 'Never saw it coming.'" Ostertag gave Buzz a condescending smile. "Okay? We good?"

Buzz nodded, but he wasn't feeling good.

"Here's another thing." Ostertag lowered his voice. "Those Indians? They're not like us, okay? They get out of whack about stuff that doesn't bother us, like the school mascot bullshit. They're high-strung, can't handle their liquor. Who knows what sets them off half the time. Tomorrow, I'll take a drive out and tell the family the pathologist's findings. It isn't what they want to hear, but you learn in this job that you can't argue with the evidence."

Ostertag turned and walked off, wing tips tapping on the linoleum. Buzz wondered if it was guilt for having told Earl and Nettie Kanasket that he'd find their daughter that was driving him to find something that might not exist. Maybe Ostertag had a point. Maybe you couldn't argue with the evidence.

Except in this case, Buzz Almond still thought you could.

Judging from the fledgling foliage next to the sidewalk and in the yards, Tracy surmised that the development where Tommy Moore lived had been built within the past year or two. Unlike Earl Kanasket's neighborhood, the address for each of the one- and two-story homes here, cut from the same cookie-cutter architectural plan, was prominently displayed on the wall between the garage and the front door.

Tracy turned on her truck's headlights and slowed as she approached the house she had stopped at earlier that afternoon. A heavyset man in jeans, work boots, and a winter jacket stood in the yard spiking at the ground with a bladed shovel, but with one eye seemingly watching the street. Parked in the driveway was a white truck, the bed filled with gardening tools, rakes, a mower, and gas cans, and the words "Golden Gloves Landscaping" stenciled on the doors and tailgate.

Tommy Moore stopped pretending to be picking at the ground when Tracy pulled to the curb. He approached her truck before she had a chance to step out. Tracy instinctively moved her right hand to her Glock. "You the detective from Seattle?" he asked.

Little remained of the Golden Gloves boxer Buzz Almond had described in his report as looking "like a Hawaiian surfer." Moore had fought as a welterweight, which had a weight limit of 147 pounds. The man before her was considerably heavier, with fleshy features and nub-short gray hair.

"Tracy Crosswhite," she said.

"Élan said you would be stopping by."

"You two still talk?" Tracy said.

"No," Moore said, shaking his head. "We don't."

"Getting kind of dark for gardening," Tracy said.

Moore glanced at the house. "I have a wife and two girls. They don't know anything about Kimi. I'd like to keep it that way."

"I understand. I saw a bar in town."

"I don't drink."

Tracy recalled Moore's Triple I criminal background check and the lack of any convictions after 1982. "How long have you been sober?"

"Twenty years."

"Congratulations. How about coffee?"

"Can't drink it at night. Keeps me awake. Let's

go for a drive. I know a place." Moore left the shovel on the lawn, walked around the bed of Tracy's truck, and got in the cab. "Head back out to the main road. There's a park," he said. "I take my kids there."

Three turns later they came to an open field with a playground structure. At the moment, the park was deserted. Tracy shut off the engine, keeping her right hand near her Glock, though Moore showed no signs of aggression. To the contrary, he looked and sounded tired.

"You mind if I smoke?" Moore asked.

"Let's step outside." She walked around the hood to where Moore leaned against the front fender shaking a cigarette from its pack. He pulled it free with his teeth and cupped the tip with his hand to light it. The breeze quickly caught the smoke and caused it to dissipate.

"Not a day goes by I don't regret going into the diner that night," Moore said, slipping the cigarettes and lighter into the pocket of his wool-lined jean jacket and looking out at the playground like he'd already mentally slipped forty years into the past.

Tracy thrust her hands into the pockets of her jacket to warm them. "Why did you?"

Moore shot her a lazy glance. "Why do you think? I was angry at Kimi for breaking up with me. She was heading off to college at the end of the year. Said she wanted to spend her

171

final year in high school with her friends, but that wasn't it."

"What was it?"

"She could do better." He shrugged and took another drag.

The wind kicked up the dust and caused the swings to shake and sway on their metal chains. "So why do you think she went out with you in the first place?"

"I was better-looking back then." Moore smiled, but his smile quickly waned. "You know how it is. I was a boxer, and I played that . . . you know? The brooding, silent type. I was also older, and Élan put in a good word. That doesn't work for long on girls like Kimi."

"You told Buzz Almond the breakup was mutual.

He flicked the ashes. "Who's Buzz Almond?"

"The deputy who came and interviewed you."

"I probably did. But that was just pride talking. I probably also told him I didn't care about her. That was also pride. I wouldn't have gone into the diner that night if I hadn't cared."

"What happened?"

"I was mad, so I took a girl in with me, thinking I'd get even."

"Cheryl Neal?" Tracy said, recalling the name from the file.

"That's right. She and Kimi didn't get along. Cheryl was a cheerleader and had a reputation of

172

sleeping around, and she didn't much care for Kimi."

"Why not?"

Moore took another drag on his cigarette, the tip glowing red. He didn't exhale, just let the smoke escape his mouth and nostrils. "Jealous," he said. "Like I said, Kimi was smart and athletic. She had a lot of guy friends, without having to sleep with them." Moore's gaze was focused on the ground. "Kimi acted like it didn't even bother her when I walked in with Cheryl. And that just made me more angry." Moore glanced at Tracy. "I was angry a lot back then, at just about everyone and everything. My job. My boxing career. It didn't take a lot to set me off."

"Did Kimi set you off that night?"

Moore didn't hesitate. "Yeah, she did. I grabbed Cheryl and left. Took her home. I didn't even walk her to the door."

"Where'd you go?"

"A bar in Husum."

"You told Buzz Almond you went back to your apartment."

"I was twenty, and I'd already had one DUI. Another one and I'd have lost my license and probably my job. I made it back to the apartment, but my roommate said Élan and some of the others had come by looking for me, that Kimi was missing. I didn't like the sound of that, so I left for my mom's. She lived here on the rez. But I drank too much, and I fell asleep and smashed my truck into a tree."

Tracy felt another gust of wind and a chill on her neck that ran down her spine. "Was there a police report?"

"I wasn't about to call the police. I got the truck running enough to get to my mom's and spent the weekend banging it out so I could get back. I had to work Monday."

"Did you crack the windshield?"

"Probably. Had to have."

"Where'd you get it fixed?"

Another shrug. "I don't know."

"Columbia Windshield?" Tracy asked, recalling the name on the invoice in the file.

"I don't remember."

"How'd you pay?"

"What do you mean?"

"Would you have paid with cash, a credit card, a check?"

He took another drag. "Probably cash. I don't remember. That was forty years ago."

"Where'd you get the bodywork done?"

"Friend of mine did it in his garage."

"So you first heard about Kimi missing from your roommate?"

Moore dropped the cigarette on the ground and crushed it with the toe of his work boot. "Only that he said Élan came by saying Kimi didn't come home and wanted to know if she was with

174

me. I read in the newspaper—Monday, I think—that she'd killed herself."

"You didn't sound like you cared much when Buzz Almond interviewed you."

Moore pinched the bridge of his nose, and Tracy realized he was fighting his emotions. "I'm not proud of the man I was, Detective. I was already on my way to being a drunk, but when I found out what happened to Kimi, that put me over-the-top. I lost my job and had to move home with my mom. I cared, okay? I cared."

"Your criminal record indicates that wasn't the end of your problems."

"No, it wasn't. Like most drunks, I had a ways to go before I hit bottom."

"What changed?"

"I met my wife. She wouldn't go out with a man who drank. Her father drank. If I wanted to marry her, I had to get right. So I started going to AA meetings and taking a hard look at myself. It took a while to get sober. It took longer to stop blaming myself for what happened to Kimi, but like I said, it's a rare day when I don't think about her and about what part I might have played in it. It nearly ruined my life, Detective, thinking she killed herself because of me; are you here to tell me she didn't?"

"I don't know yet. But you were one of the last people to see her alive. You were angry at her, you have no alibi after you dropped off your date, and your car was damaged."

"All true," he said. "But if someone did kill Kimi, it wasn't me."

"With forensics we can determine things we couldn't determine back in 1976."

"Then I hope you find something."

"I intend to."

Moore might no longer look like the fighter Buzz Almond had confronted, but he still had a boxer's confidence—or a good bluff. Tracy wasn't going to be able to intimidate him. She ended the interview and got back in her truck, blasting the heat. She drove Moore back to his house and stopped at the curb. Twilight had become night, and light peeked out from behind the curtains. Inside, a woman apparently loved Moore enough to look past his faults, and two girls of his flesh and blood awaited him.

Moore stepped down from the cab. "I have my own daughters now," he said before closing the door. "I know how Earl must have felt, and it rips me up inside."

Tracy nodded but did not comment.

"Forty years I thought I killed Kimi, Detective. I thought she jumped in that river because of me," Moore said. "I hope you do prove me wrong. Not for Kimi—she's in a better place. Not even for me. I hope you find out for Earl, so he can finally put his daughter to rest."

CHAPTER 14

Tracy drove back into town and pulled over beside one of the murals, writing down everything she recalled about the interview while it remained fresh in her mind. After, she spent the drive back to the farmhouse going over her conversation with Tommy Moore another time, uncertain what to make of his final request. Moore looked and sounded sincere, but she knew from experience that his sincerity could be due to a lack of remorse, like Bundy and other psychopaths. It was also possible that Moore killed Kimi but over the years had convinced himself he had not; Tracy had seen other criminals do just that. The third option was that Moore was innocent, as he proclaimed, and someone else had killed Kimi, though the evidence seemed to dictate otherwise—notably the damage to his truck and the invoices to the auto repair and windshield companies, which had to be in Buzz Almond's file for a reason. Moore also had a motive, and usually the person with the motive committed the crime.

Tracy was even more uncertain what to think of Élan, a brother who seemed decidedly disinterested in getting answers about what had happened to his sister. Then again, maybe Tracy was just comparing Élan to herself, which wasn't fair.

Tracy had admittedly been obsessed with finding out what had happened to Sarah—so obsessed she'd nearly let it ruin her life. She remembered vividly that moment when she'd boxed up all the trial transcripts and witness statements, along with her notes, and shoved them into the closet of her bedroom because she knew she'd go crazy if she didn't. For months she would glance at the closet door the way, she assumed, a recovering alcoholic like Tommy Moore glanced at a bottle of vodka: with a deep longing for just a small sample.

Maybe Élan had long ago slid the memories of his sister's death into his own mental closet so that he could get on with his life, and he had no desire to go back. If that was the case, he hadn't gotten far, at least not from the looks of his current living situation. Or maybe Élan, too, was trying to forget something *he* did that night, something born out of animosity and jealousy toward a sister who was everything he was not—smart, athletic, and motivated to do great things.

The fourth option, of course, was that Kimi had committed suicide, but every time Tracy considered that possibility, she became less convinced that had been the case. She just couldn't articulate why. At least now she had Earl Kanasket's blessing to try to find out.

A sudden glare of high beams caused her to quickly steer her truck to the shoulder. A large flatbed blew by her in the opposite direction, the rush of wind shaking her truck. The encounter had the same effect as if she were a boxer administered smelling salts in between rounds; she sat up, more focused. When she did, she spotted a one-room log building along the side of the road, and it triggered something she'd read in Buzz Almond's file. She drove to a crude gravel parking area. From the building's dilapidated condition, Tracy could tell the establishment had long since closed, but she had no doubt that it was the Columbia Diner.

She opened the file and skimmed Almond's report of his conversation with the waitress, Lorraine. After speaking to the waitress, Almond had made this note: *I drove in the direction Kimi Kanasket would have walked home, and came to a turnout 100–150 yards past the café.*

Tracy pulled back onto the road and continued at a slow rate of speed, frequently checking her rearview mirror for headlights. After driving a little more than the length of a football field, she spotted a half-moon-shaped escarpment, about the size of a car, carved out of the otherwise encroaching brush.

She parked, reached into her glove box for her Maglite flashlight, and confirmed it worked. Then she grabbed her coat and pushed open the cab door to a rush of cold air. She stepped out, quickly zipped her coat and shut the door, but she did not immediately turn on the flashlight. Without the cab's dome light or the benefit of any street lamps, and with a low cloud layer preventing any natural light, it was "darker than dark," as her father liked to say—probably as dark as the night Kimi Kanasket went missing and Buzz Almond described as "dark as ink."

Tracy flipped on the flashlight and started along the edge of the road, directing the beam over the brush. It was cold enough that she could see the white vapor of her breath in the stream of light, and the chill caused her fingertips and cheeks to tingle. She switched the metal cylinder to the other hand, blowing into her free hand. She'd gone less than ten yards when the beam seemed to pierce through an initial wall of foliage. Stepping closer and using the Maglite to push aside branches, she found an overgrown path that conjured the image of the deer paths her father had taught her to use when hunting in dense brush. If this was the path Buzz Almond had written of in his report, Tracy wasn't surprised he hadn't seen it that first dark night.. She'd been specifically looking for it and still had almost walked past it.

Common sense told Tracy to go back to her truck and come back in the morning when it was light, but common sense was taking a back-seat to curiosity—and her desire to retrace Buzz Almond's footsteps in the same conditions he'd encountered. Besides, the dark had never bothered her. Maybe because Sarah had been so afraid of the dark, Tracy, as her big sister, never allowed herself to be afraid. Tracy and her friends used to play hide-and-go-seek at night in the woods behind their home, and they'd pitch tents on the back lawn and turn off all the lights and tell ghost stories. Sarah never lasted long before rushing inside, but Tracy enjoyed it. Beyond that, she had the Maglite and her Glock.

Tracy stepped from the road into the brush, kicking at encroaching vines snagging her jeans. A hundred yards down the path, the foliage became less dense and the footpath more defined. Recent rains had made the ground soft but not sloppy. Farther along, the grade steepened, enough that Tracy's breathing became more pronounced from the exertion. The foliage changed to scrub oak and pine trees, the ground covered with pine needles. Tracy used her jacket sleeve to protect her face from the branches, snapping off the smaller limbs as she went. The grade continued to steepen until she was bent forward, driving with her legs, feeling the cold in her lungs. At least the effort had warmed her and stemmed the chill.

Sensing she was nearing the top of the grade, she bent under a branch, pushed through a final tangle of tree limbs, and came out atop a hill looking down at an open patch of ground—what had to be the clearing Buzz Almond had written of and Earl Kanasket had described. She was surprised to feel a strange sense of accomplishment at having found it. She turned off the Maglite. A break in the cloud layer allowed sporadic moonlight, and the clearing appeared as both men had described it, barren of any tree, sapling, bush, or shrub. It looked like one of those crop circles in the middle of a field that you see featured in tabloid magazines—a compressed area people said had been made by alien space-ships.

As Tracy started down the hill, she quickly realized she'd misjudged the grade. The ground, slick from the rains and the drop in temperature, made keeping her footing like navigating a thin sheet of ice. The soles of her boots slipped and slid, and she feared she'd lose her balance and tweak an ankle, or snap a leg or an arm. She had to angle her body and sidestep to better control her descent. Halfway down, she gave in to gravity and allowed herself to stumble to the bottom.

A noise, what she first thought to be the low, drawn-out hoot of a barn owl, drew her attention to the top of the hill. But it wasn't an owl. The limbs of the trees, stripped of their fall foliage, began to whip and sway, and she watched the blades of tall grass fold over as a gust of wind shot down the hill. It sounded just as Earl Kanasket had described it, like a man moaning. The wind rushed at her, strong enough to blow the hair back from her face, and felt as though it was passing right through her. She turned and directed the beam of her flashlight to the edge of the clearing, following the wind as it flowed in a clockwise direction, the branches of the pines dancing and swaying. She felt as though she were standing in the eye of a tornado and wondered whether the swirling wind, and not some hanged man's curse, was the likely reason nothing grew here.

As she followed the wind's progress, the beam of light fell on something moving at the edge of the clearing. From its brown coloring, Tracy first thought it was an animal—a deer or a bear. But deer and bears didn't walk upright on two legs.

"Hey," she yelled, starting across the field. "Hey!"

The man looked back over his shoulder before disappearing quickly into the tree line. Tracy ran after him. "Hey. Stop. Hang on a minute."

The man didn't stop, and Tracy gave chase. At the edge of the forest, she unholstered her Glock and used the beam of light to search between the trees, but she didn't see the man or a defined path he might have taken. She stepped farther in, ducking and bending and picking her way carefully over fallen trees. She thought she caught a glimpse of the man off to her left and continued another fifty yards, but she saw no sign of him. She was about to turn back when she sensed the brush and the trees beginning to thin, so she kept going, and soon stepped out onto a power line easement. Electrical cable strung between metal towers continued up and over the ridge.

But no one was there.

She wondered if her eyes had played a trick on her, or maybe she *had* seen Henry Timmerman's ghost, as Élan had warned. She directed the flashlight to the ground, searched a moment, and found what looked to be bootprints and the tread of a thick bicycle tire, likely a mountain bike of some sort. Both appeared to be fresh. The tire tread followed the path of the electrical cables up the hill to the ridge.

Ghosts didn't ride bicycles. Not to her knowledge, anyway.

She took a few pictures with her phone before making her way back through the trees to the clearing. There, she spent a few minutes shining the beam of light over the ground looking for shoe imprints, but something else caught her eye—a small shrub. She bent to a knee, touching the freshly tilled soil.

Nothing grows in the clearing, Earl Kanasket had said.

Maybe not, Tracy thought, looking back to the edge of the clearing where she'd seen the man, *but someone's trying anyway.*

CHAPTER 15

In the morning, after another early run, Tracy headed out to get a pulse on the town. Downtown Stoneridge was an odd mixture of alpine architecture, reflecting German and Scandinavian immigration to the area, and the more traditional nineteenth-century Pacific Northwest stone and brick buildings that reminded Tracy of Cedar Grove. Whereas Cedar Grove had one stoplight, Stoneridge had only a stop sign at the end of a long block of businesses—a general store, pharmacy, hardware store, and post office, among others, on the north side of the street, and a pizza and brew pub, flower shop, and art gallery displaying Northwest Native American pieces on the south side. It should have been quaint, a town that quietly exuded history and tradition, but something about the tableau was unsettling, something that made the town seem as fragile as a Hollywood set—a façade lacking depth, a town that did not exude its history but seemed intent on hiding it.

As she drove down the block, a white sedan slowed its approach as it drove toward her from the opposite direction. Tracy considered the blue lettering and shield on the door panel identifying it as a Stoneridge Police Department vehicle. She waved and briefly considered stopping to introduce herself but instead continued to the end of the block. When she checked the rearview mirror, the police car had pulled to the side of the road and parked.

She turned left and drove past several churches, Baptist and Methodist, and a building that housed some fraternal order. The homes were small, mostly one-story, with yards going dormant for the winter, lawns a little ragged, and cut wood stacked neatly beneath overhangs. Her GPS directed her to a tree-lined street, and she pulled to the curb at the base of concrete stairs leading up to the red brick Stoneridge Library, which resembled something out of colonial America, with two white pillars and a pediment over the entrance.

She climbed the steps and felt the warm air as she pulled open the door. Inside, Tracy interrupted a middle-aged woman applying makeup while sitting behind the reference desk.

"Sorry," the woman said, slipping a compact into her purse and sliding the purse beneath the counter. "I didn't get a chance to put my face on this morning."

"Not a problem," Tracy said.

"How can I help you?"

"I'm hoping to review some old high school yearbooks and newspaper articles from the

Stoneridge Sentinel," Tracy said. "Would that be possible?"

The woman grimaced. "How far back are you looking to go?"

"1976."

"Are you writing an article on the reunion?"

No point in lying. Having lived in a small town, Tracy knew word of her presence would spread quickly, no matter how low a profile she kept. "Actually, I'm a police officer from Seattle," she said, showing the woman her ID and shield. "I was hoping to review some articles written back then. I assume the library keeps them on microfiche?"

"We did," the woman said. Tracy didn't like the sound of that. "We had a fire in 2000, and what the fire didn't burn, the sprinklers ruined. We don't have any archives before that."

Tracy considered this a moment, then asked, "Would any other libraries in the area have kept copies?" She thought it doubtful but worth a shot.

"Not likely the *Sentinel*. That was primarily local Stoneridge news. They might have some of the bigger newspapers, like the *Columbian* and the *Oregonian*. You could try the library in Goldendale. It's about an hour northeast of here."

Tracy didn't see the point in that. "How long have you lived here?"

"Me? My entire life."

"Have you heard of a couple of companies

called Columbia Windshield and Glass, and Columbia Auto Repair'?"

"Sure."

"You have? I couldn't find either one online. I was assuming they're out of business?"

"Oh, yeah. They've been out of business for some time now," she said. "Shortly after Hastey Senior passed."

Tracy recalled that name from the article on the reunion and pulled out the newspaper, finding the photographs and the caption. "Hastey Devoe?" she asked, handing the woman the newspaper.

"That's young Hastey. The father owned both businesses. They were side by side, out on Lincoln Road. His wife closed both businesses shortly after Hastey Senior died."

"Is his wife still alive?" The chance that Devoe's wife would have any information about two incomplete invoices was slimmer than none, but Tracy knew that small businesses in small towns were often family affairs, and the wife could have also been the bookkeeper.

"I really don't know. Last I heard she was living in a nursing home in Vancouver and had Alzheimer's or dementia."

"What does the son do now?"

"Hastey Junior? He works for Reynolds Construction, I believe. At least I've seen him driving one of their trucks around town. Don't ask me what he does though."

Tracy considered the newspaper photograph and caption. "Would that be Eric Reynolds's company?"

"That's right."

"Does Hastey Junior still live in town?"

"In the house he grew up in, over on Cherry."

Tracy made a note on her notepad and thanked the woman. As she stepped away, the woman said, "You might try Sam Goldman. He might have copies of the paper."

"Who's he?" Tracy asked.

"Sam was the publisher of the *Sentinel*. Publisher, reporter, photographer. He and his wife, Adele, did just about everything. He's retired now. We call him Stoneridge's unofficial historian."

"Where would I find him?"

"They live over on Orchard Way," the woman said, already reaching for a pen and a pad of paper to jot down an address and directions.

Minutes later, directions in hand, Tracy descended the front steps of the library. As she did, she noticed the white police vehicle parked around the corner, only partially hidden behind the trunk of a cottonwood tree.

Following the librarian's directions, Tracy took a right at the end of the block. Rather than stay straight for a mile, however, she took the next right, then turned right a third time and slowed. She stopped behind the cottonwood, which the police

189

vehicle had vacated. It was now parked in the spot where Tracy had parked, at the foot of the library stairs. A Stoneridge Police officer was shuffling up the concrete steps, hands on his utility belt.

Her presence in town had been duly noted.

She pulled from the curb and drove out past the elementary school, occasionally glancing in the mirrors, though she didn't expect to see the police car. The officer didn't need to follow. He'd know soon enough where Tracy was going, and why.

Orchard Way was a quiet street of barren trees and wires sagging between telephone poles, but no street lamps or sidewalks. It wasn't unusual for the older towns. As residents moved farther away from the city center, they focused on essential utilities like electricity, phone, and gas and sewer. Street lamps and sidewalks were far down the priority list, and often never installed.

Tracy parked just off the asphalt, alongside a white picket fence that would need painting after another winter. The fence enclosed a narrow stretch of lawn, split in two by a concrete walk leading to a single-story A-frame home. A satellite dish protruded from the roof like one large ear.

She pulled open the screen and knocked, then closed it and stepped back. There was a window to the left, but no one looked out before the door rattled open. A woman Tracy estimated to be in her late sixties or early seventies pushed open the screen. "Can I help you?" Her voice was tentative—strangers did not likely come knocking often—but not unfriendly.

"I'm looking for Sam Goldman," Tracy said. "Evelyn at the library gave me this address. She said he might be able to tell me about Stoneridge back in the seventies."

The woman frowned, but not in a displeasing manner. "Well," she said, "Sam would know."

"Who is it, Adele?" The man who came to the door was no more than five six, with a head of curly dark hair, graying at the temples. He adjusted his sturdy black-framed glasses as he looked at Tracy with a bemused, curious expression that made his eyes sparkle as if he held the world's biggest secret.

"Evelyn over at the library said you could help this woman," Adele said.

Sam Goldman peered at Tracy. "What's this about, friend?"

"I was hoping to get some background on Stoneridge—what it was like here in the seventies. I understand you're sort of the town historian since the fire in the library."

"September 16, 2000," Goldman said, his voice becoming more animated. "A three-alarm blaze. We could see the smoke from our offices on Main Street. I thought Timmerman's ghost had returned and the whole town was going up in flames again. Most excitement we've had since Dom Petrocelli punched out Gordie Holmes at a town council meeting in 1987."

"I understand it wiped out all the back copies of your newspaper at the library."

"Burned the copies and melted the microfiche," Goldman said. "They were in the process of raising funds to scan and convert the microfiche to discs, but their dreams went up in smoke faster than the Pony Express."

"I'm sorry to hear that," Tracy said.

"Old news," Goldman said, grinning. "I have everything stored up here." He tapped his temple. "Best computer north of the Columbia. Are you a reporter, hero?"

"I'm a police officer."

Goldman's eyes widened, along with his smile. He turned to his wife. "The plot thickens, Adele." He pushed the screen door fully open. "Come on in so we're not heating the neighborhood."

The home was modest but tasteful, with well-used but clean furniture. Tracy noted that Goldman had been watching ESPN on a flat-screen TV. He reached for the remote control on the coffee table and shut it off.

"I hope I'm not interrupting anything," Tracy said.

"The only thing you're interrupting is our forced retirement," Goldman said. "We can rest at the funeral home. Have a seat."

Tracy sat on the couch. Goldman sat in a cloth chair that swiveled to face her. Two folded TV dinner trays leaned against a brick fireplace beneath a painting of a coastline. "Can I get you some coffee or tea?" Adele asked.

Sensing that Adele wasn't sure what to do with herself, Tracy said, "Tea would be wonderful, thank you."

Adele stepped from the room, and Tracy heard her opening and closing cabinets and filling a kettle at the sink.

"Where do you want to start?" Goldman asked.

"How about the state championship game," Tracy said, wanting to give his memory a point of reference, which turned out to not be needed, before diving immediately into Kimi Kanasket.

"Saturday, November 6, 1976."

"What was it like around town back then?"

"Like Christmas and the Fourth of July rolled into one," he said, animated. Tracy had clearly picked a topic that excited him. "The town was so puffed up it was bursting at the seams. Up until then, Stoneridge couldn't have won a one-legged race with two legs. That was the start of it."

"The start of it?"

"The championships. Football mainly, but also swimming, basketball, baseball, soccer."

"So what happened? What changed?"

"Ron Reynolds rode into town like John Wayne in *Rio Bravo*. He changed the culture. The kids were used to losing, and content to do so. Reynolds put an end to that."

"How'd he do that?"

"You paid in sweat to play sports for Ron Reynolds. If the kids weren't playing games, they were practicing or conditioning. Initially, some parents moaned about the time commitment interfering with schoolwork, but Ron just charged ahead like Teddy Roosevelt up San Juan Hill. He didn't care what people thought of him. The complaints stopped when the banners started flying in the gym and people started reading their kids' names in my paper. Then a few started getting scholarships. Money talks, friend. The complainers got quieter than a nun in the confessional."

"He was the football coach?"

"They hired him as the football coach. They made him the athletic director, and he stayed on thirty-five years. They had a big retirement party for him in the school gym a few years back."

"He's still alive?"

"Lives in the same house he bought when he moved here."

"I read in the paper they're naming a stadium after him."

"That's the son's doing. His company's providing the material and labor. The town isn't going to look a gift horse in the mouth."

Tracy wasn't much of a football fan. She'd

grown up listening to Mariners baseball games with her father, but sensing Goldman's excitement for the topic and hoping to establish a rapport, she asked, "You covered the championship?"

"They would have lynched me and burned the Sentinel building if I hadn't. The town was all caught up that year in the Four Ironmen."

"The Four Ironmen?"

"Eric Reynolds, Hastey Devoe, Archie Coe, and Darren Gallentine."

Tracy recognized the names Devoe and Reynolds from the recent articles in the newspaper. "Why were they called 'the Four Ironmen'?"

"Never missed a down in three years of varsity football, and they played both ways."

"Played both ways?" Tracy asked.

"Offense and defense," Adele said. She'd entered the room carrying a tray with a teapot and ceramic mugs. She made a face that conveyed, *You'd be surprised what you learn after fifty years.*

"Reynolds was the all-American," Goldman said as Adele handed Tracy a cup of tea. "He was the straw that stirred the drink. Without him, they don't win. Devoe opened the holes on the offensive line, and Coe and Gallentine ran through them. Coe was fast and shifty. Gallentine was the hammer. On defense Devoe played nose tackle, Gallentine played linebacker, Coe was the cornerback, and Reynolds was the free safety. He had five interceptions his senior year."

Tracy took a sip of her tea, which had a mint flavor. She set the cup on a coaster and retrieved the file from her briefcase. "I saw a photograph in the paper." She showed Goldman the picture of the four young men hoisting the trophy into the stadium lights, and this time noted the names in the caption.

> Red Raiders senior cocaptains and Ironmen Hastey Devoe (far L), Eric Reynolds (L), Darren Gallentine (R), and Archibald Coe (far R) hold aloft the Washington State 2A Championship trophy.

"I took that," Goldman said. "I got the four of them together right after the game; didn't see the steam rising off their heads until it was developed in the darkroom."

"It's a great shot," Tracy said. "Sounds like the whole town was wrapped up in the winning."

"They filled the stadium every home and away game. It didn't matter if you had a kid playing or not. That trophy belonged to every man, woman, and child in Stoneridge."

"I know how that is," she said.

"Where're you from?"

"Cedar Grove. It's in the North Cascades—a thousand people on a good day."

"So you do know what it's like."

Feeling as though she'd made a connection, Tracy turned to the reason for her visit. "So I'm wondering—what impact, if any, did Kimi Kanasket's death have on the celebrations?"

Goldman smiled, and the glint returned to his eyes. Tracy could almost see the wheels spinning inside his head. He pointed a finger at her. "I figured you'd get around to her eventually."

"How come?"

"I figured a cop who didn't know what 'both ways' meant wasn't here to relive the glory days of the local football team."

Tracy smiled. "Do you remember the story?"

"Kimi? It was my story."

"What do you remember?"

"A tragedy of Shakespearean proportions."

"How well did you know her?"

"Everyone knew Kimi. She was a track star. In the fall she ran cross-country, and in the spring she ran the high hurdles and the one hundred— back then it was still called the hundred-yard dash. She finished second in the state her junior year and was the odds-on favorite to win both races senior year."

"What kind of kid was she off the track?"

This time Goldman didn't hesitate. "Great kid. 'A' student. Polite. She worked at a diner just outside of town to earn money for college."

"The Columbia Diner."

"That's the one. The family didn't have much.

Kimi was going to be the first to graduate high school and go to college. I intended to do a feature on her." Goldman sighed. "Like I said, a real tragedy."

"I noticed the diner is closed—"

"It went the way of the dinosaur long before I closed the *Sentinel*."

"What about the people who owned the diner— are they still around?"

"Lorraine and Charlie Topeka, spelled like the city in Kansas. Charlie was the cook. Lorraine was the boss. They made a go of it for many years."

"You know where I might find them?"

"Charlie's playing pinochle with the worms. Lorraine, I'm not sure. Heard she moved south somewhere with a daughter. She'd be pushing eighty."

"Mr. Goldman, you strike me as a pretty intuitive guy."

"I've fooled a few people in my day. And call me Sam. I'm old enough. I don't need to be reminded."

Tracy smiled. "Fair enough, Sam. Let me ask you straight up. When you heard the news that Kimi Kanasket killed herself, what was your first thought?"

"First thought?" He paused, eyes closed.

"We couldn't get anyone to talk to us," Adele said.

"She's right," Goldman said, opening his eyes.

"Facts were tucked away as tight as a pound in Churchill's knickers."

"Why do you think that was?"

"People didn't talk about those types of things back then."

"They didn't want to spoil the mood," Adele said before catching herself. "But I'll let you two talk." She went back to sipping her tea.

"So what did you think, Sam? What was your first thought?"

"I guess my first thought was the same as everyone else's," Goldman said. "I was shocked. Kimi didn't strike any of us as a kid who would do that. The brother maybe, but not Kimi."

"Her brother had some issues?"

"Élan was his name. He clashed with the white kids at school and got himself expelled."

"What was he fighting about?" she asked, though she suspected she knew the answer.

"The local tribes were protesting the school's use of the name 'Red Raiders' and the Indian mascot—a white kid wearing war paint would ride onto the field and bury a spear in the grass. The tribes said it was historically inaccurate and degrading. Looking back, they were ahead of their time."

"How big a deal was it?"

"At first, not very. The tribal elders brought their concerns to the school administrators and to the city council. It was all very respectful until they got no response and felt they were being ignored. They changed tactics and started to protest outside the football games. That's what got feathers ruffled."

"I understand Earl Kanasket was a tribal elder and one of the leaders of the protest. Any of that fallout ever hit Kimi?"

"Not that I ever heard," Goldman said. "Kimi wasn't like Élan. Like I said, she was a quiet kid, polite. She kept more to her studies." Goldman leaned forward, looking at Tracy over the top of his glasses. "Are you saying otherwise?"

"I don't know yet," Tracy said. "But something about what happened back then didn't sit right with a young deputy sheriff—"

"Buzz Almond."

Tracy nodded. "You really do have a computer up there, don't you?"

"Use it or lose it, friend; that's what my doctor says. I intend to use it." Goldman sat back again. "Buzz was a good man and a great sheriff. If Buzz thought something was up, it likely was."

"So tell me, what was a great kid like Kimi doing with someone like Tommy Moore?"

"Tommy got all the girls back then. He was our James Dean—smoldering good looks. He could charm a rattlesnake into not biting him."

"How well did you know him?"

"Not well. Never spoke to him. I covered his fights when he fought Golden Gloves. He could have been a good boxer; he had a heck of a left hook."

"What happened to him?"

"He drank too much, and the town more or less ran him out after the story broke about Kimi. They blamed him for her death. I heard he moved back home to the reservation. Hasn't been seen or heard from since, far as I know."

Tracy switched gears to the two receipts in Buzz Almond's file. "How about Hastey Devoe? I understand he owned a windshield repair company and an auto repair shop."

"That's right, just off 141 on Lincoln Road, I believe."

"What kind of guy was he?"

"What do you mean?"

Tracy struggled to rephrase her question. "I don't know. Was he honest? Did he go to church? You know what I mean?"

"I never had any direct business with him, but I never heard anything to indicate he wasn't a stand-up guy."

"Any connection to Tommy Moore you're aware of?"

"Not to my knowledge."

"Sounds like it was an interesting time around here, Sam."

"It was like Dickens wrote in *A Tale of Two*

Cities, 'It was the best of times, it was the worst of times.' "

"You wouldn't know of any place else that carries copies of old newspapers I could go through, would you? Evelyn thought I might try the library in Goldendale."

Goldman smiled again. "Friend, I know the best library around, and it's a lot closer than Goldendale."

Tracy followed Goldman through a spotless kitchen that held the faint odor of lemon-scented bleach.

"Where're you going now, Sam?" Adele asked.

"Back to the future," he said, leading Tracy into a tiny mudroom off the kitchen and turning the deadbolt on a curtained back door.

"You're not taking her out to that awful shed are you?" Adele looked at Tracy like Sam was taking her to a horror film. "He's got more stuff in there than the thrift store in town. You'll get dust all over your nice clothes."

Tracy smiled. "I'm not wearing anything that can't get dirty," she said, though she'd thrown on her blue cashmere sweater that morning.

Goldman led Tracy down wooden steps into a sun-drenched patch of grass enclosed by a six-foot redwood fence. The yard looked to have been buttoned down for the winter, benches stacked upon a picnic table and stored beneath a lean-to extending off the roof of the freestanding shed. The shed doors were secured with a sturdy padlock. Goldman removed it, swung the door open, and used a five-gallon bucket to keep it propped. Inside, he flipped a switch, and two bare bulbs hanging from overhead rafters shone golden light upon Sam Goldman's treasures—bicycles, garden tools, baseball bats, a bucket of tennis balls, tennis rackets, file cabinets, and dozens of ties adorned with Disney and Peanuts characters and other trinkets. Adele hadn't exaggerated; a thrift-store owner would have been duly impressed.

Goldman slid aside and rearranged his treasures as he made his way to the back of the shed. With each movement, more dust motes danced in the shafts of light, spinning and swirling. At the back of the garage stood a wall of Bekins boxes, six or seven high and extending the width of the building. Each box had been neatly labeled with the month and the year in black marker and stacked in chronological order, starting with "7/1969" and ending with "12/2000." Goldman moved a few boxes until he reached the box labeled "6/1975–1/1977."

"This would be it." He removed the lid, revealing neatly folded newspapers.

"You kept every newspaper?" Tracy asked.

"From the day we opened our door until the day we closed. I was like the milkman. I delivered regularly."

Goldman thumbed through the papers. "August, September, October . . ." When he got to November, he pulled out four of the papers and set the lid back on the box, using it as a table. "These are the issues leading up to and following the game," he said. "This is where you'll find the articles on Kimi Kanasket, and they'll give you a feel for what it was like around here."

"Front-page news," Tracy said, reading the headline of the first paper.

Stoneridge Wins Region!
State Championship Saturday

"Like I said, they'd have lynched me if I hadn't covered it."

The half-column article on Kimi Kanasket's death was pushed to the bottom of the front page.

Local Girl's Body Pulled
from White Salmon River

The article did not mention the word "suicide."

"I take it there weren't any follow-up articles?" Tracy asked.

"Nothing to follow up. She was cremated in a private service on the reservation. The detective told me the coroner concluded she'd jumped in because Tommy Moore broke up with her. I had a copy of his report at one time, though I don't believe I kept it. Didn't see any reason to make that public, though everyone knew soon enough."

"You spoke to the detective?"

"Jerry Ostertag."

"Is he still around?"

"I wouldn't know, chief. Last I heard he'd retired and moved someplace in the Midwest to fish. Montana, maybe."

Jenny had said that Ostertag had died, but even if Ostertag was still around, Tracy doubted he would recall many of the details of Kimi Kanasket's death. Kimi Kanasket was a black mark on an otherwise joyous occasion, like the drunk uncle who causes a scene at a family wedding. You didn't acknowledge or talk about the incident. You quietly escorted him from the building so others could focus on the celebration, and when the family got together to remember that day, the blemish was never discussed, until, as the years passed, the incident was forgotten completely.

CHAPTER 16

Tracy and Sam Goldman made copies of the relevant pages of the newspaper at the copy machine in the drugstore in town, a task that took longer than it otherwise should have. Goldman stopped to talk to just about everyone, calling each person "chief," "friend," or "hero."

Tracy sensed Goldman was enjoying the break from a daily routine likely forced on him by the Internet and twenty-four-hour news programs, which had rendered so many small-town newspapers obsolete. Goldman was a perpetual ball of motion; though retired, his blood still ran black with newspaper ink, and his nose could still sniff out a news story. He was on the trail of one now.

After dropping Goldman back at home, Tracy called and gave Jenny an update, thanked her again for allowing her to stay at her mother's home, and said she'd be in touch when she got back the forensics. She decided to make one more stop on her way out of town, and as she drove along State Route 141, her cell phone rang. She put the caller on speakerphone.

"Detective Crosswhite? It's Sam Goldman."

"Yes, Sam."

"I thought you should know that after you left I had another visitor."

"A Stoneridge Police officer?"

"You got that right, friend. He came by asking what we discussed. I told him you were interested in the parade."

Tracy chuckled. "How'd he take that?"

"He puffed up his chest a bit, asked a few more questions, and moved on. I just thought you'd like to know."

Tracy could hear the excitement in Goldman's voice. "I appreciate it, Sam. It's probably just a jurisdictional thing. The sheriff let them know I'd be in town. Next time down I'll stop by and introduce myself, but I appreciate the heads-up."

"Not a problem, friend."

Tracy was about to disconnect when she passed the small turnout and the path leading to the clearing. "Sam?"

"Yeah."

"You know anything about the clearing that's just off 141? The big open field a few miles out of town?"

"You want the local legend?"

"I've heard that story. I'm more interested in recent news."

"High school kids used to go out there at night, usually on the weekends."

"Not anymore?"

"Police cracked down a few years back, after a couple of alcohol-related accidents."

"You ever hear anything about anyone trying to plant things there?"

"What do you mean?"

"Someone trying to grow plants or shrubs. Anything."

"Nothing grows there."

"That's what I hear, but do you know of anyone *trying?*"

"I don't. I did a story on it years back and looked into its history. Nothing definitive, but there used to be a phosphorous mine in the foothills not far from there. The suspicion is, that's where the mining company illegally dumped its mining sludge, and the ground is contaminated."

"I take it nobody has ever tested the soil?"

"Nah. Nobody cares enough to find out."

"Okay. Thanks again for your time."

"Not a problem, chief. Keep me posted. You have me interested."

Tracy disconnected and drove another mile, slowing at the wooden sign for Northwest Park. She turned right, descending the tree-lined road for about a mile and slowing at a narrow concrete bridge that spanned the river. She stopped on the bridge. To her right, the river was an iron gray with hundreds of white ribbons where the water flowed over submerged rocks. To her left, the river continued its path to the Columbia.

Just after crossing the bridge, she turned left into a parking lot. The park next to it was nothing more than a tiny patch of lawn with a few picnic tables along the river's edge. She got out and considered a kiosk of concrete and metal that provided a pictorial and written history of the White Salmon River. Apparently, it had been dammed for hydro-electric energy for decades, until the recent push to restore the natural runs of the Chinook salmon and steelhead migrating from the Pacific Ocean to their spawning grounds.

Tracy stepped onto the lawn and approached the river. The water flowed gently here, lapping over the rocks along the shore. Her eyes were again drawn upstream to where the water flowed more forcefully, water that had carried Kimi Kanasket's body downstream until the outstretched limb of a sunken tree caught her somewhere near this spot.

A car engine and the sound of tires hitting speed bumps drew Tracy's attention back to the bridge, and she watched a white-and-blue Stoneridge Police SUV slow as it crossed, not the same patrol vehicle that had been following her trail. The driver peered down at her from behind sunglasses. Seemed the officer really was interested in what Tracy was doing.

She didn't follow the SUV's progress, turning her gaze back to the river, but she heard the gravel crunching as the car entered the parking lot and came to a stop. The engine shut off, and a car door opened and shut.

"Excuse me?" This officer looked more seasoned

than the officer at the library. He was older and heavier, with a head of gray hair and the stern expression of someone officious. The sun glinted off his sunglasses and the gold badge attached to the grommet just above the breast pocket of his beige short-sleeve shirt. "I'm chief of police here in Stoneridge," he said. "Lionel Devoe."

There was that name again.

Devoe hooked his thumbs in the belt of his pants, which hung below his gut. "You must be that detective from Seattle who Sheriff Almond said would be in town. I would have appreciated the courtesy of a call to let me know you'd made it."

"The officer checking up on me in town never gave me the chance to introduce myself," Tracy said. "I was intending to stop in and visit, but the day got away from me."

Devoe removed his sunglasses, slid them into his shirt pocket, and stepped to the side so he wasn't looking directly into the sun. "So what's of interest to a Seattle police detective here in Stoneridge?"

Tracy knew Jenny had already informed Devoe of her interest. She figured the other officer hadn't followed her on his own, but likely had been told to do so when he pulled to the curb after he first encountered Tracy in Stoneridge that morning. Through experience she'd learned that sometimes if she stirred the pot, something unexpected bubbled to the surface. "Devoe?" she said. "Where have I heard that name before?"

"I wouldn't know."

She snapped her fingers. "Hastey Devoe. Didn't he have an auto repair shop back in the day?"

"That was my father," Devoe said, clearly surprised by the question. "That's a long time ago. Why would you want to know about that?"

"Name just popped up in conversation. I understand that was a special time around here in Stoneridge. I read about a big forty-year celebration coming up."

"Sheriff said you're interested in Kimi Kanasket."

"That's right. I am."

"Kimi killed herself," Devoe said. "Jumped in the river."

"Yeah, that's what I read."

Devoe looked past Tracy to the river, and he seemed to realize why she'd come here. "This is where they found her body."

"I know. I thought I'd take a look."

"Why?"

"I just like to see things for myself."

"So what's your interest in Kimi Kanasket?"

"Sheriff asked me to take a look at the file and see if there might be anything there."

"The file?" Devoe sounded more surprised than curious, like someone who'd maybe gone looking for the file and thought it had been destroyed.

"That's right. Buzz Almond kept a file."

"So what do you expect to find?"

"I have no expectations. I like to go into these things with an open mind."

"Well, I think you'll find that Kimi jumped in the river. Or fell. It was pretty open-and-shut, as I recall."

"You recall it?"

"Not really, no. Just a general recollection. Talk. You know."

"I'm assuming you weren't a police officer back then?"

"No, not back then."

"What were you doing?"

"Why are you asking, Detective?"

"Just trying to get a handle on the town back then, what people recall it was like. Were you around?"

Devoe smiled again, but now his expression had the unease of a man trying to get out of a conversation. "Like I said, when a fellow law-enforcement officer comes to town, I appreciate a courtesy call."

"I'll remember that."

"You on your way out?"

"I am."

"Will you be coming back?"

"I don't know yet. I guess that depends."

"Depends on what?"

"What the forensics tell me." Tracy made a show

of checking the time. "I got a bit of a drive ahead of me. Thanks for stopping and introducing yourself, Chief."

She walked past him to her truck. When she backed out, Devoe remained where she'd left him at the water's edge.

When Tracy reached State Route 141, she called Sam Goldman again. Adele answered, but Sam was quick to get on the line. "That was fast."

"I'm sorry to keep bothering you, but I have another question."

"No bother. Fire away, hero."

"What can you tell me about Lionel Devoe?"

"He's been chief of police in Stoneridge going on thirty years now."

"What did he do before he became a police officer?"

"What all the Hastey boys did—worked for his father."

"How many brothers were there?"

"Three, but the oldest, Nathaniel, died in a hunting accident."

Tracy considered the information. "Any idea why Lionel left the family business to join the police force?"

"Nothing you could quote in the paper, but I can speculate."

"Please do."

"Like I said, the oldest of the three was

Nathaniel. He was the most like his father, a hard worker with a good business head on his shoulders. I think Hastey Senior intended to leave him the business, but then Nathaniel died. Hastey Junior and Lionel weren't like their old man, or their brother—neither had the work ethic or the brains. It caused a lot of friction."

"They didn't get along with their dad?"

"Hastey, the father, tried giving the business to Lionel after Nathaniel died, but Lionel nearly ran it into the ground, and the old man took it back. I imagine getting away from his father and the enticement of the police department's benefits package were more motivation to join the force than any desire to serve the good citizens of Stoneridge. Down here, it's mostly small stuff. We don't get a lot of excitement unless one of the meth-heads blows up his lab. Basically, if you don't screw up, it's a job for life."

"So it's an elected position?"

"You could say that, but it's really a matter of default. There's never been a lot of competition for the job," Goldman said. "And Lionel is tight with Eric Reynolds. That name goes a long way here in Stoneridge."

"Eric Reynolds the contractor?"

"That's right."

"Doesn't Hastey Devoe work for him also?"

"He does."

"Did Hastey ever take over the family business?"

"Young Hastey isn't like his old man. Maybe he had one too many concussions. Only chance that boy had of getting a college education was football, but he drank his way out of school and had to move back home."

Tracy thought it all very incestuous, but having lived in a small town, she knew that friends helping friends wasn't uncommon, and it could be nothing more than that. That didn't explain why Lionel Devoe had been so guarded, however, and she didn't for a minute believe he had his panties in a bunch just because Tracy didn't drive to his office and curtsy.

"What else can I tell you?" Goldman asked.

"I think that's it for now," she said, though she had more questions now than when she'd started the day.

CHAPTER 17

Tracy arrived back at the Justice Center late in the afternoon, but she didn't stay long. Kins had set up a meeting with Tim Collins's divorce attorney in the University District. Faz had gone home early to celebrate a family birthday. As they drove, Kins filled Tracy in on conversations he and Faz had with two of Tim Collins's coworkers and his supervisor at Boeing, names not on the list provided by Mark Collins. They'd also spent time talking with a person from Boeing's IT department who had been tasked with downloading Tim's e-mails and compiling a history of his recent Internet searches.

"They all said he was a good guy and a hard worker. Never saw him lose his temper and never had a bad thing to say about his wife. They said he'd seemed depressed the past several months and attributed it to the breakup of his marriage, but he wasn't the kind to air his dirty laundry."

"What about his relationship with Connor?"

"They said he was a proud father who talked about his son often. He kept photographs in his cubicle of the three of them, like it was still one big, happy family."

"Maybe he was having trouble letting her go."

"Maybe. The brother did say he'd become very codependent."

"What about the kid? You talk to his classmates?"

"No real friends to speak of, according to his counselor and two of his teachers. They all described him as quiet and reserved. Said he doesn't participate much in class or show much interest in any extracurricular activities."

"Any indication he lies?"

"Nothing. I got the impression he's one of the many faceless high school students who show up for class, do enough to get by, and leave."

"So no problems?"

Kins shook his head. "None."

"Anything on social media?"

"A few photos. Nothing alarming. We got the phone records. The father sent a text at 5:10 that evening saying traffic was bad, and he'd be a few minutes late."

"Any response?"

"One letter. *K.* Overall, it's been slowgoing."

"Well, at least it gives you a little more time to spend at home," she said, fishing.

"Yeah, there's that," Kins said, not sounding excited.

"Things not going well?"

Kins shrugged. "About the same."

"I thought things were better after Mexico?"

Kins and Shannah's relationship had hit a rough

217

patch when Kins and Tracy were working late nights and early mornings on the Cowboy investigation; the case had taken a physical and emotional toll on everyone on the task force. When the investigation ended, Kins took Shannah to Mexico, without kids, and said it helped them remember why they'd married each other in the first place.

"It was, for a while. You'd think me being around more would be a good thing, but it seems like we just get on each other's nerves."

"What about?"

"Name it," he said, offering a sad laugh. "It feels like she's paying me back for being gone so much. She leaves to play tennis or go to her book club. And she's at the gym all the time."

"You could join her."

He gave her a look, one eyebrow arched. "Tennis? With my hip? And her book club, as far as I can tell, is just an excuse for the wives to drink wine and rag on husbands. I don't think I'd fit in."

"You can't fault her for having a life, Kins. We're gone so much."

"I know."

"What about counseling?"

"Been there."

"What about more counseling?"

"I don't know."

Anthony Holt's office was on the second floor of a building not far from the University of

Washington. He specialized in family law, and his partner specialized in wills and estates. Holt met Kins and Tracy in a modest lobby, and they walked across the hall to a conference room he shared with other lawyers on the floor. Tracy estimated Holt to be in his midforties, though prematurely gray, which gave him an authoritative appearance. He was marathon-runner thin.

"You were Mr. Collins's divorce attorney," Kins said after they'd settled into chairs.

"I was. I was sorry to hear about what happened to him."

"How did you hear?"

"Angela's divorce attorney called and advised me."

"When was that?"

"It was the day after the shooting."

"What time?"

"It was in the afternoon. I could get you a specific time, if it's important."

"What did the attorney tell you?"

"She said Angela had called her and told her what had happened. She wanted to file the paperwork to dismiss the divorce and begin probating the estate."

Kins shot Tracy a glance. Angela must have called first thing after leaving jail. "Do you know when that paperwork got filed?"

Holt smiled. "I do. Bright and early Monday morning."

"That surprised you."

"Surprised?" He smiled again. "Nothing surprises me in this area of the law. Just . . ." He paused to choose his words. "Just seemed quick, given the circumstances."

"Like the fact that she was in jail until Friday afternoon?"

"That thought crossed my mind, yes."

"And she was facing a murder charge and the prospect of a long sentence?"

"That also."

"Any thoughts why she'd be in a hurry to file the paperwork?"

"The sooner the divorce proceeding is dismissed, the sooner the estate can be probated and the sooner she gets the money. But I tend to be cynical about these things."

"How contentious was the divorce?"

"Scale of one to ten, this was a six, but only because Tim did a lot to not escalate things."

"Can you explain what you mean?" Kins asked.

"Angela was pushing for fifty-eight percent of the assets. In the interim she was blowing through a lot of the money. She kept asking Tim for more and chiding him when he refused."

"Do you know how she was spending the money?"

"No. That was the problem. She claimed it was everyday living expenses, but in three months she'd spent close to forty-five thousand dollars, and every time we asked for receipts we got the runaround. Her attorney couldn't explain it either. Tim suspected she was squirreling it away or using it to fix up the house."

"How close were you to getting a resolution?"

"Not close. We went to mediation, but it didn't last long. I didn't see it resolving without a trial."

"Most cases settle, don't they?" Kins asked.

"Ninety-five percent or more."

"So why not this one?"

"Again, I'm probably biased, but from my perspective Angela had dug in her heels and wasn't going to budge. I'm also not sure she wanted to settle."

"What do you mean by that?"

"As long as the divorce continued, she had something to hold over Tim's head."

"But I'd imagine going to trial would be expensive for both parties," Kins said.

"It already was expensive, but, yes, once you step foot in court, the price escalates quickly. Since the fees come from the estate, though, Tim would bear much of that burden."

"How big was the estate they were fighting over?"

"Not all that much in the scheme of things. Roughly a few million dollars. Tim owned a rental property before they got married and never put Angela on the deed of trust, but Angela was alleging they'd used community funds to fix it up and that she was entitled to a percentage. She also accused Tim of hiding money."

"Was he?"

Holt smiled again. "No. Tim wanted to get this resolved. He was reaching a breaking point emotionally. I was the one telling him to hang on."

"What do you mean, 'reaching a breaking point emotionally'?"

"Angela had worn him down pretty good. Tim was ready to just throw in the towel, give Angela what she wanted, and move on with his life. It isn't uncommon in divorce proceedings, but often the person who caves ends up regretting it. I kept telling him not to rush, that it would play out, that he'd already given Angela the house."

Tracy had been taking notes. Upon hearing the latter comment, she sat up. "What do you mean, he gave her the house?"

"Tim had agreed to let Angela keep the house so Connor wouldn't be displaced from his home until after graduating. He was worried about Connor's emotional well-being."

"He was just giving her the house?" Tracy said.

"No, not exactly. We were proposing a settlement in which Tim would get the rental unit outright and be compensated for his share of ownership in the house with other assets. Basically, it's just a matter of how you balance the assets in each spouse's column."

"The home wasn't being sold?" Tracy asked, remembering that the night she'd arrived she'd gotten that distinct impression from the condition of the yard and the interior.

"Not that I'm aware of," Holt said. "That would have gone directly against Tim's wishes and the interim agreement we'd reached pending final resolution."

"What agreement?"

"Angela had to get Tim's consent to sell, and anything obtained over the appraised value at the time of separation would be split at the time of sale."

"You have a copy of that agreement?"

"I do, and I can get a copy to you."

Tracy nodded to Kins to let him know she was through. He said, "We understand that Mr. Collins was also redoing his will."

Holt slid documents across the table. "My partner was creating a trust for Connor. It isn't uncommon in a divorce. Tim was also changing his personal representative from Angela to his brother, Mark, and appointing Mark as the trustee of his estate."

"Practically, that means that if anything happened to Tim, his estate would go to Connor, with the brother keeping a watch on it, not Angela," Kins said.

"Correct."

"Angela wouldn't have any right to any portion

of that trust or control over how the assets were distributed'?"

"None. The brother would serve as a trustee until Connor reached the age of thirty-one, or he deemed the trust was no longer necessary."

"Thirty-one?" Kins said. "That seems really old."

"Tim didn't want Angela to have any ability to get at the money, if anything were to happen to him. Connor isn't the strongest personality. Tim wanted his brother to remain involved to ensure the money went to Connor—for his school, a down payment on a house, whatever. Tim wanted restrictions. By thirty-one, most of the estate would have been distributed."

"But that new will and trust were never finalized?" Kins asked.

"No. Tim was coming in that Friday to sign everything and have it witnessed."

"The day after he got shot?"

Holt nodded. "Yes."

"So what happens now?"

Holt shrugged. "Everything goes to Angela as the surviving spouse, and she remains the personal representative."

"Even though they were separated?"

"Even though they were separated."

"And it is against Tim Collins's express wishes."

"His express wishes don't matter without a signed and witnessed new will."

• • •

Kins was quiet on the drive back to the Justice Center, appearing to be deep in thought.

"We should call local real estate agents," Tracy said. "To find out if Angela spoke to any of them and when. When are we supposed to get her cell phone and computer files?"

"Cerrabone said Berkshire promised them any day now." Kins looked at her. "You think that's where the forty-five thousand dollars went?"

"Sure looked like the property was being fixed up to sell," Tracy said.

"She was depleting the estate to fix up her asset."

"One way to get more money out of him, and if she turned around and sold that asset, she'd get the full benefit."

"Except that would have been in violation of the agreement they'd reached," Kins said.

"Not if Tim was dead," Tracy said.

CHAPTER 18

K ins left the office right away after their meeting with Tim Collins's divorce attorney. Tracy planned to stay a little later, playing catch-up after being away two days. When her cell phone rang, she smiled at the caller ID.

"I was hoping it would be you," she said.

"We finished early," Dan said. "It was a miracle on par with Jesus raising Lazarus from the dead. I'm on an earlier flight."

"That's the best news I've heard all week. When do you get in?"

"If there aren't any delays, I should arrive right around nine."

"And will you be spending the night?" she asked, teasing. West Seattle was only about twenty minutes from the airport. They'd already discussed Dan spending the night before he drove to Cedar Grove to care for his two dogs, Rex and Sherlock. Knowing he'd be exhausted after a long and trying week, Tracy wanted to surprise him by cooking him a late dinner.

"Do you give a discount for Triple A members?" Dan asked.

"No, but we do for AARP members."

"Ouch."

"I think we can negotiate something."

"Then I'll see you when I see you."

Tracy hung up and grabbed her coat, in a hurry to go shopping, when her desk phone rang. She contemplated not answering but saw it was her private line.

"I'm thirsty," Kelly Rosa said, "and it's been a hell of a week. My husband has the girls at a soccer practice and is taking them out to dinner, so I have a couple hours' reprieve. Buy me a beer, and I'll spill my guts about Kimi Kanasket."

Rosa chose a Capitol Hill bar called the Elysian. Tracy found her at a table in the back by interior floor-to-ceiling windows that allowed patrons to see the brewery's large metal beer tanks. Tracy never could quite reconcile Rosa's physical appearance with what she did for a living. Only five feet tall and dressed in comfortable clothes, Rosa looked more like a PTA parent or a soccer mom than someone who spent her workdays trudging up mountains and navigating forests and swamps to recover and examine the remains of bodies often in advanced and horrific stages of decay. Rosa had once explained to Tracy that she thought of her job as a forensic anthropologist for the King County Medical Examiner's Office to be as much historian as scientist. She said she looked at each new case as a puzzle that required her to journey back in time, and it was her job to solve the puzzle.

Rosa sipped a beer with one hand while texting with the other. With two teenage daughters, she had to be a model of efficiency.

"Those things will be the death of society," Tracy said, reaching the table and pointing to Rosa's phone.

Rosa stood, phone still in hand, and gave Tracy a hug.

"How're you doing?" Tracy asked.

"Still living the dream. Hang on. I'm actually texting my husband to confirm he's taking the girls out to dinner after their soccer practice."

"I'm sorry you're missing out," Tracy said.

Rosa scoffed. "Ha. If I wasn't here having a beer, I'd be standing in the cold and rain watching a ball get kicked all over the field. You've saved me from a nasty cold." Rosa hit "Send" and set the phone down. "Okay. The ringer is off and so am I. How are you?"

"Can't complain." The legs of Tracy's chair scraped the terrazzo tile floor as she sat.

"It's been a while," Rosa said. "That's a good thing."

Tracy took a moment to look around and smell the rich aroma of hops. "Interesting place. I like it."

"Paul and I used to come here after I got off work," she said. "BK."

"BK?"

"Before kids—though my kids still think the

two of us have never been to a bar in our lives. I told my oldest about a Rolling Stones concert we went to in college, and I don't know what shocked me more—that she didn't know who the Rolling Stones were or that she refused to believe we ever went to a concert. Wait until the day I tell them I once died my hair purple."

A waitress approached. "What are you drinking?" Tracy asked.

"The Immortal."

"It's an IPA," the waitress said, handing Tracy a menu with beers named Loser Pale Ale, Men's Room Red, and the Wise. "I could use a little wisdom," Tracy said, "but who can pass up immortality?"

Rosa sipped her beer. "I see way too much mortality at work."

If the demands of Rosa's job ever wore her down, she didn't show it. At least Tracy had never seen it. Rosa packed a lot of positive energy into her small frame.

"How's that boyfriend of yours?" Rosa asked.

"Good," Tracy said. "But right now neither of us seems to be able to get out from under work."

"Screw that." Rosa slapped the table loud enough to draw the attention of a woman seated at the next table. "The work will always be here. People are always going to die. Take him someplace exotic, where you don't have to worry about anything except what cocktail to drink and how many times a day you can have sex."

"Sounds good to me," Tracy said. "Help me solve this one and I might find that time."

"I think I can help with that," Rosa said, "but I'm waiting for someone." She glanced over Tracy's shoulder to the door.

Tracy noticed a third chair at the table and recalled Rosa mentioning she might ask for help. "So who is he?"

"Trust me. He's worth the wait." She glanced again to the door. "And there he is." Rosa stood and waved at a ruggedly handsome man scanning the crowd. When he saw Rosa, he returned her wave and flashed a mouthful of white teeth.

Rosa spoke under her breath. "Is it sexual harassment if I just *think* about grabbing his butt?" She stuck out her hand and gave the man a one-armed hug, then made the introductions. "Tracy, meet Peter Gabriel."

Tan, lean-muscled, and dressed in a pair of loose-fitting khakis, an open-collared shirt, and a lightweight raincoat, Gabriel looked like he'd just walked off the pages of a J.Crew catalog. His curly brown hair fell nearly to his shoulders. Tracy was guessing he was a rock climber or an extreme skier—definitely something outdoorsy.

"Peter Gabriel, like the singer?" she asked.

"Spelled the same," he said, offering a firm handshake. His other hand held a single manila file. "Good taste in music."

He set the file on the table, took off his raincoat, and pulled out a chair.

"About a year back, Peter and I worked another river-drowning case together," Rosa said. She paused to let the wailing sound of a siren pass before continuing. "I thought he might be of help with this one."

"Okay," Tracy said, turning to face him. "What do you do, Peter?"

Gabriel was unbuttoning his cuffs and rolling up his shirtsleeves. He wore two colorful woven rope bracelets on his left wrist. A hefty sport watch adorned his right. "I work as a consultant for REI, but my passion has always been white-water river rafting and canoeing."

The waitress returned with Tracy's beer and offered Gabriel a bright smile. Gabriel surveyed the beer menu for a moment, then said, "Okay, I cannot pass up the opportunity to try a beer called 'Loser Pale Ale.'"

Tracy liked him already.

"Peter has guided white-water excursions on just about every major river in the state," Rosa said. "Everything from Class Two to Class Five rapids. Did I get that right?"

"You did," Gabriel said before turning to Tracy. "My dad owned a white-water rafting company on the Rogue River in Oregon. It was a family business. My brothers and sisters and I could navigate a river about the same time we could walk. I guided my first white-water trip when I was twelve."

"About a year ago, I needed some help with a body pulled from the Skykomish," Rosa said, referring to a river about an hour northeast of Seattle. "We were trying to determine whether or not the injuries were inflicted by the river. Peter was recommended to me."

"I appreciate the help," Tracy said.

Rosa flipped open her manila folder, and Gabriel mimicked her, opening his. "Let's start with the coroner's finding that the deceased was alive when she entered the water," Rosa said. "First, drowning is one of the most difficult causes of death to get a handle on, because there is no true definitive sign of drowning. A drowning person actually dies from a lack of oxygen. Having said that, I concur with the pathologist who prepared this report that the person was likely alive when she hit the water."

"You do?" Tracy asked, surprised and disappointed by the conclusion.

"Based on what's in the coroner's report, yes. The coroner found water in her air passages, including the lungs and stomach. Now, a person can get water in both locations passively if there is a strong current, but in this instance I believe the intake of water is consistent with a person still breathing upon impact."

"Why?"

"I'm going to let Peter answer that."

"The White Salmon in November runs just around forty-two degrees," Gabriel offered. "A person hitting water that cold, if alive, will have a gasp reflex. I know. I've done it. If the victim wasn't wearing a life jacket or wet suit, she'd go under and take that gasp, ingesting a large volume of water."

"Which is what we have here," Rosa said. "The bruising on her body is another indicator she was alive when she went into the water—that is, that her blood was still circulating to those areas," Rosa said. "When you have antemortem bruising, you expect swelling, damage to the skin, coagulation at the site of impact, and infiltration of the tissues with blood, resulting in color changes, which is what the coroner noted in his report and documented in photographs. You don't find that in postmortem bruising."

Tracy sat back from the table, feeling deflated, though she also knew as well as anyone that most cases were exactly what they seemed. The "whodunits" were a lot rarer than the grounders. "So she committed suicide."

Rosa started to answer, but the waitress had returned with Gabriel's beer, setting it on a coaster.

"Can I get you anything else?"

"I think we're good," Tracy said.

After the waitress departed, Rosa sipped her

beer and set the glass back down on the coaster. "Actually," she said calmly, "I don't believe she committed suicide."

"What? Why not?"

"Three things." Rosa held up a finger as she raised each point. "First, pattern recognition with respect to the bruising. Second, the nature of the recorded injuries. And third, river dynamics. I'm going to let Peter start with the river dynamics."

Gabriel handed Tracy and Rosa each a document. "Let's start with terminology. The flow of a river is measured in cubic feet per second. That flow is going to vary based on the particular river, the month, and seasonal factors, such as the depth of the snowpack in the mountains that year, and the number of inches and the severity of spring rains—those sorts of things. What I just gave you is a document from the USGS website, which records water flow on just about every river. NOAA provides similar information—historical data on things like inches of rain, temperature, and river flow. For fishermen and river guides, this is our bible. It's no different than people commuting to work checking traffic cameras to determine the traffic flow before going to work or driving home. River guides and fishermen check river flow."

"How far back do these records go?" Tracy asked while trying to decipher the document on her own.

"About eighty years," Gabriel said. "Your body was found in November 1976. November and February are wild-card months in my business. The water flow can be highly unpredictable. It can be at its absolute peak one day and at its absolute low just days later. We refer to them as transition months. In September and October, the water level is traditionally at its lowest flow because the spring and summer runoff from the snowmelt in the mountains has ordinarily ebbed by then, but if we've had a particularly good snowpack, the river can run high all the way into December. If we've had a poor snowpack, like the past two years, or we've had an Indian summer and the warmer temperatures extend into October, the water levels will be low. But even then, if we get early November rains or maybe a light snow in the foothills that melts, the water flow can go from superlow to superhigh extremely quickly, a matter of days."

"Okay. So you're saying you really have to look at it day to day," Tracy said. "But when you say the river has a high flow rate, how fast are we talking? Can you put it in layman's terms?"

"In November?"

"Right."

"In November the water flow in the White Salmon can peak at two hundred twenty cubic feet per second, which is the equivalent of about eight to twelve miles an hour. Doesn't sound like much for a car, but on a river it's really, really fast, and the water is really high," Gabriel said. "When the water is that high, the boulders are covered; a river guide can literally just point the raft downstream and steer it into and over big waves."

"And a body would go over them also?"

"A body in the river with a life jacket would go over them. A body *without* a life jacket or wet suit is likely to get pulled under, especially if the person is already hurt or inexperienced in that type of survival situation. I've been there, though I always wear a life jacket and a helmet and I'm experienced. It isn't a lot of fun. You don't see the rocks and boulders coming, so you don't have time to brace for a hit or the chance to try to avoid it. It's like getting hit with a baseball bat. The pain is excruciating."

Tracy looked to Rosa. "So, swift enough to cause the type of impact injuries the coroner noted on his report?"

"Maybe," Rosa said, nodding again to Gabriel and taking another sip of her beer.

"If the river is low, the flow is maybe five hundred to six hundred cubic feet per second, which equates to four to five miles an hour. The water flow isn't as intense, but then the water isn't as high, and there are more exposed boulders and rocks to navigate. A person in the water at low flow won't absorb the same impact, but she'll hit more rocks and boulders. It's more a rat-a-tat-tat," he said tapping on the table, "instead of thwack." He slapped his palm for emphasis, causing Tracy to reach for her glass.

"Sorry," he said.

"No worries." Tracy reconsidered the document Gabriel had handed her, which included a graph with data points. "Help me out here. It looks like from this document that the water flow for the first week of November 1976 was a little over five hundred cubic feet per second. Am I reading that correctly?"

"You are," Gabriel said, using a pen to circle the information on Tracy's document.

"So," Rosa said, "some of the injuries identified in the coroner's report would be consistent with what you would expect to see on a body being forced down a river with a four- to five-mile-per-hour flow—bruising, cuts and scrapes, some abrasions."

"But not all of them?" Tracy said.

"In my opinion, your victim suffered what are called 'crushing injuries,' injuries more consistent with blunt-force trauma. What I would expect to see as a result of a high-speed impact."

"Like if the river was at a high water flow," Tracy said.

"Not necessarily," Rosa said, "but possibly. If she was slammed into a boulder and then crushed by, say, a log or other debris, yes."

"Which we did not have," Tracy said, looking to Gabriel.

"Not according to the USGS report," he confirmed.

"So how did she sustain her injuries?" she asked Rosa.

Rosa picked up her copy of the coroner's report. She'd scribbled all over the margins, circled words, and drawn arrows. "In my opinion, the fractured pelvis, bilateral rib fractures, and the fractures to the pubic rami, as well as the cracked sternum, are consistent with the type of injuries I've seen when a person is crushed by a car traveling at a high rate of speed."

Tracy's adrenaline pulsed. She thought of Tommy Moore and the damage to his truck. "She was run over," she said, needing to hear the words spoken out loud.

"Which brings us to the third factor, pattern bruising." Rosa handed Tracy one of the photos from the coroner's report. It took Tracy a moment to determine that she was looking at bruising on Kimi Kanasket's back and right shoulder. Gabriel picked up his beer and looked away.

"Intradermal bruises occur where the blood accumulates in the subepidermal area," Rosa said, "and a pattern emerges when the skin is distorted by being forced between ridges or grooves, like you'd find on a car tire." Rosa used her finger to outline some of the bruises. "The more pronounced the ridges and grooves, the easier it is to discern a pattern from the bruising. It is highly unlikely that your hospital pathologist in 1976 would have recognized this, but we are much more attuned to it now. In my opinion, this is a classic example of pattern bruising from a tire. I'd have Mike Melton take a look and see if he can match the bruising to a particular tread from the State Patrol Crime Lab."

Tracy had already made a mental note to do just that. "Okay, what else?"

"Her face and chest suffered lacerations and abrasions, indicating the body was impacted, forced down, and shoved forward by the blow."

"Wait a minute," Tracy said. "Are you saying you believe she was knocked down and dragged, or that she was already on the ground?"

"If she had been hit and dragged, say on pavement, I would have expected to see a lot more abrasions, skin and muscle torn from bone, those sorts of injuries."

Tracy thought of the clearing. "What if she was standing on grass and dirt at the time of the impact?"

"Maybe, but I think it more likely she was already on the ground because of the nature of the injuries and the location of the most prominent bruising."

Tracy thought of her visit to the clearing. The

weather conditions and temperature had been, according to Buzz Almond's report, similar to the night Kimi disappeared. The ground had been soft from a recent rain, but the back side of the hill leading down to the clearing had been slick from the moisture and drop in temperature. Tracy had nearly fallen.

"So . . . you're saying what . . . ?" Tracy leaned over the table to demonstrate as she spoke. "She was on the ground, facedown, and a car came down on top of her, then went over her?"

"I'd say she was on the ground," Rosa said, "and she tried to cover up to protect herself, which is why the bruising is on the right side of her back and shoulder. That would be the natural instinct."

"So the bruising on her forearms isn't necessarily from impacts with rocks and boulders. It could have been from the impact with a car."

"Could have been," Rosa said.

Tracy sat back. "How sure are you?"

Rosa gave it a moment of thought. "That she was hit by a car? Ninety to ninety-five percent. That all the injuries are attributable to a car and not the river? Not as certain."

Tracy slowed the conversation. Her mind was spinning with questions. "So you're saying she was run over, but she was still alive when she went into the water."

"Correct."

"Given the nature of her injuries, could she have walked to the river on her own?"

"Highly unlikely," Rosa said, "but I don't know the distance we're talking about."

"Considerable," Tracy said.

"Not very likely. In fact, I'd say no way."

"So the only way she could have made it to the water would have been if somebody carried her there."

"That would be my theory." Rosa turned to Gabriel. "Do you agree?"

"I do," he said. "And here's another thing to maybe consider. If she'd been capable of walking to the river on her own, I would have expected her to have had the physical capability to protect herself as she went downriver, and I don't see that was the case, at least not from what's in this report."

"What do you mean?" Tracy asked. "What would you have expected to see?"

"What we discussed earlier—scratches and abrasions on her forearms and hands as she tried to protect herself," Gabriel said. "Also, the coroner's report noted that the body was found with both shoes on and that she was still wearing her coat."

"Why is that significant?"

"If a body is found in the river missing both shoes and articles of clothing, it's usually an indication the person was fighting for their life and still had clarity. One of the first things a person will do is remove clothing weighing them down."

Tracy looked again to Rosa. "Assuming she was hit by a car, in your opinion were those injuries life-threatening? Would she have died from them?"

"It would have depended on how much time passed before she received medical attention. And remember, this was 1976 and in a remote area that didn't have a trauma center," Rosa said. "Bottom line, the longer she lay there, the more likely she wouldn't have survived. But if you're asking me *could* she have survived *had* she received immediate medical attention, I'd say yes. I think she would have."

CHAPTER 19

Tracy remained alone at the table, feeling light-headed, in a fog that had nothing to do with the beer; she hadn't finished her one glass. She needed a moment alone to consider what Rosa and Gabriel had told her and to consider it in conjunction with what she knew. Kimi Kanasket had been run over, almost certainly in the clearing in the woods. That's what Buzz Almond had suspected. That's why he'd taken all those photographs, why the ground was chewed up. She was kicking herself for not having kept copies of the photographs, or at least the negatives, before she gave the packets to Kaylee Wright, and now she had the irrational fear that Wright had somehow lost them.

She recalled at least three photographs of the damage to Tommy Moore's white truck, but she couldn't recall if those photographs captured the tires, or only the damage to the hood and front right fender.

She tried Wright's cell phone, but the call went straight to voice mail. She left a message and tried the King County Sheriff's Office, but she was having trouble hearing over the increasingly animated crowd at the Elysian. She put a finger in her ear to cut down the ambient noise.

"She's where?"

"Tacoma," the woman on the phone said. "She's working a missing-person case."

"She's back from Germany already?" Tracy said.

"That would appear to be the case," the woman said.

Tracy left a voice-mail message on Wright's desk phone. Until Wright called her back, Tracy would just have to be patient, which wasn't one of her better-developed character traits.

She gathered her purse and the materials Rosa and Gabriel had left her. As she stood to leave, her cell phone rang. She hoped it was Wright, but when she checked caller ID she got that terrible sick feeling that accompanied the realization she was supposed to be someplace and had completely forgotten.

"Dan," she said, answering.

"Hey. I'm at your house. Where are you?"

"I'm sorry. I got tied up. I'm on my way."

"I can hardly hear you."

"I was just in a meeting," she said, trying to navigate the crowd to get outside and escape the noise.

"This late? Sounds like you're in a bar."

"I'm done. I'll explain when I get there. I'm on my way."

"Maybe I should just go?"

"No. I'm on my way. Just let yourself in." She disconnected and hurried to her truck.

It was drizzling by then, and traffic was heavy getting to the freeway because of some construction. On I-5, traffic remained heavy all the way to the off-ramp for the West Seattle Bridge. She tried to think of grocery stores along the way to buy something to cook, but nothing was leaping to the forefront of her mind and, given how late she was, she thought it best to not keep Dan waiting any longer than she already had. A mental inventory of her refrigerator contents consisted of a carton of milk, cottage cheese, yogurt, condiments, and various serving containers from leftover takeout.

As she turned down her street, the drizzle had become a steady rain. Dan's Tahoe was parked at the curb outside her gated front patio, and Tracy saw that Dan remained sitting in the driver's seat. She parked in the garage and went back outside, using her jacket as a makeshift umbrella to deflect the rain. Dan lowered his window.

"Why are you sitting in the car?"

"The combination to the gate isn't working," he said, sounding irritated.

Tracy had a second sinking feeling. "I'm sorry. I changed it again." She'd been obsessive about changing the combination since a stalker had assaulted her inside her house.

"Maybe I should just head back to Cedar Grove," Dan said. "I really should make sure Sherlock and Rex are okay. I told the dog sitter I'd be home tonight."

"Don't do that. Please."

"We've both had a long week. Maybe this isn't a good night."

"It is, Dan. I got a late phone call from Kelly Rosa about the case in Stoneridge. I met her for a beer to discuss it. I'm sorry. I . . . ."

"Forgot," he said.

"It's been crazy." She looked up at the sky. Water was dripping down her back. "Can we get out of the rain?"

He raised the window and got out, following her through the garage to the door leading to the kitchen. He did not carry his suitcase.

Inside, Roger mewed loudly. "Let me get him fed to keep him quiet." She grabbed a can of food from the pantry and popped the lid. "How'd the depositions go?" she asked, fending off Roger and spooning the food onto a plate.

Dan shrugged. "Some better than others; the president of the company isn't telling the truth. I caught him in a few lies. Unfortunately, I have to go back next week. I'm really not looking forward to it."

"We had a crazy development in that murder in Greenwood," Tracy said. "The son walked in alone and confessed."

"I thought the mother confessed."

"She did."

"Wow. So what now?"

"At the moment we're sorting through it."

"Unless one of them recants, you have reasonable doubt no matter what."

"That's the conclusion the prosecutor reached." Tracy went to the pantry, searching for pasta but not finding any.

"So what did Kelly Rosa want?"

Tracy spoke from behind the wall. "She doesn't think that girl in Stoneridge committed suicide. She thinks somebody ran her over with a car and then dumped her body in the river."

Dan came around the corner into the kitchen. "My God. Really?"

"I know. Can you imagine someone doing something like that?"

He shook his head and leaned back against the counter. "Your week makes mine look like a picnic. Can Rosa prove it?"

"She can prove the girl was run over and still alive when she went into the river."

"Still alive?" Dan said, thinking like a lawyer. "Would she have lived?"

"Rosa thinks it's possible, but there are a lot of factors to consider." She walked to him and wrapped her arms around his waist. "I missed you." She kissed his lips. "Should we get takeout from Thai Kitchen?"

Dan gave her a thin-lipped smile. "Given the contents of your refrigerator, I'd say takeout's a necessity."

She groaned. "I'm sorry. I meant to get home earlier."

"Don't worry about it," he said. "Takeout is fine."

She stepped back and leaned against the counter, suddenly feeling overwhelmed and emotional. She couldn't help but equate what had happened to Kimi Kanasket with what had happened to Sarah. "I know, but I wanted to make you dinner."

"Seriously, it's fine."

Her eyes watered.

He stepped closer. "Hey, what's wrong?"

Tracy thought of Angela and Tim Collins and about what Kins had said his and Shannah's relationship had become, and she couldn't help but think that at one time they had been just like Tracy and Dan, feeling intoxicated each time they saw one another. "Are we ever going to find time for one another? I know you must feel like you're always an afterthought."

"I'm a big boy, Tracy. I understand the demands of a job when you're not punching a clock."

She sighed. "Last weekend you seemed frustrated."

"Disappointed," he said. "I told you, I just had expectations that maybe weren't realistic. I get it—this is your job, and mine isn't much better at times. We're always going to have conflicts."

"So what do we do?"

"Well, for the moment, I'm not sure there's much we can do about it."

"That doesn't sound optimistic."

"Listen, if either of us reaches a point where this isn't working, then we need to be honest and let the other person know. We were friends, Tracy. We should always remain friends."

"Is that what you want?"

"No. I don't. Is that what you want?"

"No."

He placed his hands on her hips. "I was married for twelve years. Being together in the same house doesn't mean being with someone. My wife and I shared the same bed, but we found a lot of excuses to not be together. Eventually, I found reasons to work, and she found reasons to have an affair. So let's just make a deal that when we are together, we'll appreciate that time and try to maximize it."

Tracy looked up at him. "I imagine you've been feeling underappreciated lately."

He smiled. "Like I said, I'm a big boy. I'll let you know if it comes to that. Let's order. I'm starving."

She leaned in to him. "We'll have at least twenty minutes before the food arrives. How about I show you how much I appreciate you."

"Twenty minutes? You're talking to a man who made love once in the time it takes to boil noodles."

"I recall. But I don't think that's something to be proud of."

"You did then."

"Let's use the full twenty this time."

CHAPTER 20

It had poured during the night. Tracy and Dan had lain in bed eating Thai food straight out of the cartons and listening to the rain. It rushed against the roof shingles and pinged like coins from a slot machine paying off as it funneled down the gutters and downspouts. By morning the rain had subsided, but a suffocating gray cloud layer had settled over the city.

Dan gave Tracy a kiss at the front gate. "Are you sure I can't convince you to come to Cedar Grove and help me fend off two hundred eighty pounds of frenzied dogs?"

"I'd love to see them," she said, "but it sounds like you'll have most of your day full preparing for next week, and I can use the time to go over some things and hopefully talk with the tracker."

"Coward," he said. "You've left me alone to the beasts."

After Dan left, Tracy cleaned up the living room. She was about to jump in the shower when her cell phone rang.

"Sorry I missed your calls last night," Kaylee Wright said, sounding tired. "We were trying to find a body in Tacoma."

"I heard. What happened to Germany?"

"Cut short when they found the body and thought it could be related to Ridgway," she said, meaning Gary Ridgway, the Green River Killer. "Had to take a red-eye back."

"Any luck finding the body?"

"No. It got too dark, and the weather turned on us. I'm waiting to hear if we're going out again today."

"No rest for the wicked."

"Tell me about it. I'm still jet-lagged. The last thing I needed was an evening romp through the woods in the rain."

"Well, I won't add to your workload. I was just hoping I could stop by and take a look at the photographs I gave you. You don't even have to meet me. Just tell me where to find them."

"Actually, I have them here with me at home. I was hoping to finish my report this weekend, but I'm not sure I'll have the time now."

"You've gone through them?" Tracy asked. She'd assumed Wright hadn't even started.

"I took them with me on the plane to Germany; I told you I like a challenge, and you had me interested. I haven't typed up anything formal, but I got a good start."

"When will you know if you're headed back to Tacoma?"

"They're supposed to let me know by ten. I could meet you for a lot of coffee while I'm waiting. Can you come my direction?"

They met at a coffee shop near Wright's home in Renton. Like Kelly Rosa, who technically worked for King County but whose unique skills were available to every county in the state, Wright's abilities were in high demand. She'd been with the King County Sheriff's Office for nearly thirty years, including stints as a CSI detective and a homicide detective, but her claim to fame was becoming the county's first certified tracker, a skill she'd since cultivated over many years. Among the detectives who used her services, the consensus was that Wright didn't see as much as the camera lens; she saw more—things that even seasoned investigators walked right past.

The Pit Stop looked to have once been an automobile repair shop before some enterprising soul with a greater imagination than Tracy turned it into a coffeehouse. The concrete floors had been painted rust brown, and the walls were adorned with metal auto-part signs and posters of scantily clad women draped across the hoods of cars and lounging on motorcycles. Slabs of wood had been fitted onto the lifts, turning them into customer tables and a barista counter, from which emanated the rich aroma of coffee.

Wright had set up in a corner near one of three roll-up garage doors. Glazed windows atop the doors provided murky light. The sky outside had darkened to a charcoal gray, giving every indication it would again rain hard. On the table, beneath a cone-shaped lampshade dangling from a wire, Wright had arranged Buzz Almond's photographs in multiple stacks. She was standing there, flipping the pages of a legal pad. Tracy nodded to Wright's half-full porcelain mug of coffee, a latte judging by the foam and swirl. "You need a refresher?"

"I'm good for now. I'll probably be injecting it later today."

They greeted one another, and Tracy rested on a barstool across from Wright. She considered the stacks of photographs arranged on the table. "Looks like you've put in a lot of work already," she said.

"Like I said, you got me curious. I want to find out if I'm on the right track. I typed something up for you to follow." She handed Tracy a copy of a draft report. "I'm assuming the person who took these photographs had some law-enforcement training or some well-developed instincts."

At the time she'd given Wright the photographs, Tracy had no idea what the pictures were meant to depict, beyond the obvious. After speaking to Kelly Rosa and Peter Gabriel, however, she suspected she knew what had happened, though she was still a long way from proving it: Tommy Moore had run down Kimi Kanasket, then tossed her body in the river.

"Tell me why," she said.

Wright remained standing. She looked like a blackjack dealer at a casino table. "The photographs were taken in a linear fashion." She reached for one of the stacks and flipped to the first page of her report. "It took me a while to figure it out, but once I did, it made sense. Let me walk you through it."

Wright removed a rubber band from the first stack and methodically handed photographs to Tracy as she narrated from her report. "The photographer took the first photographs at the road, where this path started. I've marked it with a number one on the back. He, or she—"

"He," Tracy said.

Wright nodded. "*He* then proceeded to take photographs as he walked down the path." She pointed out that in her report these photographs were numbered two through twelve, and methodically went through them with Tracy. Wright set down number twelve, removed a rubber band from a second stack, and began handing the photographs to Tracy. "When he reached this open area of dirt and grass, he photographed the site in a clockwise pattern, starting along the perimeter and working his way into the center." These were photographs thirteen to thirty-two. After going through the second stack, she handed Tracy a third stack. "Then, he took photographs as he worked his way out. Judging from the direction of the shadows on the ground as these photographs progress, I'd estimate it was mid- to late afternoon and early fall to the middle of fall."

"November," Tracy said.

"When he walked in, he was heading east or southeast," Wright said. "He walked out facing north or northwest." She handed Tracy photographs thirty-three to forty-five. "So I'm assuming your guy had some law-enforcement training, though it's doubtful he or anyone in his office had any real training in interpreting these. If they had, you wouldn't be sitting here."

"He was a sheriff's deputy," Tracy said, "but he was a newbie, just on the job. Why do you say I wouldn't be sitting here?"

Wright held up a photograph as if admiring a work of art. "These are some of the best tire impressions I've seen captured by a camera."

"Why do you think that is?"

"I'd venture to guess it's because the ground was moist when the tracks were made, probably from a light rain. If it rains too hard, it can turn everything into slop. If the ground is too hard, you don't get a good impression. The conditions when these were taken were perfect." Wright handed Tracy three pictures marked forty-six to forty-eight. "These are almost as good as if someone made a cast of the tire tread."

Tracy knew that was a good sign. "Can you identify the type of tire from the tracks?"

"Someone could. I don't have that database, but the crime lab does," Wright said. She drank what was left of her coffee and set her hands on the table. "Okay. Was there something in particular you wanted to know?"

Tracy looked at the different piles, but she didn't pick them up for fear of disrupting Wright's carefully arranged system. "There were a few pictures of a white truck . . ."

"I saw those." Wright reached for a stack and thumbed through the photos. "Here they are." She laid three out on the table facing Tracy.

"Any thoughts whether that could be the truck that left the tire track?"

"I thought that might be the reason these were mixed in here." Wright leaned on her forearms and used the eraser end of a pencil as a pointer. "He didn't capture the tread, but he got the side of the tire. Someone in the lab could blow up the negative and see if you can read the tire make and model. If so, they can pull up the tire on the computer and compare it to the tread in these photographs."

Tracy would have Michael Melton do just that. She set aside the photographs of Tommy Moore's truck. "I know you don't have a lot of time; can you walk me through your opinions and conclusions?"

Wright sat back on her barstool and took a second to reorganize the photographs. "Your deputy was following tire tracks that entered and exited the same path. The tire treads go in both directions."

"That would make sense."

"What he also may have suspected was that the truck was following someone. I can tell you the truck was chasing that person, but the deputy may or may not have figured that much out."

Tracy looked up from the document as Wright removed another rubber band from a stack of photos and began placing those on the table. She again used the eraser as a pointer. "Do you see those? Those are shoe impressions made by someone moving quickly."

"Running?"

"Running is subjective. What you consider running I might consider a jog. What I can tell you is that the average woman's walking stride length is about twenty-six to twenty-seven inches. The average stride length of a woman running can be anywhere from fifty-eight to eighty inches depending on her height, the terrain, and whether the person is a distance runner or a sprinter. I was able to take two measurements and extrapolate out the distance. This person's stride length was between sixty-two and seventy-three inches. The difference is probably because of the terrain more than anything."

"And if it was night, would that play a factor?"

"Definitely. She would have had to pick her path

more carefully, but I can tell you she wasn't too uncertain. She was, for the most part, booking it, which is another indication she was being chased."

"You keep saying 'she.' You believe it was a woman?"

"A woman or a small man."

"Tell me why."

"Well, the imprint was made by someone wearing a heel, and . . ." Wright took back the stack, flipped through it until finding what she was looking for, and handed a photograph to Tracy.

"This imprint is the equivalent of a woman's size-seven shoe, and the thickness of the heel and the shape of the sole indicate that it wasn't a boot but more like the type of shoe someone who worked on her feet all day would wear. I had the computer spit out a few examples of shoes worn back in 1976."

Wright fumbled through a stack of papers and handed Tracy a few loose pages. Tracy knew from prior cases that Wright had access to a computerized "shoe bank" at the Washington State Patrol Crime Lab, which contained literally thousands of different shoe treads. The operator entered the shoe impression pattern, and the computer searched for matches. The shoes Wright had printed out as potential matches were the durable type Tracy could see a waitress wearing.

"That takes us to this open space," Wright said. "And that's where the scenario gets truly frightening."

Wright handed Tracy another stack of photographs, but Tracy had to set it down and wipe her palms on her jeans. As in the kitchen the night before, the thought of what had happened to Kimi was causing a visceral reaction. Tracy felt light-headed and hot.

"You okay?" Wright asked.

Tracy took a moment. "Give me a second." She went to the counter and asked for a glass of ice water. Seeing the photographs of the ground chewed up, while knowing from her discussion with Kelly Rosa what had likely transpired there, had cast everything in a different light. After a few sips of water, she felt the dizziness pass.

Back at the table she said, "Sorry. Something about this case is hitting home."

"No apologies necessary," Wright said. She set out several photographs and again used the pencil eraser as she explained. "To make that significant of a depression, the vehicle had to have been traveling at a very high rate of speed when it landed."

"Landed?"

"The vehicle that hit here came down at an angle," Wright said, confirming Rosa's opinion that Kimi had suffered "crush" injuries. "Given the direction of the tire tracks, we can assume the truck crested the hill." Wright thumbed through the photos and set out another photograph. "Here. This is what I was looking for." The photograph appeared to have been taken from the clearing looking up the sloped hillside. "I think, from this, that your deputy made the same assumption—that the vehicle crested that hill, went airborne where the tracks stop, and crashed down bumper-first right there, making that deep depression."

"Why would the ground be so torn up?"

"I would surmise from the circumstances—the driver going at a high rate of speed and not expecting to suddenly be airborne—that his instinct was to take his foot off the accelerator and jam on the brake. When the truck landed, it would have bounced and fishtailed. If he was experienced with off-road driving, he would have hit the gas, causing the back tires to tear up the ground in a counterclockwise direction, which is what we have here."

Tracy's heart hammered in her chest. "You said this was 'truly frightening.' Why?"

Wright set down the photographs and took a moment to pick through a stack and lay out a few others. "Because there was someone on the ground."

"Where?" Tracy's mouth and lips were dry. She took another sip of water. "I mean, how can you tell?"

Wright handed Tracy another photograph. "The

impact when the car landed obscured some of the impressions, but not completely." Wright pointed with the eraser. "Do you see these three depressions where the grass blades are lying flat, all in the same direction?"

"Not really."

Wright flipped through the other photographs and handed Tracy a second one along with a small magnifying glass for Tracy to use. "This one is a little better. Here. You see where the grass is lying flat?"

Tracy could. "Yeah, I see."

"Your deputy, without training, never would have recognized these. In fact, I'm amazed he was able to capture them with his camera. He likely wouldn't have, except he was so thorough. He might have thought they were shoe impressions. It was overkill, really, but it was also fortuitous. I've seen this a hundred times. Those are impressions made by someone's head, shoulder, and hip."

"Someone lying on her side?"

"Yes. And judging from the deep impression made where the vehicle landed, it struck her just below her hip."

Again, Wright's analysis was in keeping with Rosa's opinion that Kimi Kanasket's pelvis had been fractured.

Wright collected those photographs and began setting out rows of other photographs. "Your guy also captured a lot of shoeprints. I'd say these were made by at least three people and as many as five."

Tracy felt suddenly numb. "More than one?"

"Oh, definitely more than one," Wright said. She leaned over and pointed to the first photograph in the top row. "These are Converse, which was a popular brand for boys during that time period. Size twelves."

"So we're probably talking about a young man as opposed to a boy," she said.

"Yes." She handed Tracy a second photograph of a shoe impression. "These are also Converse, also size twelves, but the impression is deeper than the other impression. I can't say with any certainty, but the depth of the impression could mean these were made by someone heavier."

"But again, a young man."

Wright handed Tracy a third photograph. "Also Converse, but these are smaller. Size nine to ten."

"So a second, and possibly a third person," Tracy said.

Wright shuffled through the photographs and set another on the table. "Puma," she said. "Also popular at that time with kids, also size ten."

"So that's definitely three and maybe four," Tracy said.

Wright handed Tracy another photograph, but this one captured a pattern much different from that of the Converse or the Puma—inverted *V*s above three rows of multiple slash marks, with the second row slanted in the opposite direction from the first and third rows. It looked like a row of backslashes between two rows of forward slashes on a computer keyboard.

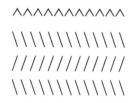

"Also size twelve," Wright said.

"Doesn't look like an athletic shoe," Tracy said.

"It isn't. It's from a rubber boot," Wright said. "I did a little research. The pattern is distinct for boots made by the United States Rubber Company. They were popular in the 1970s and highly sought after because they were rubber, which meant waterproof, but also because they were lined with fur, which meant they were warm. They were originally made for soldiers in World War II and became popular with hunters, but the plant closed when rubber was needed for more pressing war purposes." Wright handed Tracy another photograph. "Something else."

Tracy held it up to the light. "What is it?"

"I had to look at it under a microscope," Wright said. She handed Tracy the magnifying glass. "It's chewed-up tobacco leaves. I'm totally hypothesizing now, but if someone was chewing tobacco in a car that went airborne like it appears it did and slammed back down . . ."

"They would have swallowed the tobacco and threw it back up," Tracy said.

"Or spit it out involuntarily," Wright said. She laid out the photographs of the shoe impressions on the table, recreating the clearing. "Now, what do you notice about the shoe impressions?"

"They're all over the place," Tracy said. "They're facing in every direction."

"Some are smudged. Some are elongated," Wright said. "There's no pattern to them. They were clearly not moving with any deliberate intent."

"They were panicked, worked up," Tracy said.

"Scared. Confused." Wright said. She handed Tracy photographs numbered forty-nine to fifty-three, which captured impressions made by the boots.

Tracy brought the photographs closer. "These impressions look to be around the area you said the body was on the ground."

"Not just around it. Under it."

Tracy looked to Wright for clarification. "Under it?"

"The person wearing those boots picked the body up," Wright said, confirming Rosa's opinion—Kimi Kanasket had been moved after sustaining her injuries.

"You see that rounded impression in the mud?" Wright said.

"Yeah."

"And this one here, where you can see only the inverted *V*s and the first row of slash marks?"

"Okay."

"The distance between the two is just eighteen to nineteen inches. The rounded impression is the impression made by someone dropping to a knee. The second is the ball of that person's foot. Now, you see these shoe impressions that are twisted and staggered?"

"Yeah."

"Those were likely made when the person stood, but he was bearing the weight of someone else, maybe staggering to adjust the weight and regain his balance," Wright said. "People don't realize how heavy a person is when they're deadweight. Even a hundred pounds is difficult to lift."

"A hundred and twenty-five," Tracy said.

Wright looked up from the photographs. Then she straightened.

"A seventeen-year-old girl," Tracy said. "She was five seven and a hundred and twenty-five pounds, and she was a runner, and she had the rest of her life ahead of her."

Wright took a moment. She spoke softly. "What did they do to her?"

"I'm not fully certain yet," Tracy said. "And I'm starting to wonder, whoever it was, whether they had any idea what they *actually* did."

The likelihood that four, and maybe five, young men, had been in the clearing the night Kimi Kanasket died changed things in Tracy's mind. It could still have been Tommy Moore, except that would have meant that Moore would have had to have enlisted the help of others quickly, possibly too quickly for the timeline Buzz Almond's investigation revealed. If you believe Moore and his roommate were telling the truth, after leaving the diner, Moore drove his date home, then drove back to his apartment. He couldn't have enlisted his roommate's help because the roommate had spoken with both Élan and his posse and to Buzz Almond that night.

As for Élan, he was out that night and already had a group of young men with him, but those young men had arrived to *help* Earl Kanasket, and it was difficult to consider a scenario where they suddenly turned and went after Kimi, though it could have been an accident.

What had first come to mind when Wright said at least four young men had been present were the newspaper articles on the high school football championship, and that made Tracy think that maybe Buzz Almond hadn't included them in the file just to help witnesses recall that weekend.

Tracy had punched in the number on her cell phone before she finished crossing the parking lot back to her truck. Sam Goldman's home phone rang six times, and Tracy thought it would go to voice mail, but he answered in the middle of the seventh ring. "Sam, it's Detective Crosswhite from Seattle."

"How are the bad guys, hero?"

Tracy climbed into the truck cab and shut the door. "Still bad. Sam, I'm sorry, but I have a few more questions for you."

"Fire away. If I can answer them, I'm happy to help."

Tracy heard Adele in the background. "Who is it, Sam?"

"It's the detective from Seattle," he said before quickly reengaging Tracy. "What can I help you with?"

"The Four Ironmen," she said, fumbling in her briefcase to grab her notepad and flipping back through her notes. "Reynolds, Devoe, Coe, and . . ."

"Gallentine."

"Right. What can you tell me about them, Sam?"

"What is it you want to know?"

"What kind of kids were they off the field?"

Goldman paused, and Tracy heard Adele say, "They were full of themselves," indicating that she was listening in on the conversation.

"How so?" Tracy asked.

"They weren't bad kids," Goldman said. "You know how it is. None of them came from much, and suddenly they were getting a lot of attention and seeing their names in the paper every week. Adults would stop them in the street to congratulate them and want to talk all about the upcoming game. It went to their heads a bit."

"They ever get in any trouble?"

"If they did, friend, I never heard about it."

"You sound uncertain."

"Rumors. Nothing I could ever print."

Tracy watched Kaylee Wright leave the coffee shop and head to her SUV. Tracy gave her a wave. "Sometimes there's truth in a rumor," she said.

"And lawsuits," Goldman said with a burst of a laugh. "I'm like Joe Friday. I print just the facts."

Tracy decided to push it. "Who might have sued?"

"Like I said, kids start reading their names in the paper, getting slaps on the back—sometimes they think they can do no wrong. High school stuff, you know?"

"Drinking? Smoking pot?"

"Here's the thing. Little Timmy gets caught with a beer, the police drive him home, and nobody cares. One of the Ironmen gets caught, and the police still drive him home, but everyone in town knows, and now they're worried he's going to get kicked off the team and their undefeated season is going to go up in smoke."

"Right, but you had your finger on the pulse. Any truth to those rumors?"

Goldman sighed. Then he said, "Not a lot to do in a small town."

"Any of them have any romantic involvement with Kimi Kanasket that you're aware of?"

Goldman paused, and Tracy knew he was connecting the dots between her questions. "If there was, I wouldn't have known about it."

"You never heard anything like that?"

"Nothing of the sort."

"Any connection at all you can think of?"

Again there was a lengthy pause. "Coe and Gallentine ran track. That's the only thing I can think of."

"What can you tell me about Arthur Coe?"

"Archie Coe," Goldman corrected. "Nice kid. He was probably the least heralded of the four. He joined the Army after high school, but he washed out, came home with a medical discharge."

"Do you know what for?"

"Officially, he hurt his back."

"Unofficially?"

"Unofficially, he had some type of nervous breakdown. He lives in Central Point now. Works in the nursery—at least he did fifteen years ago when I last tried to speak to him."

Tracy thought of the man she'd seen in the clearing and of the freshly planted shrub. "Was he married? Did he have any kids?"

"Divorced. His wife and kids moved to

somewhere in California. Palm Springs maybe."

"Why'd you try to speak to him fifteen years ago?"

"I was writing an article on the twenty-five-year anniversary of the championship. It turned out to not be the celebratory piece everyone was expecting."

"Why not?"

"Eric Reynolds is the only one of the four who made anything of himself. He played four years at UW, but he blew his knee out during practice sophomore year. If he did it now, it'd be no big deal, but back then it was the kiss of death. He never reached the kind of stardom he did in high school. Still, after he graduated, he moved home and started his construction and cement business. Any public-works job this side of Seattle, you're likely to see a Reynolds Construction banner."

Tracy again considered her notes. "What about Darren Gallentine?"

"He shot himself. He was living in Seattle."

"When?"

"Sometime in the late nineties, I believe."

"Do you know why?"

"Not a clue, friend," he said. "The last of the four was young Hastey, who is universally considered the town drunk. Like I said, not exactly a feel-good story. We shelved it."

"What does Hastey do for Reynolds?"

"He *drove* a cement truck until he got his third

DUI. Now I think he shines a seat in the office."

"Sounds like Reynolds is pretty loyal to him."

"Old ties run deep in a small town."

"Yeah," Tracy said, thinking of Cedar Grove. "I'm going to need to come down and take another look at your newspapers, Sam. Would that be all right?"

"Anytime, friend. We're not going anywhere."

CHAPTER 21

Monday morning Tracy drove to the squat cement building on Airport Way that was home to the Washington State Patrol Crime Lab. She'd left the coffeehouse Friday feeling both energized and sick. She had definitive forensic proof that Kimi Kanasket had not thrown herself into the White Salmon River. Far from it. She'd been run down and run over, her body unceremoniously dumped like a piece of garbage.

And Tracy's focus had now shifted squarely to the Four Ironmen.

She refrained from calling Jenny. She'd learned not to prematurely express her conclusions every time she thought she had a significant break in a case. Too often that break turned out to be a false lead, and she had to go back and explain why she'd been wrong.

Michael Melton's office was located on the first floor. A level five forensic scientist, Melton was at the top of the pay chain, which was a testament not only to his longevity, but also to his skill and dedication to his job. Melvin could have earned three times his salary working for a private forensic company—which many chose to do after getting the training and resume boost of working for the crime lab. Melton, however, remained—

year after year, even when he was in the midst of paying college tuition or funding weddings for his six daughters. The detectives knew Melton stayed out of a sense of obligation to the victims and their families. He sat on the board of directors of the Seattle chapter of Victim Support Services, and he and three other crime-lab scientists played in a country-western band called the Fourensics to raise money for that organization. A bear of a man with a full head of graying brown hair and a matching beard, Melton had nimble enough fingers to strum a guitar and a surprisingly soothing voice.

Tracy met Melton in his office, which contained an eclectic mix of family photographs, ball-peen hammers, combat knives, and a cast-iron skillet—evidence from cases Melton had helped to solve.

"To what do I owe the pleasure of seeing my favorite detective?" Melton said. "Let me guess—the Tim Collins case."

"Actually, different case," Tracy said.

"As long as you don't need it tonight. Got a gig at Kells."

Kells was a popular Irish bar in the Pike Place Market that Tracy occasionally frequented. "And you didn't tell me?"

"Just found out. We're subbing for an Irish folk band."

"No, nothing I need by tonight," Tracy said. She set down her briefcase and pulled out the photographs, thumbing through the packets until she found the shots of the tire-tread impressions in the ground. "I'm hoping you can tell me the make and model of the tire that made this impression. You'll need to go back a ways. These were taken in 1976."

Like shoes, tires made unique impressions. Even tires of the same make and model could be differentiated by tread wear and the differing amounts of damage in the form of tiny cuts and nicks in the rubber. The latter could be accomplished only if the tread in the photograph could be compared to the actual tire, which was beyond unlikely. However, knowing the manufacturer and model of the tire would be extremely helpful if, for instance, it matched the tires on Tommy Moore's truck, or another vehicle Tracy might come across upon her revisit to Sam Goldman's personal library.

"Computer doesn't go back that far," Melton said.

His response caught her off guard. "Is there any other way to do it?" she said.

"I got a buddy who's a genius at this stuff. Let me ask him."

"This might help." She handed Melton the three photographs of the white truck. Buzz Almond had focused on the body damage to the truck, but in two of the pictures he'd managed to capture a portion of the front tire. "Hoping you can work your magic and blow these up enough to make out the make and model of the tire."

"You want to know if it matches the make and model that left these impressions."

"Or if it doesn't," she said.

"Then these will help." Melton lowered his glasses to the tip of his nose and held up the photographs of Tommy Moore's truck, considering them. "You have the negatives?"

"They're in the packet."

Melton removed the strip of negatives from the front pouch of one of the Kodak packages and also held it up to the light. Then he reached into his drawer and pulled out a magnifying glass, running it first over the photograph, then over the negatives. He lowered the glass without comment. "I take it this isn't an ongoing investigation?"

"It's a cold case from 1976, and it's a bad one, Mike."

"Aren't they all?"

"Seventeen-year-old girl went missing on her way home from work. They found her body in the river the next afternoon and concluded suicide. Evidence indicates that wasn't the case. Someone ran her down."

That gave Melton pause, as Tracy thought it might. He shook his head. "How do people live with themselves?"

Tracy thought of Sam Goldman telling her he'd

scrapped the article on the twenty-five-year anniversary of the state championship when he realized it wouldn't be the celebratory piece he'd anticipated. "Maybe not very well," she said.

When she got to her cubicle at the Justice Center, Tracy e-mailed the Department of Licensing in Olympia for a vehicle check on Tommy Moore's truck. Buzz Almond's photographs had captured the license plate. She also ran the names Eric Reynolds, Hastey Devoe, Lionel Devoe, Darren Gallentine, and Archibald Coe through Accurint, as well as the National Crime Information Center. And she sent a second e-mail to DOL, seeking the make and model of every vehicle registered to those men or, since they were in high school in 1976, their fathers.

She received return e-mails that afternoon. DOL had been able to use the vehicle identification number from Tommy Moore's truck to determine that the truck was sold in January 1977 to a buyer in Oregon and had since been scrapped. The fact that Moore had sold the truck just two months after Kimi's death made Tracy question his statement that he'd had the windshield and body damage fixed. Why bother if he was going to sell it? On the other hand, maybe that was the reason for the cash invoices—Lionel Devoe, who was running his father's business at that time, could have cut Moore a deal for paying cash, which Devoe didn't have to show on his books or otherwise pay a business tax.

The second report revealed that Hastey Devoe Senior's businesses owned several trucks, including tow trucks that likely would have been fitted with all-terrain tires. Earl Kanasket owned a 1968 Ford truck. A 1973 Ford Bronco was registered to Ron Reynolds. Bernard Coe, who Tracy assumed to be Archibald Coe's father, owned a 1974 Chevy truck. Any of them could have also had all-terrain tires. In fact, Tracy suspected they did. She also suspected that the chances any of those vehicles remained in circulation were slim to none. The chances they'd have the same tires as in 1976 was ludicrous to even consider.

The Accurint report confirmed that Hastey Devoe lived in Stoneridge, and an electricity bill indicated that Archibald Coe lived close by, in Central Point, as Sam Goldman had said. The address looked like it would be for an apartment. Eric Reynolds's address was also Stoneridge, though a Google map and satellite search revealed the property was far out of town and surrounded by orchards. Tracy didn't find a utility record for Darren Gallentine, but she wasn't expecting one, since Sam Goldman had said Gallentine had killed himself.

Other than Tommy Moore, only Hastey Devoe had a criminal record. He'd been arrested three times for driving under the influence—the first arrest in 1982, the second in 1996, and the most recent in 2013. Tracy could only imagine how many times a career drunk had driven impaired and *not* been caught, or had been caught but received the benefit of having a brother serving as the chief of police.

Tracy ran Gallentine's name through the Washington State Digital Archives and got a match. Darren John Gallentine died October 12, 1999, at age forty-one. The death certificate from the Washington State Department of Health listed the cause of death as a self-inflicted gunshot wound to the head. She located a short obituary in the *Seattle Times* archives. Gallentine had worked for nearly two decades as an engineer for Boeing after graduating from UW in 1981. He was survived by his wife, Tiffany, and his two daughters, seventeen-year-old Rebecca and fourteen-year-old Rachel. In lieu of flowers, the family had asked for donations to an organization called Evergreen Health Clinic Northwest. Tracy Googled the name and found that the clinic still existed and had been serving the Puget Sound region since 1973. Searches using the name Tiffany Gallentine produced no results. Gallentine's wife could have died, remarried, changed her name, or simply not done anything to warrant a Google hit. The names Rebecca and Rachel Gallentine produced multiple possibilities on Facebook of women who would have been about the right ages. However, given that the sisters would be in their early thirties, they also could have married and legally changed their last names, making the hits for "Gallentine" even more suspect.

Deciding to go after the lowest-hanging fruit, Tracy called the clinic referenced in Darren Gallentine's obituary and asked to speak to the director. She knew she was treading on thin ice. Under federal HIPAA laws, the confidentiality of a patient's health information continued even after the patient's death, and the law was particularly touchy about psychotherapy notes. She was connected to an Alfred Womak, who confirmed that the clinic had treated Darren Gallentine but wouldn't reveal for what. Tracy said she was in the area and would appreciate a few minutes of the director's time. Womak agreed to see her for twenty minutes starting at two.

Evergreen Health Clinic Northwest was located in a chic shopping complex off Northwest Gilman Boulevard called The Village at Issaquah, a thirty- to forty-five-minute drive east of Seattle. Once nothing but hills of virgin forest, the plateau was now looked upon by many in Seattle as an illu-stration of urban desecration of the environment. In the past decade, developers had clear-cut and bulldozed large swaths of forest for tracts of homes, shopping centers, schools, and sports facilities. The population had quickly tripled—predominantly white middle-class families with young children, who'd rushed to buy large homes at affordable prices.

The buildings at The Village at Issaquah, interconnected by wooden and brick walkways, included restaurants, a hair "studio," an upscale kitchenette store, art galleries, and a yoga studio, in addition to the clinic. It gave Tracy a better sense of Evergreen's likely typical clientele— overextended husbands, stay-at-home moms feeling unfulfilled and underappreciated, and the children of those parents sent to counseling for ADD, anxiety, and stress-related disorders.

Tibetan bells announced Tracy's entrance as she stepped into a reception area of soft colors and soothing music. Womak met Tracy in the lobby and escorted her to his office, which resembled the inside of a yurt but with plate-glass windows for walls that provided an eastern view of the hills. She estimated Womak to be in his early sixties, with the mandatory mental health professional's beard. His was salt and pepper. Balding, he wore round wire-framed glasses.

"As I indicated on the telephone, Detective, federal laws prohibit me from telling you any-thing about Mr. Gallentine's treatment."

Tracy pushed forward. It was why she preferred face-to-face meetings. It was easier to hang up a phone than to ignore a person sitting across from you. She'd also learned to avoid debate and just get the witness answering questions. "I understand. You were able to confirm he was a patient of this clinic?"

"Yes, he was."

"And for how long?"

"Just under two years."

"Did he come regularly for those two years?"

"His billing records indicate he did."

"And you still have a copy of his records here?"

"Not his physical file. We move physical files older than five years to a storage facility and maintain electronic files."

"Someone scanned in the contents of those files?"

"Correct."

"So you can access them, search them, that sort of thing."

"Correct."

"Do your records indicate whether anyone has ever asked to see Mr. Gallentine's records before my request?"

"There have been no prior requests."

"Mr. Gallentine was married?"

"According to his file, yes."

"His wife didn't ask for the records?"

"There's no indication in the file that she did."

Tracy thought that odd, given that Darren Gallentine had committed suicide. She would have thought a spouse would have wanted to know if his psychotherapy records revealed why. Then again, maybe Tiffany Gallentine knew why. Tracy certainly knew why her father had shot himself—grief and depression brought on by the disappearance and presumed death of Sarah. "He had minor daughters at that time?" Tracy asked.

"Two."

"Neither has asked to see the file?"

"There have been *no* requests by *anyone* for any purpose," Womak said, sounding officious.

"Did Mrs. Gallentine or either of the two daughters seek any treatment?"

"Our records indicate they came in for family grief counseling after Mr. Gallentine's death."

"How long did that continue?"

"Just a few visits."

"And Mr. Gallentine's therapist no longer works here?"

"She does not."

"Was she fired?"

"I won't answer questions related to our employees' work history."

"What I'm trying to determine is whether your clinic did any type of an investigation or inquiry as to why one of your patients, while undergoing regular treatment, killed himself." Sometimes when she challenged a person's decision making, particularly doctors, Tracy found they would get their significant ego feathers ruffled and endeavor to defend their actions, giving away information they might not otherwise.

Womak, however, remained calm. "We have staff meetings every week to discuss patient treatment and, yes, we do have discussions in the event a patient chooses to end his own life."

"It's happened before, besides Mr. Gallentine?"

"Unfortunately."

"How could I get a copy of the file?"

"The only way is if Mr. Gallentine designated a personal representative, and that individual notified us that he or she was waiving his privacy."

"Do you have a last known address in the file for Mr. Gallentine?"

"I do." Womak provided the address.

"Do you know if Mrs. Gallentine has remarried or if she still lives in the area?"

"I'm afraid I don't."

"What about either of his two daughters, Rebecca and Rachel?"

"I'm sorry, I don't. It's been many years."

"Do you know if Mrs. Gallentine worked outside the home when Mr. Gallentine was seeking treatment?"

"Again, I don't know and would have no way of knowing."

Womak looked at his watch and started to rise from his chair. "I'm afraid I'm out of time."

"He killed himself in what year?"

"October 1999."

Gallentine's obituary indicated that he worked at Boeing until 1997. "What about billing records? Was his therapy paid through his insurance at Boeing?"

Womak sat again. His fingers clicked the keyboard on his desktop, and he raised his nose to read through his bifocals. "The file indicates his therapy was paid by insurance. But it wasn't Boeing's. It was paid through his wife's insurance as an employee at Microsoft."

When she left Evergreen, Tracy called Ron Mayweather and asked that he pull up property records and run the address Womak had provided for the Gallentine family home. She also tasked him with doing a search of King County records to determine if a will was probated for a Darren John Gallentine in 1999, and if it named a personal representative. Then she dialed information and asked for the number for Microsoft.

"Any particular department?"

"What do they have listed?"

"How much time do you have?"

"Human Resources," Tracy said.

CHAPTER 22

Tiffany Gallentine had become Tiffany Martin, a director of business development at Microsoft, and Tracy heard the unease in Martin's voice when she introduced herself on the telephone as a Seattle detective—she left out the word "homicide"—and asked for a few moments of Martin's time.

"What's this about?" Martin had asked.

"I have a few questions about your late husband, Darren Gallentine."

"What?" Martin sounded both relieved and confused, and maybe a bit irritated. No doubt her initial concern upon hearing the words "Seattle Police" and "detective" had been for her current husband and/or her daughters. Still, getting a call out of the blue from a detective wanting to talk about your husband who committed suicide was not likely at the top of anyone's list of fun things to do. "My husband shot himself fifteen years ago."

"I understand the topic is probably painful, Mrs. Martin, and it isn't my intent to inflict any undue pain, but I have some questions that might be relevant to a matter I'm looking into in Klickitat County."

"I don't understand how that could be. My husband shot himself in our home in Issaquah."

286

Martin's tone was a mix of relief and befuddlement.

Tracy was honest. "I'm in the initial stages of an investigation and was hoping for just a few minutes of your time."

This was the moment people found an excuse to say "Now is not a good time," but Tracy was betting Martin—a professional woman likely used to difficult conversations and with limited free time—would prefer to rip off the Band-Aid and get the conversation over with rather than spend an afternoon or day stewing about it.

"I have a few minutes at three thirty," she said. "After that, I'm on conference calls the rest of the afternoon, and I leave tomorrow on a business trip."

Martin's office was located in one of the buildings on the company's West Campus in Redmond. After stopping at the visitor center for a map and directions, Tracy parked in a designated visitor's area and hurried along a footpath. She had never been to Microsoft headquarters, a sprawling complex of buildings and acreage that very much reminded her of college, with fountains, a lake, grass playing fields, and young people walking around dressed in jeans and tennis shoes and carrying backpacks.

Tiffany Martin was not so casual. Dressed in cream slacks and a gold top, she met Tracy in a glass-and-concrete lobby. Though she had to be at least midfifties, Martin's hairstyle and makeup made hcr look younger.

She handed Tracy a visitor's pass and said, "You need that to get in." She then escorted Tracy into the building as quickly as if she were trying to get a crazy relative out of public view.

Martin chose a conference room with a modern theme, not surprising for a technology company whose success depended on being forward-thinking. The walls were white and covered with what looked to be Japanese prints, the carpet a utilitarian gray. Martin pulled out a chair at the glass conference table, but Tracy walked to the windows with a view of the heart of campus.

"I wouldn't get any work done with all these distractions."

"You learn to tune them out," Martin said in a crisp tone. "And you don't have a lot of free time."

Tracy had not been looking for an answer. She was hoping small talk might help Martin relax. Her eyes and mouth were pinched so tight Tracy thought something might pop.

"Must be nice to have it available, though," Tracy said.

"It helps people to be more efficient," Martin said, joining Tracy at the window.

"Tell that to my bosses. Our amenities are a decade-old coffeemaker."

"I have to tell you I was dismayed to get your

phone call, Detective. I don't see how Darren's death could have anything to do with anything."

"I understand." Tracy rolled back one of the black leather chairs from the table, and the two women sat. "And I'm sorry to bring up a difficult topic."

Martin favored silver and gold bracelets that rattled each time she moved her arm or lowered it to the glass table. "It was a long time ago, Detective," she said. "But you never really move on from something like that. You try, but there are always reminders."

"How long were you married?" Tracy asked, hoping to put Martin more at ease by asking a simple question.

"Twenty-one years."

"You met in college?"

"At the University of Washington; we were in the engineering department together."

Martin's answers continued to be short and direct. Tracy decided to cut to the chase. "It appears your husband had a good job at Boeing. You have a good career here. I'm guessing from your address at the time that you had a nice home."

"Darren had demons," Martin said, anticipating where Tracy was going. "I wasn't aware of them when we got married, and he kept them in check during the early years of our marriage."

"What kind of demons?"

"He didn't sleep well, for one." She paused. "He didn't sleep. He didn't *like* to sleep. He stayed up late, and it wasn't uncommon for him to get up again at three. Three to four hours was a good night for him. Eventually, that takes its toll."

"Do you know why he couldn't sleep?"

"He *said* he just didn't need that much."

"But you believe there was something more to it?"

"He suffered nightmares. He'd wake me moaning and thrashing. When I'd wake him, he'd be in a lather of sweat, trying to catch his breath. It became progressively worse."

"I noted from his obituary that he worked at Boeing until 1997."

"They laid him off." She shrugged. "He did it to himself. He became self-destructive. He started drinking at night to help himself fall asleep. Then he started drinking at lunch. There were a few incidents at work—inappropriate comments to his colleagues. I had to go pick him up several times. I finally told him I wouldn't raise our children in that environment. I told him I'd leave him if he didn't get help."

"Did he?"

"He went to counseling, but given the outcome, I guess you can conclude he never got the help he needed."

"Did he ever discuss what the nightmares were about?"

She shook her head. "Not with me. He said he didn't know. He said when he woke up he couldn't remember anything."

"But you said they got progressively worse?"

"Just judging from his reactions when he woke. I don't know what they were about."

"When did they start?"

Martin took a moment, bracelets rattling as she raised her hand and ran her index and middle finger across her bottom lip. "Not long after our first daughter was born. I spoke to his counselor about it once, after Darren was gone. She said that things from childhood could be triggered by the birth of a child. Abandonment issues, for instance . . . or abuse."

"Did the counselor say what it might have been with respect to your husband?"

"No. And at that point I really didn't want to know."

"How old were your daughters when your husband took his life?"

"Rebecca was seventeen. Rachel was fourteen."

"And you've *never* found out why?"

"You mean other than depression and substance abuse?"

"Did you ever ask to see his counseling records?"

She sighed. "Why? What would be the point?"

"To see if he ever said what was troubling him, what was keeping him awake at night, why he drank?"

Martin continued to rub her lower lip. "Why would I want to know?" she said, voice and demeanor soft, but her eyes almost challenging Tracy to give her a reason. "What good would come from knowing, *if* it was anything?"

"You'd have an answer."

"Maybe not an answer we want."

"I understand—"

"No." Martin raised a hand. Her blue eyes bore into Tracy. She sounded tired. "I don't think you do, Detective. No offense, but I've had a lot of people over the years tell me that, and until you've been through it, you have very little credibility making that statement."

"My sister was murdered when she was eighteen. I was twenty-two. Two years later, my father, overcome with grief, shot himself." She paused just a moment. Her intent was not to make Tiffany Martin feel bad, but to find common ground. "I went twenty years not knowing what happened to my sister. Finding the truth was painful. Not knowing the truth was more painful."

Martin caught her breath and looked out the window, seemingly on the verge of tears. She turned back to Tracy. "I'm sorry. I guess I shouldn't assume I'm the only person who's been through this."

"Don't be sorry; you couldn't have known."

"That's the thing, isn't it? We don't know. Do you know how many people came up to me after and told me they'd lost someone they loved to suicide?"

"A lot," Tracy said. "Too many."

Martin nodded. Tracy gave her the moment. "You said this has something to do with an investigation?"

"It might," Tracy said. "I really don't know yet."

"What's the investigation about?"

Tracy saw no way to soften the facts. "A seventeen-year-old girl who went to the same high school as your husband went missing in 1976—"

"Oh God." Martin dropped her head into her hands. "You think he killed her? Is that what his nightmares were about?" It struck Tracy that Martin had to have thought about what had troubled her husband, or at least speculated.

"No. No, I can't say that. Mrs. Martin, this is really preliminary. The sheriff's office concluded that the girl committed suicide."

"And?"

"With advances in technology, we can review old cases in ways that weren't possible in 1976. We can evaluate the evidence differently. That's all I'm doing at this point."

"And does the evidence indicate she didn't commit suicide?"

"Some experts think that it might."

"And you think Darren might have had something to do with it?"

"Let me back up. The case was investigated by

a young deputy sheriff. He left behind a file. In that file were a couple of articles and a picture of your late husband with some of his classmates."

"What was the picture of?"

"Your husband and his teammates in their football uniforms."

"Why would that be in the file?"

"I don't know. That's why I'm here, to see if there's a reason."

"Did you ask the deputy?"

"He's dead. I'm trying to follow up on what he left behind. Your husband's name was one of the names I ran through our computers. That's all it is at this point." Tracy didn't tell Martin that she was the low-hanging fruit because she was local. She tried to quickly get the interview back on track. "Did your husband visit Stoneridge often?"

"No. Never."

"Never?"

"I don't recall a single time."

"Were his parents still living there while you were married?"

"Until they died."

"And he never expressed a desire to go and visit?"

"We had holidays at our house in Issaquah. Our home was bigger and could better accommodate the family. They could spend the night. His parents' house wouldn't have fit everyone. They were simple people. His father worked for city maintenance. They liked to come up here and see the kids."

"What about to visit his high school friends? Did your husband ever see any of them?"

"No."

"Did you ever meet them?"

"He said he wasn't close to any of them."

"So he didn't communicate with any of them?"

"I'd never met them."

"What about reunions?"

"He never went."

Tracy found all of this odd, given that Sam Goldman had described Gallentine as one of the four conquering heroes who would have remained a minor celebrity in his hometown. In her experience, things like winning championships also could forge lifelong friendships.

"Did your husband ever mention to you that he won the state football championship his senior year?"

Martin's face was blank. "I knew he played football. He never said anything about winning a state championship."

"Does it strike you as odd that he wouldn't mention that?"

"I don't know. Not really. Sports weren't really Darren's thing. I mean, he liked to watch, go to an occasional game, but he wasn't a fanatic."

Tracy thought about that a second, which was a mistake, because it gave Martin a chance to look at the clock on the wall. "I need to go," she said, standing quickly. "I have a conference call."

"I'm assuming you were the personal representative of your husband's estate," Tracy said.

"I was."

"You would have access to his counseling records."

Martin shook her head. "I'm not going there, Detective."

"Maybe you wouldn't have to. If you could just get them—"

"For what—to possibly ruin my children's recollection of their father more than it's already been ruined? You don't even know if there's a connection. I'm not going to do that to my kids and grandchildren without good reason. Darren's death was traumatic for them. They were just kids. I'm not taking them back there."

Tracy was down to her final argument. "There's another family to think about, Mrs. Martin. A family who didn't get to see their daughter grow up, a family who is still without all the answers."

"They'll have to find their own closure, Detective, just like we did. It's a horrible thing, and I'm sorry, but I won't do that to my daughters and to my grandchildren. Now, I'm sorry, but I'm out of time. I'll walk you out."

Tracy left Martin a business card and drove back to the Justice Center. Foremost on Tracy's mind was Martin's statement that Darren Gallentine had never mentioned winning the state football championship, though they'd met just a few years after that historic feat, and at a time when Tracy would have thought it would remain a bragging point in any young, testosterone-driven athlete's life. Darren Gallentine wanted no part of it, apparently, and he wanted no part of Stoneridge, not even to visit his parents, and despite having departed a hero. Darren Gallentine's mind seemed to have no room for glory-days reminiscing, too cluttered with whatever nightmares tormented his sleep, made him turn to the bottle, and eventually led him to take his own life. Tracy wondered if those nightmares had to do with what happened to Kimi Kanasket.

Tracy's cell phone rang, interrupting her train of thought. Caller ID indicated it was Michael Melton at the crime lab.

"I just sent you my report," he said. "I thought I'd give you the *Reader's Digest* version."

"I appreciate that."

"The tire that made those impressions was a B.F. Goodrich 35x12.50R15," Melton said. "It was an all-terrain tire popular back then for trucks and off-road vehicles, so there were millions in circulation. Now, you want the bad news?"

"I thought that was the bad news. Let me guess—the make and model of the tire on the white truck in the photographs is different than the tires that made the impression," Tracy said.

"We were able to work with the negatives you provided for the truck," Melton said, "but I could only get a partial on the model, nothing on the make."

"What can you tell from the partial?"

"The size of the tire on the truck matches the size of the tire that made the impression, but there wasn't enough to determine the make or the model."

"So we don't know."

"I'm sorry. I wish I could be more definitive."

Kins turned from his computer the moment Tracy stepped into the bull pen, stood, and handed her two sheets of paper.

"Bingo," he said, pointing to the first of two e-mails. "Angela Collins was talking to a real estate agent about selling the house. He e-mailed her appraisals."

"When was this?" Tracy asked, searching for the date of the e-mail.

"The same week she bought a gun."

"Did you talk to this guy?"

"Just got off the phone with him; he says she asked for an appraisal *and* said she was thinking of selling first thing after the holidays. That would have been within days of the trial date," Kins said.

"Maybe before the divorce was even final," Tracy said. "I *knew* she was fixing it up to sell."

"Which would have violated the agreement."

"But only if Tim Collins was still alive. This could show premeditation."

"Maybe," Kins said. "I'm going to take a drive over there. I want to lock this guy down. You want to go with me?"

Tracy's cell phone rang. "Hang on." She fished through her purse and retrieved her phone. Caller ID indicated Jenny Almond.

"You're probably calling for an update," Tracy said.

"Actually, to give you some news," Jenny said. "I just heard through the grapevine that Earl Kanasket is in the hospital."

Jenny wouldn't be calling to tell her Earl had a stomachache. "What happened?"

"I heard he had a seizure. The son took him in, but apparently against Earl's wishes."

"How do you know that?"

"I called the hospital and spoke with his doctors."

"How bad is he?"

"He's breathing on his own now, but he's refusing any extraordinary lifesaving measures. Doctor said Earl told them he's prepared to leave this world and be with his wife and daughter."

Tracy thought of Élan Kanasket saying that

his mother had gone to her grave not knowing what had happened to Kimi, and his prediction that his father would do so as well. She didn't much care about proving Élan wrong; she cared more about putting Kimi to rest for Earl while he was still breathing. The window to do that had just narrowed significantly.

"Reunion activities start this week, don't they?" Tracy said.

"They do."

"I have something to take care of this afternoon, then I'm going to come back down. Is your mother's house still available?"

"Yeah. She doesn't get back until next week. You want to get together and talk about what you've found?"

"I'll likely be late tonight. Why don't I fill you in tomorrow?"

CHAPTER 23

The following morning, despite getting to the Almond farmhouse late and having a difficult time falling asleep, Tracy was out of bed before the rooster started crowing. She'd been unable to quiet the swirling thoughts she'd taken to bed with her, and when she awoke, they started again.

Running often helped clear her mind. When she stepped outside in her winter running gear, it was 5:15, dark, and according to the thermometer mounted near the front door, a brisk thirty-seven degrees. She set out on what had become her regular path, along the ridge of the foothills, intending to complete what she estimated to be a six-mile loop. It was disorienting running in the dark, but she had a headlamp, and the footing was solid.

When she reached the top of the ridge, she stopped to get her bearings. The state route was to the west, Stoneridge to the south. Her usual course was to follow the foothills east, then loop back north and west to the farmhouse. But a thought came to her, and instead she ran due south, following a less worn path and keeping 141, her point of reference, on her left. The foliage grew denser as she continued, and several times she considered stopping and turning back, but she pushed on, sensing she was heading in the right direction. She ran down an incline, feeling the impact on her knees and shins, continued on flat ground for another half a mile or so, and came to another grade, this one steeper. She powered up it, her breathing labored, arms and legs pumping. When she reached the top, she intertwined her fingers behind her head, pacing as she struggled to catch her breath. Below her was the clearing.

She always did have a strong sense of direction.

She walked down the hill, each breath marking the air. The first signs of dawn, a pink sky, inched just above the foothills, shedding shadowy light on the clearing and the surrounding trees.

Tracy walked to the spot where Kaylee Wright said Kimi had fallen, the spot where someone had planted a bush—the tips of the leaves already looked to be turning brown. She took a moment there, saying a silent prayer for Kimi, for her sister, Sarah, and for other young women like them. When she'd finished, a thought came to her, and she turned to consider the location where she'd seen the man the night she'd first come to the clearing. She crossed to the tree line and entered. In the daylight it was easier to pick her steps.

Farther in, she noted what looked to be a dead plant on the forest floor, its root ball still intact.

She bent to pick it up and noticed several more similarly discarded, each also with a root ball. She followed the trail and found a pile—dozens of different kinds of plants in various stages of decomposition.

Nothing grows in the clearing.

That hadn't stopped someone from trying.

She continued through the forest until she emerged onto the easement beneath the electrical lines. Her curiosity now piqued, she walked up the hill in the same direction as the tire tracks to the ridge of the foothills. From there she surveyed her surroundings but didn't see anything that stood out. She ran along the ridgeline for another mile and was about to turn back when she found herself looking down upon a sprawling plot of land with a large redwood storefront, multiple glass hothouses the size of warehouses, and what appeared to be acres of rows of potted plants, vines, shrubs, and juvenile trees.

A nursery.

She looked at her watch and started quickly back to the house.

At the farmhouse, Tracy called the Central Point Nursery and confirmed that Archibald Coe worked there, though the woman she spoke with said Coe wouldn't be in until eleven. Coe had to be the man Tracy saw the night she'd visited the clearing, which meant he must be the person planting different plants and shrubs in the place where Kimi Kanasket had been run over, and judging by the pile of plants Tracy had found, he'd been doing so for years.

She called Jenny, filling her in on what she'd recently learned and telling her she was going out to Central Point to speak to Archibald Coe. She'd also like to speak to Hastey Devoe, but she suspected that might be difficult unless they could catch him alone. Jenny suggested they put a loose tail on Hastey and said she'd let Tracy know if anything came of it.

Just before eleven, Tracy jumped in the truck and headed out into a heavy mist. When she arrived at the nursery, a woman behind a counter inside the sprawling redwood building advised her that Archibald Coe managed the nursery's garden center, which consisted of annuals, perennials, and foliage. Tracy would likely find him in one of the large glass hothouses out back. The woman offered to call Coe over the nursery's intercom system, but Tracy declined the offer and said she'd find him on her own. The woman suggested that Tracy try the farthest glass warehouse on the lot.

Crossing to it, Tracy raised the hood on her Gore-Tex jacket against the increasingly steady rain and stepped around puddles so as not to spend the rest of the day in wet shoes and socks. An ominous dark sky was the harbinger of a quickly worsening weather system, and Tracy hurried to get inside before what felt like an imminent deluge.

Inside, she lowered her hood and shook off the rain. Overhead fluorescent tubes shone above tables of perennials in various stages of gestation, and rows of potted plants and small trees. The warehouse was significantly warmer than outside, the air muggy and infused with the tart smell of fertilizer.

It wasn't hard to find Archibald Coe. He was the only other person in the hothouse and closely resembled his most recent driver's license photo—balding with just wisps of gray hair. Coe was sickly thin, gaunt through the cheekbones, with dark circles under sunken eyes. Dressed in knee-high rubber boots and a weathered Army-green rain slicker, Coe was working his way down a row of saplings sprouting in orange ceramic pots, watering them with what looked like a showerhead at the end of a metal pole. As Tracy neared, he lowered the wand and considered her with a flat expression and an almost vacuous gaze.

"Archibald Coe?"

The wand stopped spraying, though the water dribbled for a moment longer before stopping all together.

"I'm Tracy Crosswhite. I'm a detective from Seattle." She showed him her shield, which did nothing to change his impassive gaze. "I'd like to ask you a few questions."

"I'm busy," he said softly, sounding apologetic and looking like he'd already put in a full day. "I have to work."

"I won't take up much of your time, Mr. Coe. We can talk while you work, if you like."

Coe looked momentarily uncertain, then raised the wand and watered the next tree in the row, dragging the hose behind him.

"Did someone tell you to expect me?" Tracy asked, puzzled at Coe's seeming lack of interest.

Coe shook his head. "No."

"Some people would be concerned if a detective showed up unannounced and wanted to ask questions."

Coe looked up at the glass roof as a hard rain began to peck the panes, making a sound like bird beaks trying to shatter the glass.

"Are you curious what this is about?" Tracy asked.

Coe lowered his gaze. "What is it about?"

"Kimi Kanasket."

The pecking increased in intensity, hail now hitting the glass and sliding to the corners of the metal frames. Coe again lifted his gaze, and Tracy took a moment to study him. What she'd thought to be indifference she now saw as fragility. Coe, the young running back Sam

Goldman had described as shifty and fast, shuffled about with the tenuousness of an old man uncertain of his balance and afraid of falling. Each movement was so deliberate and methodical it made her wonder if Coe was sedated.

"Do you remember Kimi Kanasket?" she asked.

Coe nodded. "We went to school together. We ran track. She was very fast." Coe put down the wand and shuffled back to the beginning of the row. He picked up a box and shook out sticks the color and shape of cigarettes and began pressing them into the rich soil of each pot.

Tracy decided to try a different approach. "What types of trees are these?"

"Lemon," he said.

"Here in the Northwest?"

"We have a buyer in Southern California, but you can grow them here. You just have to know how to take care of them."

"How did you get started with plants?"

"My dad owned a nursery." Coe continued pressing the fertilizer spikes into the soil. "He used to say that plants are like children."

"Really? How so?"

"They come from a seed, sprout limbs, grow taller, stronger—but you have to nourish them."

"Do you have children?" Tracy asked.

Coe nodded.

"A boy? Girl?"

"Yes."

"One of each?"

"Yes."

"How old are they?"

Coe paused, staring at the ground. "I don't know anymore."

"You don't see them?"

Coe shook his head. Then he picked up the watering wand and started down the next row of saplings.

Recalling Tiffany Gallentine's statement that Darren took his own life when his daughter turned seventeen, Tracy asked, "How old were your kids when you and your wife divorced?"

This time Coe answered without hesitation. "Fifteen and ten."

"Who's older?"

"My daughter."

"So you know what it's like to be a parent, Mr. Coe."

Coe stepped to the next plant without responding.

"You know that sometimes kids don't always do the right thing." The watering wand hovered over the same tree before Coe directed it to the next tree in the row. "But we forgive them. If they come to us and tell us they've done something wrong, we forgive them. We all make mistakes." It was a speech Tracy had given to many suspects.

"I don't see them," Coe said. "They're grown now. We don't talk."

"Kimi Kanasket didn't jump in the river, did she, Mr. Coe?"

Coe didn't respond. He looked momentarily paralyzed, the water beginning to puddle in a pot. "What happened in the clearing in the woods, Mr. Coe?"

"I don't know," he said as if coming out of a trance. He pulled the hose behind him to the next plant.

"Who would?"

"I don't know." Coe again tugged at the hose, but it had become wedged along the bottom of one of the ceramic pots and he had to go back to free it. Rain cascaded down the glass panels, blurring the view outside.

"Earl Kanasket has gone forty years not knowing what happened to his daughter," Tracy said. "You have children. You have to know how that would feel—to lose one of your children and never understand why."

Coe began to shift from his heels to the balls of his feet, rocking. "I don't see them," he said. "I don't see my kids."

"I can help you, Mr. Coe," Tracy said. "If you tell me what happened, I can help you."

Coe shuffled to the next plant, dragging the hose behind him. "I have to work," he said. "I have to water the plants."

"Why do you put plants in the clearing, Mr. Coe?"

Coe didn't answer.

"I saw you that night, in the clearing, didn't I? You're the one who brings plants there, aren't you?"

"Nothing grows in the clearing. Everything dies."

"But you've planted things there, at the spot where Kimi was run over. You've tried many times. Why do you put plants there, Mr. Coe?"

Coe's complexion, already sickly, had become ghostly pale. He looked on the verge of tears.

"Kimi was still alive," Tracy said. "She didn't die in the clearing."

Coe looked up, and for the first time met and held Tracy's gaze.

"Whoever hit her with the truck didn't kill her, Mr. Coe. She was still alive when she was thrown into the river. Tell me what happened. You've been a solid citizen for forty years. You've never committed a crime. People are forgiving, Mr. Coe, but they want accountability. I get a sense you do too. You've been carrying this around for forty years. It's time you unburdened yourself and got it off your chest. Tell me what happened in the clearing that night."

"Nothing grows in the clearing. Everything dies," he said, and he turned and directed the wand to the next tree in the row.

CHAPTER 24

As Tracy left the nursery, Jenny called. "Looks like Hastey Devoe is getting a head start on celebrating the reunion. He's drinking his lunch at a restaurant bar near Vancouver. I suspect he'll be getting back in his car soon enough to drive home."

"Jail is as isolated as it gets," Tracy said.

"That was my thought exactly. I'll tell my guys to pull him in before he reaches Stoneridge and give you a call when they do."

"Stall him if he asks to make a call."

"Will do. What did Coe have to say?"

"Not much, unfortunately." She summarized her conversation with Archibald Coe as well as her impressions of the man and what she thought it could mean in light of Darren Gallentine's own emotional fragility and suicide. "I'm sure he was the person I saw in the clearing that night and that he's been planting things in that spot for years. I found dozens of dead plants discarded in the woods."

"A memorial," Jenny said.

"A would-be memorial. Nothing grows there. Everything dies. That's what he said. We're on the right track now, Jenny. I know it. And I got a very strong sense Coe knows what happened and that it still bothers him. I just have to find a way to get him to talk to me. If I can get him to tell me what happened, then all the circumstantial evidence becomes not just relevant, it becomes corroborating, and possibly damning."

"I can speak to the DA about it; maybe we can offer Coe some sort of deal in exchange for his testifying."

"I don't think that's the issue," Tracy said. "He's not being recalcitrant. He's emotionally fragile. It's like going back to what happened is a door he can't open or talk about. I'm going to have to think about this and be cautious about how I approach him. We can discuss it more when your deputies bring Devoe in."

"Where are you going now?"

"To look at some more old newspapers."

Sam Goldman greeted Tracy with a smile. "You must have been driving the Batmobile," he said.

"I might have broken a speed limit or two," Tracy said.

"Perk of the job, right?"

"It isn't the pay, the hours, or the praise."

Goldman roared. "You said it, friend. Teachers, newspaper reporters, and police officers—the most underpaid professions on the planet."

Goldman stepped aside to let Tracy in.

"You said you wanted to see the newspapers again?"

"If it isn't too much trouble."

"No trouble at all, chief." Goldman was already moving through the kitchen to the mudroom. Adele sat at a small table positioned beneath the window, a pencil and a Sudoku book in hand and the same half-troubled, half-curious expression, as if she were uncertain about this continued break in their retirement routine.

"*Back to the Future* two, Adele," Goldman said.

"Nice to see you again," Adele said to Tracy. "Can I get you a cup of tea?"

"Not today, but thank you. I promise not to take much of Sam's time."

Goldman was on a roll. "Places to go and people to see, Adele. She's a woman on a mission."

They stepped out the back door, and Goldman repeated the ritual of unlocking the padlock that was securing the shed doors, then placing the five-gallon bucket at the corner to keep the door from swinging shut. Inside, he turned on the light and weaved his way to the stacks of boxes containing his life's work.

He found the box Tracy had looked at previously and pulled out the issues. Tracy opened the first paper.

Reynolds' Arm, Legs Take
Stoneridge to the Brink

The front-page article carried over to an inside page containing additional articles and photographs. One photo depicted Eric Reynolds jogging off the field after the game with his helmet raised overhead and the broad smile of a kid with a bright future beckoning. Having taught high school in a small town, Tracy knew that wasn't the case for everyone. Behind Reynolds the football field was filled with teammates celebrating, girls in cheerleading outfits, and parents and students in knit hats and coats, holding pennants and handmade signs.

"That's the game that really put him on the map," Goldman said, adjusting his glasses and looking over Tracy's shoulder. "Up until then, only the smaller schools had been recruiting him, but everyone came calling after that game. He threw for more than two hundred yards and two touchdowns and ran for two more scores. When UW came knocking, that was all she wrote. The old man wanted Eric to go there, and that was it. They didn't have the big circuses back then like they do now, but we wrote a story on his decision. He signed his letter of intent at the newspaper and used our machine to fax it over to the U." Goldman thought for a moment. "That would have been February." He set the box aside and lifted the lid on the box beneath it, thumbing the papers again until he found the edition he was looking for.

"February 17, 1977," Goldman said, unfolding the newspaper. "A day that will not live in infamy."

The photograph was on the front page, Eric Reynolds seated at a desk, pen in hand. Ron Reynolds stood at his son's side, one hand braced on the desk, the other clasping Eric's shoulder. Both men looked up at the camera with broad smiles. They shared a passing resemblance. Eric had inherited the strong jawline and the smile that inched just slightly higher on the left side. Unlike Ron, who wore a crew cut and had the hard features of a drill sergeant, Eric had shoulder-length blond hair and softer features. His eyes were likely blue, though the photograph was black and white, and unlike his father's, which burned with intensity, Eric's sparkled. This was a high school kid who melted girls' hearts with just a passing glance.

"I was standing on a desk to get that shot," Goldman said with some pride.

"The mother didn't get to join in the fun?"

"The mother died before they moved from Southern California. It was just the two of them."

"No siblings?"

"Nope. Eric was the golden boy. Led the basketball team to state also that year. And he pitched well enough he would have been drafted, but Ron made it clear that football was king and young Eric intended to play quarterback and then go on to the NFL."

The article continued on the next page, accompanied by another photograph of Eric, this time wearing a letterman jacket adorned with more patches than a Boy Scout uniform, and reclining easily against the side of what was likely the precursor to the SUV—a Jeep maybe—with a cloth canopy.

Tracy held the paper up and angled it to better catch the yellow light. She realized that it was actually a Bronco with off-road tires. But her initial euphoria quickly dissipated. She could make out some of the tire tread but not much, and she could see very little of the sidewall, where she knew the make and model number were placed. "Damn," she said.

"What are you looking for, chief?"

"The tire. I need to know the make and model number of that tire."

"Let me see it." Goldman took the paper, raised his glasses onto his forehead, and studied the photograph. "We cropped this," he said.

"You cropped it?" Tracy asked.

"Sure. Had to crop it to get it to fit."

"Would you still have the original photo?" Tracy asked, cautious but optimistic, given Goldman's seeming penchant to keep everything.

Goldman gave her a knowing smile. "You underestimate me, hero." He started toward a row of file cabinets lining a side wall. Each drawer contained a white card in the front slot, the ink faded and in some instances barely visible. Goldman again raised his glasses to the ridge of his forehead, bending to read the cards in the muted light. "This one," he said, flipping the button with his thumb and pulling the drawer open. "We kept the photographs for each issue. Never knew when you might need a canned shot."

Like the boxes of newspapers, the drawer was neatly organized, with tabbed hanging green files. Goldman went through them front to back, his pace slowing as he neared the last files. "Nope," he said.

"You don't have it?" Tracy asked.

"Wrong drawer."

Goldman slid the drawer closed and pulled open the drawer beneath it, repeating the process, slowing, and pulling out one of the hanging files near the front. "This is it." He took the file back to the makeshift Bekins box table. Inside the file were loose black-and-white photos. Goldman went through them as fast as a card dealer, setting aside the photographs that had nothing to do with Eric Reynolds or his father.

"Here they are." He flipped through shots of Eric leaning against a stucco building, some with his letterman jacket on, some with it off. "It was Adele who suggested we take the picture of Eric leaning against the car, to give us better contrast." Goldman held up one of the photographs. "She said these looked too much like mug shots."

Goldman handed Tracy the shot of Eric leaning against the Bronco. Someone, likely Goldman, had used a red grease pen to draw a rectangle to delineate the area of the photo that would be used in the paper. Outside that rectangle, below the Bronco's front fender, the camera had captured more of the oversize tire than had been published in the newspaper. Tracy could see the tread, as well as a portion of the sidewall, but she couldn't see the make or model number, at least not with the naked eye.

"Sam, I'm going to have to take this picture and this negative. Copies won't work. You have my word I'll scan the photo and bring it back. The negative I have to send to the Washington State Patrol Crime Lab in Seattle."

Goldman's eyes were blazing with excitement. "Now, that's a story to tell the grandkids," he said.

Another thought came to her. "Can I see the issue covering the parade—the one with the collage?"

"That'd be the issue—Tuesday, November 9, 1976," Goldman said.

After finding the box, Goldman found the issue and opened it as if it were a centuries-old relic, carefully laying it on the box lids. Tracy studied the photographs capturing the parade. The residents of Stoneridge lined the streets, smiling and yelling, and cheerleaders carried a hand-painted "State Champions" banner at the head of a procession that included the band. Players and coaches filled trucks and convertibles. Several of the photographs were taken at angles that captured the vehicles carrying the team members in their jerseys—a station wagon, a Mustang, a pickup truck with several players standing in the bed, and a flatbed truck carrying another two dozen or so, seated with their feet dangling over the side while they waved to the crowd.

Tracy considered more closely a photograph capturing three of the Four Ironmen—Eric Reynolds, Hastey Devoe, and Archibald Coe sitting atop the backseat of a convertible Cadillac. Reynolds held a trophy aloft over his head, and Devoe had his index finger raised and a broad smile. Coe stood beside them with a blank stare, looking as impassive as he'd been at the nursery. Tracy noted Darren Gallentine's absence and scanned the other photographs, but she didn't see his face or his jersey number in any of the pictures. She also didn't see Eric Reynolds's Bronco, and she wondered why, since with its removable soft top, it would have seemed a natural for the parade.

Tracy's cell phone rang. She recognized the number.

"They just pulled over Hastey," Jenny said.

CHAPTER 25

The Klickitat County sheriff's main office remained located in Goldendale, a fifty-minute drive, but Buzz Almond had opened a "West End" office in Stoneridge to better serve that portion of the county and, if he was honest, probably to shorten his commute. When she arrived at the sheriff's office, Tracy decided to let Hastey Devoe cook for a few minutes while she and Jenny scanned and sent the photograph of Eric Reynolds leaning against the Bronco's bumper to Kelly Rosa and Michael Melton. Tracy asked Rosa to consider whether the bruising pattern on Kimi Kanasket's back and shoulder matched the tire tread in the photograph. She advised Melton that she was having the negatives driven up to him in Seattle by a deputy sheriff and asked that he compare the tread with the tread in the photographs from the clearing.

The deputies who brought Hastey Devoe in told Jenny that he had refused a Breathalyzer test in the field, didn't respond to their questions, and asked to make a phone call. Being brought in for suspicion of driving under the influence may have seemed like nothing but a minor inconvenience to Devoe, since he probably figured that his brother,

Lionel, chief of police, would iron everything out.

Tracy knew she would need to knock Hastey Devoe out of his comfort zone if she hoped to get him to talk. She would have preferred to question him after she knew what Melton and Rosa had determined, but that wasn't going to happen. She sensed they didn't have much time before Lionel found out about the arrest, and she knew they wouldn't likely get another opportunity to get Hastey alone anytime soon.

She was encouraged to see Devoe's smirk evaporate when she entered the room with Jenny. Lionel may have warned him that a detective from Seattle was in town asking questions about Kimi. But beyond that, Devoe had to know that when the sheriff showed up to interview you personally, it was a bigger deal than just another DUI arrest.

"This is getting to be an old habit, Hastey," Jenny said, sliding back a chair and sitting. Tracy took the other open chair in the room. No table separated them from Devoe, nothing to provide him a comfort zone. He smelled like a fraternity house the morning after a party.

Tracy recalled that in the photographs of Devoe as a younger man, the extra weight had given him an innocent, boyish appearance. Tracy suspected he had been the kid everyone laughed with when he took off his shirt and did cannonballs into the rivers and lakes, or belly danced as he chugged a beer. He'd likely been the class clown, one of the John Belushis, Chris Farleys, and John Candys of the world. But things didn't end well for those men—drugs eventually killed Belushi and Farley; Candy had struggled with his weight and died of a heart attack. Those men had also been trained actors, and it was possible that they created their public personas to cover their insecurities and their demons.

From the look of Devoe, things weren't going to end well for him either. Excess alcohol and overconsumption had turned his baby fat into sagging folds that overwhelmed the chair he sat in, and his boyish features had become pale and fleshy. His dress was slovenly, his khakis and blue polo shirt wrinkled and unkempt, with half-moon perspiration stains beneath each armpit and ringing his collar. His thinning gray hair was also disheveled and damp with perspiration.

Devoe's gaze flicked to Jenny. "I'd like to make a phone call."

"Just as soon as we've had a chance to talk and get you booked," Jenny said.

"I'm not saying anything." Devoe shifted his gaze to an empty corner of the room.

"Then you can listen." Tracy inched her chair closer, forcing him to look at her.

"Who are you?"

"You know who I am, Mr. Devoe. I'm the

322

detective from Seattle your brother told you about."

"What do you want?" Devoe folded his arms across his chest.

"I want to talk to you about Kimi Kanasket."

Devoe's forehead wrinkled. "Who?" he said. It was not convincing.

Tracy slid closer, leaving less than a foot between their knees. "I want you to tell me about the night Kimi Kanasket disappeared."

"I don't know who you're talking about." Devoe had the damaged, gravelly voice of a man who abused his alcohol and his cigarettes.

"Sure you do. You went to school with her your senior year, and this weekend is all about that year. Beyond that, you were there that night. You were in the clearing. You, Eric Reynolds, Archibald Coe, and Darren Gallentine were inseparable. You were the Four Ironmen. Tell me what happened."

Devoe wouldn't look at her, but his Adam's apple bobbed up and down, and he shifted and fidgeted in his chair. Though the room was air-conditioned, beads of perspiration began to trickle down the side of his face, following the contours of his sideburns. The feral odor in the room intensified.

"I don't . . ." Hastey cleared his throat. "I don't know what you're talking about."

"What size shoe do you wear, Hastey?"

"Why do you want to know that?"

"Thirteen, right?"

"Wrong," he said. "Twelve."

"You favored Converse in high school, like your buddy Eric."

"I don't—"

Tracy leaned forward. "Yes, you do, Hastey, and I'm going to prove it. I'm going to prove that you were in the Bronco when Eric ran Kimi over, and I'm going to prove that you and your brother Lionel, and maybe even your father, fixed the Bronco's windshield and front fender. So don't tell me you weren't there or you don't know anything about it."

"I want to talk to my brother."

"Your brother? I was betting that you'd ask to call Eric Reynolds," Tracy said. "He's been covering for you for forty years, hasn't he? Of course he's had little choice. The two of you share a common secret, don't you? That's why he put you on the company payroll, and that's why he keeps you there. He even helped fund Lionel's campaign to become chief of police for the same reason—to keep you quiet."

Hastey looked like a man with heartburn after eating a spicy meal. The perspiration was dripping off of him.

"Stop me anytime I'm wrong, Hastey."

Devoe didn't speak.

"The thing about a lie, Hastey, is it's never just

one, is it? You think if everyone agrees to say nothing, then nothing can happen to anyone. But soon you have to tell another lie, then another, and pretty soon, you've told so many lies you don't know what the truth is anymore." Tracy tapped her sternum. "But deep inside, the truth lingers, and that soft, nagging conscience just keeps pecking away, fighting to get out. It just keeps pecking and pecking and pecking, until you just can't stand it. You can't sleep. You can't function. You're drinking too much, eating too much. You're self-destructing. You're wondering if you're going to have a heart attack, or maybe lose it entirely, the way Darren Gallentine lost it."

Devoe looked white as a sheet.

"And then that secret that seemed so simple has suddenly become a huge anchor around your neck, and it starts to pull you under because you no longer have the strength to keep your head above water. You start to drown. You're going under, Hastey, and you know it. You're drowning. Don't you want to shake free of that anchor? Don't you want to free your conscience? You didn't kill Kimi Kanasket. You weren't driving. You were just there. You were in the wrong place at the wrong time. It happens to every kid in high school. Tell me what happened. Tell me what happened, and I'll do my best to help you."

Devoe looked to be struggling to catch his breath, as if about to hyperventilate. Tracy could picture him doing something similar in a football huddle. Tired and exhausted, not believing he could play another down, but unwilling to let his teammates down. Unlike Eric Reynolds, who was the good-looking all-American, or Darren Gallentine, who was physically fit and smart, or even Archibald Coe, who had a plan to become an Army officer, football was all Hastey had. It was how he fit in—because being the class clown necessarily meant that while people were laughing with you, they were also laughing at you, and that could be painful. So Hastey would suck it up and go back to the line and slam his body into his opponents over and over again, beyond exhaustion, because that was how he fit in, how he was accepted. And being accepted was what he wanted, which is why Tracy knew, even before he opened his mouth, that Hastey Devoe would never say anything to implicate anyone, especially not the hand that had fed him all those years. He wouldn't implicate Eric Reynolds.

"I want to talk to my brother," he said.

Lionel Devoe arrived at the sheriff's office within minutes of Hastey's phone call. Of course, he didn't have far to travel. He stalked into the conference room looking and sounding upset. He became more upset when Hastey wasn't in the room.

"He's being booked, Lionel," Jenny said. "And

he's going to spend the night in jail and be arraigned in the morning. You can post bail then and take him home."

"I'm going to call Dale," Lionel said, referring to the county prosecutor, "and let him know what this is really about."

"If I were you, I'd start calling around for a good lawyer," Jenny countered. "I've already spoken to Dale. He intends to bring felony charges against Hastey as a repeat offender, and he's not going to be offering him any type of prevention program without a suspension of his driver's license and jail time."

Lionel looked like he could spit nails. "What exactly are you doing, Sheriff?"

"My job, Lionel. You want to get angry at someone, get angry at your brother. Then get him some help before he kills himself or someone else."

"Don't preach to me, and don't tell me your deputies just happened to stumble upon Hastey, today of all days, with her in town." Lionel jabbed a finger in Tracy's direction. "That's just too Goddamn convenient. You had him watched, and you pulled him over so she could talk to him about Kimi Kanasket."

"Whose side are you on, Lionel?" Jenny said, looking and sounding completely innocent. "I know he's your brother, but he was clearly intoxicated, and he needs help."

"My concern is you facilitating a witch hunt based on some unsupported allegations from forty years ago and dragging my brother into it. This is supposed to be a celebratory weekend. This is supposed to be a celebration of a past achievement and a dedication to the future."

"Just like forty years ago," Tracy said.

"What?" Lionel said.

"Forty years ago nobody wanted a dead Indian girl to spoil their championship weekend. So Kimi Kanasket got tossed in the river and forgotten."

Lionel Devoe raised a finger and stepped closer. "Let me tell you something, Detective—"

"No," Tracy said raising her own finger. "Let me tell you something. Forty years ago those four boys conspired to keep hidden what they did to Kimi Kanasket, and I don't believe they acted alone. That windshield and front fender didn't get fixed on their own. Would you happen to know anything about that?"

Lionel shook his head, scoffing.

"You were running your father's business at that time. You know anything about two cash receipts for bodywork and replacement of a windshield?"

Lionel smiled, but it looked pained. "You're fishing, Detective. Problem is you've got a line in the water, but you got no bait on your hook." He straightened. "You think you can prove anything, then do it. Otherwise, leave my brother and me out of this witch hunt of yours."

"Oh, I'll prove it. You can count on that. I learned from fishing with my dad that you don't always need bait to catch fish. I've caught them with a fly, a lure, a net, and a spear. I've even caught them with my bare hands."

"Well then, good luck with that." Lionel started for the door.

"And when you call Eric Reynolds to report in, let him know I'm coming to talk to him next," Tracy said. Her comment caused Lionel to stop. He looked back with a searing gaze, but when he opened his mouth he apparently couldn't articulate what he wanted to say.

Jenny filled the pause. "I'd suggest you get your brother a lawyer before tomorrow, Lionel."

CHAPTER 26

Tracy passed on her run the next morning, telling herself she wanted to give her body a day to recover. In truth, she didn't feel like running. She sensed she was reaching a dead end, and that frustrated her. Lionel was right. Her bravado and accusations wouldn't get her very far, not without more. Her best bet remained Archibald Coe, but she had to find a way to somehow get him to open up.

Her decision not to run became easier when she looked out the window. A light snow had fallen during the night, leaving a sparkling silver-and-white landscape. It was beautiful, but like a high mountain lake in winter is beautiful—unspoiled and pure, but also teeth-chatteringly, spine-numbingly cold. Mike Melton further dampened her mood when he called to tell her about the photograph of the tire on Eric Reynolds's Bronco.

"The lab worked overtime," he said. "I'm sorry. I know I'm starting to sound like a broken record, but there's just not enough to be definitive. The photo didn't cover enough of the tire for me to state with certainty it's the same make and model as the tread captured in the photos taken in the field. It looks similar, Tracy. It could be the same tire, but there were other models by other

330

manufacturers made back then that are too similar to rule out."

Tracy's breath fogged the kitchen windowpane. "So you can't say it's that tire, only that it *could be* that tire."

"I can say the impressions in the ground captured in the photographs are similar to the impressions I would expect that tire would make. But no, I can't say it was *that* tire. I'm sorry. I know that isn't the answer you wanted."

And that was a problem.

Tracy thanked Melton. His answer wasn't totally unexpected, and it was certainly better than him telling her the tires were definitely *not* the ones that had made the impressions. But *similar* would not get her where she needed to go. She suspected Kelly Rosa would offer the same conclusion—the pattern of bruising on Kimi Kanasket's back and shoulder was of the type she would expect to be left by that make of tire, but she couldn't definitely say the bruising was made by that tire.

Tracy left the window and sat at the table to reassess what she knew and where that put the investigation. Certainly there was plenty of circumstantial evidence pointing to Kimi Kanasket having been chased and run down by a truck with all-terrain tires. Eric Reynolds drove a vehicle with that kind of tire, but so did Tommy Moore and Élan Kanasket, and Hastey and Lionel Devoe had access to company vehicles that could have had similar tires, not to mention the many other trucks and SUVs in the county. The same was true of the shoe impressions. Except for the hunting boots, they were made by brands of shoes popular among young men at that time.

Beyond that, as with any decades-old case, the evidence was riddled with uncertainty any defense attorney worth his salt would exploit. Jurors would question why the case was being brought now, and even convincing arguments about advances in technology could be trumped by a more practical and human argument—whether it was justified to prosecute three or four men who had never committed another known violent act against anyone on the basis of questionable evidence. Without more, the case would be near-impossible for a prosecutor to convince a jury to sacrifice those lives for the life of a young woman dead forty years.

Someone knocked on the front door. Tracy was surprised to find Jenny standing on the porch. She looked troubled. "I just came from the Central Point Nursery," she said, and Tracy felt her stomach drop. "An employee found Archibald Coe hanging in one of the hothouses."

They moved into the dining room, but neither Tracy nor Jenny sat. Tracy felt as though she'd taken a mule kick to the gut.

Jenny had driven out to the nursery upon receiving the call earlier that morning. "He wasn't answering his phone or responding to calls over the nursery's loudspeakers," Jenny said. "Someone noticed he'd never clocked out last night and took a walk over to the hothouse."

"Are you certain it was a suicide?"

"The person who found him said the door was unlocked when he tried it. I got a CSI team over there, but there's no indication of a struggle. He positioned some plants around himself in a circle, looped a rope over one of the overhead beams, stood on a ceramic pot, and kicked it over."

"A memorial. Like the clearing," Tracy said.

"Looks like that's what he intended."

"Any note?"

"Not that we've found," Jenny said. "I sent detectives to his apartment. I think it best under the circumstances that you not get too close to this. Let my office handle it. I'll let you know if we find anything."

Tracy couldn't disagree, but that didn't alleviate her frustration. She swore under her breath. "Maybe I should have anticipated this, given how fragile he seemed."

Jenny shrugged. "And what could you have done about it?"

"I don't know."

The police detective in Tracy couldn't dismiss

the thought that Coe had not willingly taken his own life, that it was all too convenient. Her civilian side was thinking that if Coe *had* taken his own life, she bore some measure of responsibility—that her questions about Kimi Kanasket had pushed an already fragile man over the edge. She felt horrible about it, but she also saw it as further validation that the cause of Coe's nervous breakdown was the same nightmare that had haunted Darren Gallentine. The similarities between the two men's circumstances could not be ignored. Each had problems when their children were born and when their daughters became teenagers. Tracy suspected that Coe, like Gallentine, had toed the ledge between living and taking his own life for years, and had only managed to subsist by following a structured routine. When Tracy disrupted that routine, it had shattered Coe's tenuous existence, and this time it had been enough for him to step off that narrow ledge—if Coe had in fact killed himself.

The only thing Tracy knew for certain was that she had just lost her best chance of finding out what had really happened that night in the clearing . . . and perhaps her last chance to prove it.

After Jenny had gone back to Central Point, Tracy's cell phone rang, a 509 area code, which she recognized as the area code for Eastern Washington, including Klickitat County. She didn't recognize the number. Still, Tracy answered.

"Detective Crosswhite?"

"Yes?"

"This is Eric Reynolds. I understand you wish to speak to me."

CHAPTER 27

Tracy had a difficult time finding a parking spot in the overflowing lot for the Columbia River Golf Course, and she eventually parallel parked in a questionable space that blocked several cars. She figured she'd be gone well before the golfers returned. The sun had burst through the cloud layer, and though it remained cold, any remnant of the dusting of snow that morning had melted. As Tracy approached the clubhouse, she noticed a large banner hanging from the roof eaves that explained the reason for the crowd—the Ron Reynolds Golf Tournament.

Eric Reynolds had explained to Tracy during their brief telephone conversation that he had an 11:10 tee time but that Tracy could find him on the driving range an hour before, and Reynolds would be happy to speak to her. He sounded like he was scheduling a business lunch, not the least bit concerned that a Seattle homicide detective wanted to question him about the death of a young woman forty years earlier. Tracy could tell this would not be like interviewing Archibald Coe or Hastey Devoe.

Tracy entered the pro shop, obtained directions to the driving range, and found golfers of varying ages from white-haired octogenarians to baby-faced recent high school graduates. Young men and women dressed in Stoneridge High letterman jackets and cheerleading outfits flittered around the area. Some drove golf carts or otherwise tried to look busy.

Tracy had a copy of Eric Reynolds's most recent driver's license photo, but she didn't need it. He was easy to find. He stood at the end of the range, alternately driving golf balls into a net 250 yards away and smiling and chatting with a group of admirers gathered behind him and seemingly hanging on his every word. He looked to still be Stoneridge High's all-American. He wasn't exceptionally tall, perhaps an inch or two over six feet, but he still had the muscular build of an athlete. The theme of the day was Stoneridge, and Reynolds wore the school colors proudly—red pants and sweater vest, white shirt and golf shoes.

Tracy held back, watching Reynolds while listening to the pings and thwacks of a dozen golf clubs striking range balls. After a few minutes, Reynolds caught sight of her at the edge of the putting green. He clearly knew who she was, but if her presence unnerved him, his reaction did not reveal it. He gave her a nod and half a wave, as if they were old friends and he'd be with her in just a minute. Reynolds said a few more words to the gathered assembly, slid the shaft of his club into his bag, and removed his white golf glove as he approached.

"Detective Crosswhite," he said, extending a hand. "I hope I didn't keep you waiting long."

"Not at all," Tracy said.

Reynolds looked up at the sky, pale blue with large white clouds. "Thankfully, it looks like we're going to have decent weather," he said. "I told the organizers you tempt fate when you schedule a golf tournament in November. We usually hold it in late spring, but this year they were adamant it coincide with the reunion and the stadium dedication."

"So this is an annual event?"

"It is. We started it to raise money for the Stoneridge High School scholarship fund." He gestured in the direction of the clubhouse. "I've reserved a room for us to talk."

They walked side by side, making small talk. Along the way, half a dozen people called out to Reynolds, and he acknowledged each by name. At the clubhouse he held the door open for Tracy, and they stepped inside. The carpeted hall was adorned with plaques and photographs and a trophy case, but it was far less ostentatious than clubhouses to be found in Seattle.

Reynolds led Tracy into a small banquet room set up for a formal lunch, with a dozen round tables covered in white tablecloths and place settings, and a podium and microphone at the front of the room. Reynolds led Tracy to a table with a pitcher of iced tea and two glasses.

"Can I pour you a glass?" he asked.

"Please," she said.

"It's unsweetened."

"That's fine," she said, sitting in one of the banquet chairs, content for the moment to let Reynolds play host.

Reynolds joined her, angling his knees away from the table, legs crossed, sipping his tea. "I understand you have questions for me about the night Kimi Kanasket disappeared."

"Who told you I had questions?"

Reynolds smiled. "We both know the answer to that question," he said. "Chief Devoe is a bit worked up about it; he thinks it will spoil the mood this weekend."

"What else did Chief Devoe have to say?"

"He said you were in town and were investigating the death of Kimi Kanasket, that you had doubts Kimi had committed suicide, and that you were intimating that I, along with Hastey, and possibly Archie Coe and Darren Gallentine, might have had some part in it."

"Are you aware that Archibald Coe hung himself this morning?"

"No." Reynolds set down his glass. His surprise looked genuine. "No, I wasn't."

"When's the last time you saw or spoke to Mr. Coe?"

Reynolds closed his eyes and blew out a breath. After a moment he shook his head and opened his eyes. "Wow." He took another moment before reengaging. "It's been a long time. Years."

"You didn't stay in touch?"

"No."

"He didn't come to any of the class reunions."

Reynolds sat up and uncrossed his legs, leaning toward Tracy. "No, he didn't. I'd heard Archie had some issues when he came back from the Army."

"What kind of issues?"

"Psychological issues—I heard he had a nervous breakdown—but I don't know the details."

"Do you remember who told you that?"

Reynolds shook his head. "No. That was a long time ago."

"You didn't reach out to him?"

"I was away at college, and with football practice every day I rarely went home." Reynolds put his hands to his lips, like a child about to pray. "The town linked the four of us together, Detective. The Four Ironmen." He sat up again, hands parting. "The truth was, we weren't all that close off the field. We were friends, but Archie and Darren hung with a different group of kids than Hastey and me."

"When did you last speak to Darren Gallentine?"

"He went to UW when I was there. I'd see him on campus and occasionally we'd stop and talk for a few minutes, but we didn't hang out."

"You're aware that he also killed himself."

"Yes. Years ago, I believe."

"But you and Hastey Devoe have remained close?"

Reynolds shrugged as if to say *What are you going to do?* "Hastey and I grew up just a few houses apart. When we got to high school, he was a bit of a lost soul. I persuaded him to come out for football. Actually, my dad took one look at the size of him and *mandated* he come out for football." Reynolds smiled. "He thought it would be good for Hastey's self-confidence and conditioning. He told Hastey he'd make him a star, and he did. Hastey could have played in college if he'd kept his grades up, but he couldn't do it. Hastey's always needed structure, a guiding hand. He didn't always get it at home."

"Why's that?"

"His father was hard on him. He was hard on all of them. They didn't measure up to his standards, except for maybe Nathaniel, but he died—hunting accident. That just seemed to make it harder on Lionel and Hastey. Hastey Senior wasn't bashful about telling his sons he was disappointed in them. He was a tough guy to like."

"So you and your father took Hastey Junior under your wing?"

"In a sense I guess you could say that. It was just my dad and me. We lost my mom to cancer when I was eight. Hastey spent a lot of nights at my house. We've stayed close."

"Isn't he a bit of a liability?"

Reynolds smiled, closed lips. "That's why we took him off driving and gave him a desk job." He sat up. "Look, despite his faults, he's good with people, affable. He's self-effacing and doesn't come on with a hard sell. Customers like him. So do I."

"You know he was arrested for another DUI."

"Yeah, I know."

"So you're not just keeping him on the payroll out of a sense of loyalty?"

"That's part of the reason, sure." Reynolds set an elbow on the table. "He's not a bad guy, Detective. He needs help. Lionel protects him and makes it too easy for him. Maybe this latest arrest will change that."

"I'm surprised Lionel doesn't listen to you, given that you were a big supporter of his campaign for chief of police."

Another smile. "First of all, Lionel is his brother, and Hastey is a grown man. Second, 'big supporter' here doesn't have the same meaning I suspect it might have in Seattle. A couple thousand bucks to buy posters, a billboard, and some bumper stickers isn't much. Life's been good to me. If I can spread some of that good to help old friends or people who can use it, I try. I'm no saint, but I try."

"Like this golf tournament?"

"Exactly like this golf tournament. It raises money for the school. Some families have fallen on hard times with the economy, and the money helps pay for books, teachers' salaries, those things."

"And a football stadium to be named after your father?"

"No. The funds aren't used for that."

"Straight out of your pocket?"

"The company's pocket."

"You drove a Ford Bronco in high school."

Reynolds looked mildly surprised at the sudden change in topic. "This *is* a trip down memory lane. That's a long time ago. Yes, I drove a Ford Bronco, back before OJ made them infamous." He smiled, seemingly at the recollection. "It was canary yellow with running lights across the roof, a roll bar and black canopy, oversize tires, a winch mounted to the front grille, and one of those foghorns. If you couldn't see us, you could hear us coming from a mile away. I'm not sure it could have been any more obnoxious. We'd pile in that thing and drive through town after games, and Hastey would blow the horn. People loved it."

"Did you hunt?"

"My father did. I wasn't much for killing animals. I liked to go four-wheeling, though, especially after a hard rain. That car would be caked in so much mud you couldn't tell the color."

"You ever go four-wheeling in the clearing?"

"The clearing off 141?"

"Yeah."

Reynolds seemed to give it some thought before answering. "Probably once or twice, but that was more of a weekend party destination. We'd get six or seven cars out there, turn on the headlights, crank the music, and drink beer." He shrugged. "It was harmless stuff."

"How'd you hear about Kimi Kanasket?"

Reynolds rocked back on the legs of his banquet chair and slid the tips of his fingers beneath his belt buckle. His gaze shifted to the ceiling, and he spoke deliberately, as if trying to recall. "I believe we heard sometime that Sunday. We played the championship game Saturday night, and after the game we all went out— players, coaches, parents. We stayed the night in Yakima. On Sunday we boarded the bus and caravanned home. I believe someone said something on the bus. I remember being shocked. But it could have been an article in the paper . . . maybe on Monday. But don't quote me. That part is a bit hazy."

"What was your reaction?"

Reynolds shrugged one shoulder. "Same as everybody else. Shock. Dismay. It's a small community, smaller back then. Everybody knows everybody. You think you're invulnerable at that age. Then you hear something like that. It's a shock. It was a shock."

"So you knew Kimi?"

"Absolutely. We all knew each other."

"What was your relationship with her?"

"Friendly. Kimi was smart and athletic. She was going to state in track, and I think she was also going to UW. We weren't great friends, but I knew her."

"You weren't romantically involved?" Tracy was taking another shot in the dark. Reynolds was far too comfortable. She was hoping to shake him up.

Reynolds chuckled. "Kimi and me? No. First of all, you didn't try anything with Kimi."

"Why not?"

"Because she had a brother and a boyfriend—I forget the guy's name, but I remember he was a Golden Gloves boxer and had a temper."

"Tommy Moore?"

"That's it. Tommy Moore."

"How do you know he had a temper?" Tracy asked.

"He and Kimi's brother got kicked out of school for fighting."

"Do you know what they were fighting about?"

"Back then there was a beef about the school's use of the name 'Red Raiders.' They said it was insensitive to Native Americans. I'm sure it was, though not as insensitive as a white kid wearing war paint driving a spear into the turf." Reynolds lowered his chair. "Things were different back then. The old people in town got upset over the protests and dug in their heels. Me? I didn't care what they called us. For me it was all about winning. I just wanted to finish undefeated and cart that state championship trophy off the field at the end of the season."

"You said you took buses to Yakima Saturday morning and returned Sunday morning."

"That's right."

"What did you do Friday night?"

"That's easy. I stayed home. You didn't go out the night before a game and play for Ron Reynolds. He wouldn't have cared that I was his son and the starting quarterback. He would have benched my butt."

"So you didn't go out at all?"

"No. I stayed at home."

"You'd be surprised then if I told you that Archibald Coe told me yesterday that you all went out together Friday night?" Again, Tracy was looking to rattle Reynolds and get him out of his comfort zone.

"Very surprised," he said, shaking his head. "You spoke to him yesterday?"

"Yes."

"How did he seem to you?"

"Fragile."

Again, Reynolds paused, seeming to give this some thought. "Maybe Archie wasn't thinking straight or got things confused in his head, given his apparent state of mind."

Tracy let Reynolds's answer linger. The detective part of her again thought the timing of Coe's death just too convenient after he'd lived years with whatever demons had tormented him. "Anyone who could vouch for you, Mr. Reynolds?"

"For what?"

"For the Friday night that Kimi died."

"Sure. My dad."

"He'll say you were home?"

"That's what he told that deputy who came by the following week."

The answer surprised her. "A deputy came by and spoke to your father?"

"Yeah. That's what I recall. He came by and wanted to know if I knew Kimi and said he was just following up on some things. He asked if I had been out Friday night and maybe had seen her. I told him what I've told you—I was home and went to bed early. Like I said, winning that state championship was foremost on my mind. I imagine he would have filled out a report or something, wouldn't he?"

"One would think," Tracy said.

CHAPTER 28

Tracy left the clubhouse feeling like she was in the middle of a game of chess and it was her move. Eric Reynolds's statement about Buzz Almond paying a visit to his home the week after Kimi disappeared had thrown her off her game. No such report existed, at least not in the file Tracy had, and Buzz Almond certainly appeared meticulous about including everything in his file. If Reynolds was telling the truth, Tracy had little doubt Buzz would have documented their encounter and kept it. And if he had, that meant someone had removed the report from his file.

Tracy considered the logic of someone doing that. *If* someone was aware Buzz kept a file, that person might be reluctant to destroy it, concerned that would draw too much suspicion. Instead, he or she could have opted to just destroy one essential element of the file, a portion that might have implicated a specific person but that nobody would have missed unless they knew it existed in the first place, a portion that might have been useful to an investigation but could not be duplicated. Lionel Devoe, Stoneridge chief of police, certainly would have known how to search for, and gain access to, a closed file.

The alternative was that Reynolds was lying, and Buzz Almond had not driven to the house to question his whereabouts that night. That would have been risky, but not if Reynolds already knew, or at least *believed,* the file—or the incriminating portion of it—had been destroyed. As for any concern that telling a detective that Buzz Almond had questioned him about his whereabouts that night could cause people to speculate that Buzz Almond considered Reynolds a suspect, Reynolds had a ready-made alibi.

Ask his father.

In which case, Reynolds could have offered the information to convince Tracy that law enforce-ment had already been down that dead end.

Still, if Buzz Almond *had* questioned Reynolds's whereabouts, it meant he at least suspected exactly what Tracy suspected. That Reynolds and the other three Ironmen had some role in Kimi's death.

—

Tuesday, November 23, 1976

Buzz Almond parked his Suburban in the drive-way of the modest one-story home at the end of the cul-de-sac. Pine needles from the surrounding trees covered the wood shake roof and over-flowed the gutters. The flower beds were barren, and the lawn was buried beneath leaves fallen from the now-bare limbs of the maple tree in the center of the yard. Parked in the dirt-and-gravel driveway was a Ford Bronco.

Dressed in Levi's and tennis shoes, Buzz zipped up his winter jacket as he approached the Bronco. The fall sunlight glinted off the windshield, which was clear but for dappled spots of sap from the trees. It didn't have a crack, chip, smashed bug, or smudge on it. The rubber bead around the glass also looked new. Buzz circled, running his hands along the fenders and doors. Despite the recent weather—rain and snow— the Bronco also looked like it had just come out of a hand car wash, with not a speck of dirt on the body or in the cracks and grooves of the oversize tires.

When he reached the passenger side, Buzz paused to remove his sunglasses, then stepped closer. After a moment he stepped back and took a different angle, comparing where the right fender met the passenger door, separated by a thin seam. He ran his hand between the two. The fender and the hood were a slightly different shade of yellow than the door.

"You interested in the car?"

Buzz Almond looked up as Ron Reynolds came out the side door of the house. Reynolds looked every bit the part of the high school football coach, in an Adidas sweatsuit and a white ball cap with the red initials *SH* woven on the front.

"How much are you asking for it?" Buzz asked. The sign in the window simply said "For Sale" with a phone number.

"Twenty-five hundred."

Buzz did his best to look disappointed. "That's a little more than I was looking to spend."

"It was the last year Ford made the half cab, and it's got all the extras—bucket seats, roll bar, running lights, front winch. Did you see the ad in the *Sentinel*?"

"No," Buzz said. "I was just driving by." He'd first seen the Bronco in the Stoneridge High School parking lot, ran the plate, and determined it was registered to Ron Reynolds. He wasn't so much interested in the car as he was the tires—oversize all-terrain tires.

"How many miles you got on it?" he asked.

"Just under forty-four thousand."

"Are you the original owner?"

"No. I bought it used."

"Looks like it's had some bodywork done," Buzz said, pointing to the front right fender.

"A little bit," Reynolds said, stepping back and considering the front fender at the same angle as Buzz. "Runs like a top though. Interested in taking it for a spin?"

"Could I hear the engine first?"

"Sure." Reynolds reached into his pocket and

produced the keys. He didn't bother climbing in; he just opened the door and leaned across the seat to insert the key in the ignition and turn the engine over.

"Starts right up," Buzz said.

"Like I said, runs like a top."

"Where'd you have the bodywork done?" Buzz asked.

"It wasn't anything, just a few dings. I just took it up to Columbia Auto Repair."

"Looks like you also had the windshield replaced."

"Decided to kill two birds with one stone," Reynolds said. "Same thing. One small crack from a rock chip."

"Where'd you get that done?"

"Same place. Actually, just across the street. Also had the oil changed, new spark plugs, air filter. I don't want any trouble for the ne owner. I'm Ron Reynolds, by the way." Reynolds stuck out a hand. "I'm the athletic director and football coach over at the high school."

Buzz shook hands. "Ted," he said. "Congratulations. I read about your big win. Quite an achievement, I'm surmising, from all the excitement around here."

"Thanks. Yeah, pretty heady stuff for such a small school, but that's just the start of things to come. That school has more championships in it. I just have to squeeze them out of the kids."

"I'll tell you what. Let me talk this over with the missus, and I'll call you back."

"You sure you don't want to take it for a spin?"

"Let me bring my wife back. She's partial to yellow. I'm hoping if she sees it, that'll seal the deal."

"I hear you. Do you hunt? Put on the all-terrain tires little over a year ago."

"No, but we like to hike."

"All right then. You need the phone number?"

Buzz pointed to the number handwritten on the "For Sale" sign. "I wrote it down when I pulled up. I'll be in touch." He started to walk away but turned back as if having thought of something else. "Would you mind if I took a couple pictures to show to my wife? If she won't let me buy it, I have a brother up north who hunts and fishes who might want it."

"No problem," Reynolds said. "But I got another potential buyer coming by later this afternoon, so you don't want to delay too long. I've priced it to sell."

"I appreciate you letting me know," Almond said. He took out the Instamatic from his coat pocket and snapped a couple of photographs, careful to get the side of the tires, as well as the tread. He put the camera back in his pocket. "Thanks," he said. "I think I've got everything I need."

When Tracy arrived at Jenny's home that evening, where they'd agreed to meet, Jenny answered the front door looking harried. She held Sarah, who was in a bathing suit, her eyes distorted behind swim goggles, and holding a red plastic squirt gun. Tracy heard Trey laughing and shrieking somewhere in the house.

"Sorry," Jenny said, stepping back to allow Tracy inside and then shutting the door. "Neil's stuck at work. He said to eat without him."

"That appears to be the least of your troubles," Tracy said, watching as Trey came running down the hall in his bathing suit, also wearing swim goggles and holding a water pistol. He came to a halt when he saw Tracy, then dashed, shrieking and laughing into another room. "I'm just trying to get him into the bath so I can get dinner on for us. The nanny fed them earlier."

"Let me give you a hand." Tracy held out her arms for Sarah, who smiled and went willingly.

"I'm free," Sarah said, holding up the correct number of fingers.

"I know," Tracy said. "May I borrow your squirt gun?"

Sarah gave it up. Trey made another appearance, and Tracy said, "Halt right there in the name of the law, mister." Trey froze. "I am a Seattle police officer, son, and I am about to arrest you for failure to stop at a four-way intersection."

Trey looked uncertainly to his mother, who kept a straight face but arched an eyebrow.

"Now, I'm going to give you until the count of three to march up those stairs into that bathroom before I arrest you and put you in the back of my police car."

Trey wanted to smile, but with Tracy and Jenny poker-faced, he dashed up the stairs in a bear crawl.

"I think you have everything under control," Jenny said with a smile. "I'll get dinner going."

After baths Tracy supervised Trey and Sarah slipping into their pajamas, and she tucked them into bed. They had separate bedrooms, but Sarah preferred to sleep in hcr brother's trundle bed, which was adorned with a bedspread to make it look like a NASCAR stock car.

She read them each a book of their choosing, held firm when they tried to negotiate a third book, and kissed Trey on the forehead, which made him scurry quickly under the covers. When she went to kiss Sarah, the little girl popped up, gripped Tracy around the neck, and gave her a peck on the lips.

"Do you have babies?" Sarah whispered, as if sharing a secret.

"No," Tracy whispered back. "No babies."

Sarah poked at Tracy's stomach. "What about in there?"

"Nope. Nothing in there," Tracy said.

Sarah released her grip and lay back, scrunching down into the covers.

Tracy went back downstairs and found Jenny in the kitchen, pouring what smelled like a potent lemon-and-garlic sauce over breasts of chicken on beds of rice with a side of broccoli.

"Smells incredible," Tracy said.

Jenny set the pan down on the stove. "An old standby. Simple but healthy. You don't look any worse for wear."

"They're great kids."

"They can be a handful, especially when one of us works late." Jenny handed Tracy a plate and a glass of wine, and they carried them into the dining room and sat at the table. Jenny let out a breath and sank into her chair like a balloon collapsing. "These are the moments of peace I treasure."

As they ate, Jenny updated Tracy on the investigation into the death of Archibald Coe. "No sign of a forced entry or struggle, and the coroner didn't find any marks on the body to indicate that Coe didn't act willingly. Nothing to indicate he didn't kill himself."

"Except the timing."

"Except the timing."

"Any note?"

"No," Jenny said.

Tracy took a sip of wine. "What about his employers? Did they notice anything out of the ordinary?"

"Nothing except you coming to speak to him, which was beyond rare. Coe didn't talk much to anyone—just came in and did his work and went home. It was actually amazing how little they knew about him."

"Nothing in his apartment?"

"I wouldn't say that," Jenny said. "We found an entire medicine cabinet—Vicodin, Zoloft, sleep aids. But he didn't have a computer or a laptop, and he didn't own a cell phone or a car. Apparently, he rode his bike everywhere."

"Further confirming he's the man I saw in the clearing that night." She set down her utensils, frustrated that she'd been that close and now the opportunity had evaporated. "Did you get ahold of his ex-wife and kids?"

"The ex-wife thanked us. She sounded saddened but not surprised and said she'd call their children. I have their numbers if you decide you want to talk to them after this dies down a bit."

"I'd sure like to ask them if their father ever confided in them about what had caused his problems."

Tracy thought of the moment upstairs when Sarah kissed her lips and asked, *Do you have babies?* Tracy didn't, but she knew enough to know you couldn't truly appreciate what others went through, their joys or their sorrows, unless you had experienced it yourself, or something similar. If her current working hypothesis was correct and the Four Ironmen had something to do with Kimi's death, Tracy suspected that neither Darren Gallentine nor Archibald Coe had fully appreciated the pain Earl and Nettie Kanasket had gone through until they had become fathers themselves, especially when their daughters had reached the same age as Kimi. That appeared to be what put them both over the edge.

Jenny pushed aside her plate. Neither she nor Tracy had finished. "Tell me about your conversation with Eric Reynolds."

"I'll tell you as we clean up." They took their plates to the kitchen, and Tracy ran them under the Faucet and handed them to Jenny, who put them in the dishwasher. "He was very polished," Tracy said. "Professional, polite. If he was anxious or nervous, he didn't show it."

"And full of shit?" Jenny asked, finishing what was left in her wineglass and handing it to Tracy.

"Maybe. He told me a deputy came by the house to talk to him about a week or two after they found Kimi."

"My father?"

"He didn't say that, but if it happened, it had to be."

Jenny set down the glass and dried her hands on a towel. "I don't recall reading anything about that in the file."

"It isn't in there."

"Did he say what my dad wanted?"

"He said a deputy came by to ask him where he'd been the Friday night Kimi disappeared, whether he'd been out."

"So my dad suspected him?"

"Maybe. Reynolds said he had the impression the deputy was just asking if anyone might have seen Kimi that night."

"What did Reynolds tell him?"

"He said he'd been at home in bed resting for the big game and that his father would vouch for him. If you think about it, if it was a lie, it's very low-risk because it's simple, it's believable, and it's unlikely to be refuted."

"Why would Reynolds lie about something like that and potentially draw attention to himself? It seems counterintuitive."

"I thought about that also. It could be he's using it to let me know someone already went down that path and nothing came of it. Or it could be that he knows, or at least he *believes,* that someone already removed that report from the file, so I can't prove him wrong or question him. And like I said, his father is still alive to vouch for him."

Jenny filled the tea kettle at the faucet. "I

wonder if that's why the system indicates the file was destroyed—if my father wanted whoever did go looking for it to believe the file no longer existed. He puts 'Destroyed' into the system and takes the file home and locks it in his desk." Jenny set the kettle on the stove atop a blue flame. "Why wouldn't he have just duplicated the report?"

"Maybe because it wasn't something that he could duplicate."

"Like what?"

"Photographs. He could have taken photographs of Eric Reynolds's car—or, more specifically, the tires."

"He was interested in whether they matched the treads he'd photographed in the field."

Jenny handed Tracy a box of assorted teas. She chose chamomile, not wanting caffeine. She was amped enough and knew she'd have difficulty sleeping.

"Can we go after Eric with what we have?" Jenny asked.

"Unfortunately, the crime lab said there isn't enough in the photograph we sent to be definitive about whether the tire treads match the treads made in the clearing. The medical examiner said the same thing about the bruising on Kimi's back and shoulder. Without more, I seriously doubt we could get a charge to stick. After forty years, there's just too much uncertainty."

"So where do we go from here?" Jenny asked, opening another cabinet and pulling out a sugar container and bottle of honey.

"That's what I've been thinking about. My focus has been on the mechanics of what happened. Maybe I need to change focus and consider *why* it happened."

"What about the animosity over the mascot?" Jenny said.

"There were a few articles about it in the newspaper," Tracy said, "but it didn't seem to be that controversial, and I don't see high school kids getting too worked up about it. That's one thing Eric Reynolds said that I do believe. He said the parents were more concerned about it than the students. I taught high school. Some of the students couldn't even tell you the school mascot, and those who could really didn't care. They're more concerned about who they're taking to the formal, where they're going after the game on Saturday night, and how they're going to get alcohol and get laid." Tracy leaned back against the counter, thinking. "Something else had to have happened that night."

The kettle whistled. Jenny poured hot water into two mugs and handed one to Tracy. "If Eric Reynolds is orchestrating this, maybe there's something on his computer or his cell phone—a text message with Lionel or Hastey. We have enough to get a judge to issue a subpoena, which would allow us to take a look."

Tracy had considered that course of action. "I don't see Reynolds being that careless. Again, if we're right, we're talking about someone who's not only managed to keep a forty-year secret but also got the others to keep it."

"Agreed, but Hastey's a drunk and Lionel's no rocket scientist. One of them could have sent Reynolds an e-mail or a text."

"Maybe," Tracy said. "But if we do look and we're wrong, we've alerted Eric that he's a suspect."

"He already knows he's a suspect, Tracy."

"True."

"What other option do we have?" Jenny asked. "He's had forty years to cover his tracks. And unless we can come up with something else, it feels like we've hit a dead end."

CHAPTER 29

The rooster did not crow in the morning, and Tracy wondered if the bird had met its doom in the jaws of a coyote or a raccoon. That was the problem with crowing too loudly. You gave away your position and made yourself vulnerable. It made her think of Eric Reynolds and his proactive decision to invite her to interview him. She'd love to find a way to use it to make him vulnerable.

She put on her running clothes and laced up her shoes, hoping the cool air would invigorate her and the endorphins would help her to think of something she hadn't yet considered.

She took the longer run to the clearing, starting to feel a connection to it. Far from being scared of ghosts there, Tracy found the place peaceful. When she arrived, she noted that the leaves of the shrub Archibald Coe had most recently planted had already started to turn brown and now were looking wilted, and not for a lack of rain.

"I can't help you without something more," she said to the spot where Kimi Kanasket had lain. "I wish I could. You don't know how much I wish I could—for your father and for so many others like you. But I need something more."

She looked up the hill, half expecting the leaves

to begin to shake and the branches to sway and the wind to sweep down the hill and hit her in the face as it had that first night. But the wind didn't come, and neither did any inspiration.

When Tracy got back to the farmhouse, she sat down at the table and wrote out her thoughts on possible motives, including romantic relationships, petty jealousies, some conflict between the Ironmen and Élan and his crew, or with Tommy Moore. She hoped that getting the possibilities on paper and out of her head would give her a new direction, but like the wind that morning, inspiration did not come.

She unplugged her phone from the charger, started up the stairs checking messages, and noticed that she'd missed a call.

The number was not associated with a name, and Tracy didn't recognize it, though it had a Seattle area code. The caller had left a message, so Tracy played the voice mail. When the caller identified herself, Tracy stopped climbing the stairs. The voice was tentative and unsure, nothing like the strong businesswoman Tracy had spoken with days earlier. Tracy didn't wait for the message to finish. Halfway through, she pressed "Call Back" and hurried up the remainder of the stairs and into the bathroom.

Sixty minutes later, Tracy was back in her truck driving north on I-5, a trip she felt like she could now make blindfolded. Her hair remained damp and felt greasy. In her rush, she'd failed to thoroughly rinse out the shampoo. She called Jenny on the drive and explained what had happened, letting her know that she would not be going into the sheriff's office to prepare the affidavit in support of the subpoena to search Eric Reynolds's home.

"Why don't you take a stab at drafting it and leave a couple paragraphs at the end. I can dictate those on the drive back, depending on what I find out, if anything. This could be a wild-goose chase."

Nearly four hours into her drive, Tracy neared Seattle's baseball and football stadiums south of the downtown skyscrapers. She took I-90 east and fifteen minutes later exited for the Highlands. Following the GPS's directions, she made the first right at the top of the hill and drove through a newly constructed shopping area, coming to a roundabout with a grass park surrounded by a waist-high wrought-iron fence. Old-fashioned street lamps and quaint two-story English colonial townhomes rimmed the perimeter. Despite the clear fall weather, the park and sidewalk were empty but for a lone man walking a chocolate lab on a leash.

Tracy found the address and parked in the street at the foot of stairs leading up to the small front porch. She was early, but she wasn't about to wait in the car. She pushed out, quickly climbed the steps, and knocked.

"Mom, she's here," a female voice inside said, followed by the sound of a deadbolt disengaging.

Tiffany Martin pulled open the door with a look of resignation and said, "Please, come in."

Two adult women in their thirties, remarkably similar in appearance, waited in the small marble entry. Like their mother, the two sisters were well put together, hair and makeup done and nicely dressed, but also like their mother, they each looked on edge. Tracy knew they were all reliving those horrible moments fifteen years ago, and she regretted having to put them through it again.

"These are my daughters, Rachel and Rebecca," Tiffany Martin said.

Tracy greeted each, and Martin motioned for them to step down into a spotless living room with white leather furniture. A sprawling palm in the corner near a game table and a large oil-based painting provided color. The room held the smell of a vanilla air freshener.

"That's it," Martin said, her voice catching as she nodded to a brown file on the glass coffee table. None of the women moved to touch it. Rachel, standing closest to her mother, wrapped an arm around her shoulder.

"We talked about it as a family," Rachel said. "We didn't want another family to suffer if they didn't have to."

Tracy said, "That's very kind of you."

"At the same time, we decided we didn't want to read it," Rachel said. "We don't want to know the details of whatever it was that led my father to do what he did. We don't see the point."

"I understand," Tracy said.

"My father . . ." Rachel had to take a moment to compose herself. She looked to her sister. "*Our* father was a good man. He was a good father. He was troubled. We recognized that as we got older, but he never let us see how much. He shielded us from it. We have very fond memories, which made this decision so difficult. We don't want to relive that pain."

"I know how you feel."

"Mom told us you did," Rachel said. "That's another reason we decided to do this; we thought you would be sensitive to what we went through."

"I am, and I will be," Tracy said. "What do you want me to do with the file after I've reviewed it?"

The three women looked to each other, and Tiffany Martin nodded to her youngest daughter to continue. "We were hoping you could review it someplace close by," Rachel said. "Someplace discreet. And we'll wait here."

"We're not prepared to read it," Tiffany Martin said, "but we thought maybe if you reviewed it and found that . . . I don't know . . . it isn't too bad, you could come back and let us know?"

"Of course," Tracy said.

"If you don't come back," Martin said, "well, we'll know. And then we'd like you to keep the file. We don't want it."

They stood in awkward silence, taking furtive glances at the file. When Tracy realized no one was about to pick it up, she stepped to the table and tucked it under her arm.

They moved collectively to the front door. Tiffany Martin pulled it open. "We'll be here until two o'clock," she said. "If we don't hear from you by then, we're going to go out together and try to eat lunch and get our mind off of it."

Without another word, Tracy stepped out onto the porch, and the door closed behind her.

CHAPTER 30

Tracy had to resist the urge to open the file and read it in the cab of her truck. Instead, she drove quickly to the Issaquah Library, which was nearby. Downtown Issaquah was buzzing. The area had seen a recent revival with the influx of young families, and the city managers had kept the downtown quaint, with mature oak and plum trees, a repertory theater with a marquee announcing the winter run of the musical *Oklahoma*, restaurants with sidewalk seating, though not on this cold November day, and a vintage 1940s Shell gas station.

Tracy hurried inside the library, anxious to find out what Darren Gallentine had told his counselor. She asked the reference librarian for a private room and was told she could reserve one for an hour. The room was the size of the hard interro-gation rooms at the Justice Center, just big enough for a small desk mounted to the front wall and two chairs. Tracy set the file on the table and retrieved a pen and notepad from her briefcase. Before opening the file, she took a moment to run her hand over the cover. It reminded her of that moment when she'd learned that Sarah's remains had been discovered after twenty years of uncertainty and she'd rushed home to retrieve Sarah's files from her bedroom closet, then found herself hesitant to open them. She had the same unsure feeling now, like stepping onto a roller coaster, excited to get started but anxious about what was to come.

She opened Darren Gallentine's file and read.

***

Friday, November 5, 1976

Hastey Devoe popped the top on another beer can. "Come to Papa," he said, touching the rim to his lips, tilting his head back and taking a long slug.

"You might want to go a little easy on the beer," Eric Reynolds said. He was reclined on the hood of the Bronco, which was at the edge of the ring of light produced by Darren's camping lantern. Eric took the final hit on a joint, held his breath a moment, and exhaled. "We do have a fairly significant game tomorrow night."

"I'm hydrating," Hastey said. "It helps keep me warm in this freaking cold."

"Just saying you might want to show a little self-control tonight," Eric said.

"It hasn't hurt me in any game this season, has it?"

"No," Archie said, "but you keep drinking a six-pack a night and you're not going to fit your fat ass into your uniform pants much longer."

He laughed the dullard's laugh, clearly stoned.

"If it wasn't for my fat ass," Hastey said, "none of y'all would have been reading your names in the paper every week."

"Shit, why do you think I run off-tackle and get outside all the time?"

"Because you're a big pussy and don't like to get hit," Hastey said.

"No, because your fat ass is stuck in the gap I'm supposed to run through," Archie said.

"Doesn't stop Darren," Hastey said. "Does it, Darren?"

Darren Gallentine sat a few feet away, on a boulder. He was neither stoned nor drunk. He'd had two beers and wasn't interested in drinking more. These nights were getting to be old. He reached out and turned the dial on the lantern, the light brightening, the propane hissing. He estimated the canister to still be half-full. He was amused by the banter and commentary, but he never participated much and, after a full season, the jibes were getting repetitious. Hastey's brother Lionel had bought them a case of beer and a couple of joints, and they'd snuck out of their respective homes and driven into the woods. It had become their Friday night routine—and some Saturday nights after games, though they usually went to the clearing after games because by the time they arrived a party was under way and half the girls were drunk. They'd make an entrance in the Bronco, Hastey blowing that stupid foghorn, and everyone would cheer as they circled the clearing. They could do no wrong those nights, especially with the girls. Eric said it was like "shooting fish in a barrel" and that he'd been laid more often that football season than a Las Vegas whore.

"Why do you think they call Darren 'the Dozer'?" Hastey said to Archie.

"Because he has to bulldoze your ass out of the way just to find the hole," Archie said.

Darren smiled but didn't respond.

"Maybe I'll just lie down next time they hand you the ball," Hastey said, tossing the empty can at Archie and missing. "Let those D-linemen pancake your ass."

"Nobody's lying down," Eric said. He flicked the butt of the joint into the underbrush and threw his beer can against the trunk of the tree not far from where Hastey and Archie stood exchanging insults. The can ricocheted and spun like a heli-copter blade, spraying beer out the top.

"Shit," Hastey said, wiping the beer from his shirt. "What bug crawled up your ass? You just wasted a perfectly good beer."

"I'm going to crawl up both your asses if you two don't shut the fuck up," Eric said.

"I'm just saying I don't need to smell like beer when I walk in the house."

"Hell, beer is your family cologne," Archie said.

"Better than roses," Hastey said, bending his wrist effeminately. "Your dad still work at the flower store?"

"It's a nursery, you idiot."

"Still flowers," Hastey said.

"Will you both just shut up," Eric said.

Darren sat up, ready to get home. He could see his breath, and the cold was starting to creep down his neck beneath his fur-lined jean jacket and seep through the soles of his Converse shoes. They called him "the Dozer" because at five eleven and 210 pounds he ran with his shoulder pads low to the ground and hit as many people as he could, shoving them out of the way. "You're just mad because Cheryl Neal is out with Tommy Moore," he said to Eric while continuing to strip bark off a tree branch.

"What?" Hastey and Archie said in unison.

"I thought that loser was dating Kimi Kanasket," Hastey said to Eric.

Eric gave Darren a look that was supposed to be a warning, but at six two and 180 pounds, Eric was no match for Darren, and he knew it. It wasn't just the difference in size. Darren was the strongest kid on the team, and he proved it every day in the weight room.

"Kimi dumped Moore's ass, and Moore asked Cheryl out," Darren said.

"And she went?" Hastey said.

" 'Course she went," Archie said. "That girl's hornier than a sixteen-point buck. You might even have a chance, Hastey."

"Why don't you just broadcast it to the whole fucking school," Eric said to Darren.

"Why'd she go out with him?" Hastey asked.

"Because she *is* a whore," Eric said.

"Yes, but she was your whore," Archie said.

"That's it. I'm going to kick your ass."

Eric slid off the hood and started toward Archie, eyes blazing. Hastey stepped between them, allowing Archie a chance to quickly retreat into the underbrush. Archie was fast, but that was because he was smaller than the rest of them and slight, maybe 150 pounds. Eric would crush him.

"You better run. And good luck getting home, you pussy."

"Don't take it out on him," Darren said, tossing the stripped piece of wood to the ground and looking for another.

"Why'd you bring it up?" Eric said.

"Because you've had your panties in a bunch all night about it, and we've got a game tomorrow night."

"Don't worry about me. I'll do what I have to do."

"Good," Darren said. "Because I'm not going all the way to Yakima to lose the last game I ever play."

"Let's just get out of here and go home," Eric said, fishing the keys from his jacket pocket. "Grab the lantern."

"Fine with me," Darren said, picking up the lantern.

"What?" Hastey whined. "We got three beers left untapped. It's not even midnight."

"Leave 'em," Eric said.

"I cannot do that." Hastey snapped to attention, his belly falling out the bottom of his shirt and hanging over his pants. He gave a mock salute. "A United States Marine will leave no soldier behind."

"Leave them," Eric said. "I don't want them in my car if we get pulled over."

"Shit, nobody's going to do anything to us. We rule this town." Hastey howled loud and long.

"Just get in the truck," Eric said.

"Shotgun." Hastey knocked into Archie, who had emerged from the brush, pushing him nearly to the ground, and grabbed the passenger-door handle. "You ride in the back."

"Need a crane to lift your fat ass into the bed, anyway," Archie said.

"You want us to get you a stepladder so you can climb in?" Hastey said.

Darren killed the lantern, plunging them into darkness, and climbed into the open bed of the Bronco. He and Archie sat with their backs to the cab, and Darren could now feel the cold through the seat of his jeans. When he flexed his fingers, they felt thick as sausages, and the joints were tight. He thought it good preparation for the game, which the weathermen were forecasting would be even colder. He hoped it didn't snow. He hated playing in the snow. Every hit felt like your bones were cracking.

"Got to get me a chew," Archie said, dipping into a bag from his back pocket and packing his cheek with a wad of chewing tobacco.

"Don't spit that shit on me," Darren said.

"And don't get any on the truck," Eric said, starting the engine. "My dad will kick my ass."

The headlights and running lights atop the roll bar lit up the area like powerful search-lights. Eric slammed the car into reverse, backed up quickly, threw it into drive and gunned the engine, whipping the steering wheel hard in the other direction, causing the big back tires to fishtail and spit gravel. It sent Archie flopping over into Darren, who had been smart enough to anticipate Eric's move and had grabbed hold of the roll bar. Eric did the same thing each time he drove, but Archie never did seem to figure it out. Then again, he wasn't the sharpest tool in the shed.

Hastey let out another rebel yell and cranked the volume on the eight-track player, blasting AC/DC's "It's a Long Way to the Top" as the Bronco pitched and bounced, the winch and grille on the front mowing down brush and vines.

A moment later the truck blew from the brush onto 141 without Eric ever taking his foot off the gas. He called it "going naked." So far this season, they'd only had one close call, crossing in front of a semitruck driving in the opposite direction, close enough that Darren heard the truck's air brakes hiss as it went past.

The wind whipped around the bed of the truck, dropping the temperature another ten degrees or so. Darren kept a grip on the roll bar where it was bolted to the bed and shoved his other hand beneath his armpit. Archie sat beside him, hunched over, knees to his chest, chin and hands tucked. He looked like a turtle trying to retreat inside his shell.

"Slow down," Darren yelled, though he knew Eric couldn't hear him over the music and the wind. Not that Eric would have slowed anyway. Eric was a hothead with a massive ego. He didn't even care about Cheryl Neal. He'd told Darren as much. He was just using her.

But then the truck slowed, and for a moment Darren thought maybe Eric had not only heard him but was actually listening for a change. Just as quickly, however, he thought maybe their luck had finally run out and a cop was ahead. He turned to look. In the truck's headlights, someone was walking the shoulder of the road, a girl in a coat with her back to them.

Eric turned down the music. "Well, look what

we have here," he said, pulling alongside the girl. Kimi Kanasket. Darren swore under his breath, sensing that this was not good.

Kimi wore a wool coat that extended to her knees; her legs were bare to her shoes.

"Hey, Kimi," Eric said, elbow out the window.

Kimi turned her head but didn't otherwise acknowledge them. She kept walking.

"Where're you heading?"

"Home."

"You want a ride?"

Darren knew what Eric was doing. If he got the chance, he'd screw Kimi just to screw Cheryl Neal and Tommy Moore. But that wasn't going to happen. No way Kimi would fall for it, which would only make Eric angry.

"No, thanks. I'll walk."

"That's crazy. It's a long way, and it's freezing out. Come on, we'll give you a ride."

"I'm good. I walk it all the time. My parents are waiting for me."

"What—you don't like us?"

Kimi didn't answer. Darren could see and sense her discomfort. She wasn't afraid. He doubted much scared Kimi, but she was clearly uncomfortable. "Let's just go, Eric," he yelled into the cab.

"Shut up. We're having a conversation," Eric said. "What is it, Kimi? You don't like us? Is it because we're the *Red* Raiders?"

Hastey leaned across the cab and let out an Indian war cry.

Idiot.

Kimi rolled her eyes.

"Eric," Darren said, "let's just go home."

"Where's your boyfriend tonight, Kimi? I heard he dumped you because you weren't a good enough lay. Or maybe you Indian girls don't put out."

Kimi stopped walking, turned, and faced the car. "You know where he is. And you know who he's screwing. Maybe *you* weren't good enough, Eric."

"Fucking bitch," Eric said, jerking the Bronco to a stop and reaching for the driver's door, but struggling to free his seat belt.

The delay gave Darren time to get up and jump down out of the bed. "Run," he said to Kimi. She looked at him, eyes wide. "Just run. Get the hell out of here."

Kimi ran.

Eric, delayed by the seat belt, stumbled out of the cab, swearing and yelling at Kimi, who'd bolted into the woods.

Darren wrapped him in a bear hug. "Let her go, Eric. Just let her go."

"Get off me."

Darren tightened his grip. "No. Not until you calm down."

After a few more seconds, Darren felt Eric

weakening. "Fine. I'm calm. Okay. I'm calm."

"Let's just go home," Darren said. "Okay? Let's go home, and let's play tomorrow night and focus on what we set out to accomplish."

"I said, 'Fine.'"

Darren released his grip and Eric shoved him in the chest, but Darren ignored it, not wanting to escalate the situation. Eric was snorting like a bull. He got back in the car and slammed the door, brooding. Darren looked at Archie, who was half standing in the bed like he might jump out, eyes wide. He contemplated grabbing him and the two of them just walking home, but it was more than three miles in the freaking cold, and it was already late. "Sit down," he said. He pulled himself up and into the bed, but at that moment he knew he was done with Eric Reynolds and Hastey Devoe. Maybe he and Archie could remain friends, but after Saturday night he was through with both those idiots. He had plans beyond football. He wanted to become an engineer and design planes for Boeing, and he wasn't about to let either of them screw that up for him.

Eric hit the gas, and the Bronco jerked forward, engine roaring, picking up speed. Just as suddenly, the front bumper took a nosedive, tires burning as they caught the asphalt. Darren and Archie were slammed against the cab. Darren's head whipped backward, striking something

380

solid. The Bronco started to spin, Eric doing a donut in the middle of the road, rubber burning. He punched it, and the Bronco shot down the road in the direction Kimi had run.

"Goddamn it," Darren shouted over the sound of the heavy-metal music and the wind. He pushed Archie off him and felt the back of his head, which was pounding. He was seeing stars.

The Bronco left the asphalt and plunged into the underbrush, pitching and bouncing. Darren had one hand gripping the roll bar and another holding Archie by the collar of his jacket, struggling to keep from being tossed out of the bed. Hastey was hooting and hollering, shouting out his dumbass war cry.

"Eric," Darren yelled, his voice a whisper compared to the wind and the radio. "Eric. Stop."

They plowed down the narrow path. The Bronco started up an incline. Darren was struggling to keep himself and Archie from sliding to the back of the bed, the muscles of his arms straining as he fought to hang on. Tree branches whipped against the bed. He ducked his head. The incline steepened, the engine straining.

Eric yelled, "Shit!" and the next instant, Darren was weightless. His butt came up off the bed of the truck, and he lost his grip on the roll bar and on Archie. It all happened so fast, and yet it seemed so slow. He was airborne, he and Archie flying out of the bed, floating for a second before he slammed down hard against the ground. A shock wave of pain passed through him. He rolled multiple times, striking rocks in a seemingly endless cycle before finally skidding to a stop. He lay there, his body and mind processing what had just happened, trying to assess whether or not he was injured, and if so, how badly. Slowly, he struggled to his feet, sore, but as far as he could tell, not seriously injured. Archie was close by, moaning and mumbling in the dark. Darren walked over to him.

"You okay? Archie, you okay?"

Archie swore and got to his knees. He looked stunned but also not seriously hurt.

Orienting himself, Darren realized he and Archie had been thrown from the bed when it went over the top of the incline. They'd landed on the back side of the hill, about halfway up from the clearing. Below them, the Bronco, with its bar of bright lights, looked like an alien spaceship that had crashed. It had spun in a circle and was now facing up the hill, though pitched off-kilter at almost a forty-five-degree angle. Darren raised his hand to block the glare of the lights and started down the hill.

He heard Hastey shouting, his voice echoing up to them. "I'm bleeding, man. I'm bleeding, Eric. Shit. Goddamn it. I'm bleeding."

Darren stumbled to the bottom of the hill.

Hastey was pacing in circles, his hand pressed to his forehead, blood oozing between his fingers and down the sleeve of his jacket. At first, Darren didn't see Eric. Then Hastey moved, and he saw Eric standing over what looked like a log on the ground but what he quickly realized to be Kimi.

"Oh God." He dropped to a knee. She lay on her side, eyes shut, not moving. "What did you do? What the hell did you do, Eric?"

Eric didn't move. He didn't speak. He stood staring down at Kimi. Behind them, Hastey continued to moan, "I'm bleeding, man. I'm bleeding."

"Shut up," Darren yelled at him. "Shut up!"

Archie finally made it down the hill, and when he saw Kimi on the ground he too started to wail. "Oh no. Oh no. Oh no." Then he turned, bent over, and threw up.

"What did you do, Eric? What did you do?" Darren repeated.

Archie continued to vomit and to swear. "Damn it. Goddamn it."

"I'm bleeding, Eric. I'm bleeding."

"Shut up," Darren said. "Everyone shut up!"

Archie straightened, stifling another wretch. Hastey stopped wailing. Darren knelt beside Kimi. She looked bent and broken.

"I didn't see her," Eric finally said. "I never saw her."

"You ran her down," Darren said. "You landed on top of her."

"Is she dead?" Archie said, crying now. "Is she dead?"

"She was on the ground. Why was she on the ground?" Eric said. "It wasn't my fault."

"Of course it was your fault," Darren said. "Whose fault is it if it isn't your fault?"

Eric lunged at him, but Darren sprung from his crouch and drove his shoulder hard into Eric's rib cage, his legs driving Eric backward and slamming him onto his back. Darren balled his fist, poised to unleash a vicious punch. He wanted to. He wanted to hit him. He wanted to beat the shit out of him, but Hastey and Archie grabbed his arm before he could take Eric's head off, pulling him off and dragging him away.

"You killed her, man," Darren said, tears streaming down his face. "You killed her."

Eric, breathing hard, got to his feet, white bursts escaping his mouth and nostrils. He had his hands entwined in his hair, as if he were trying to pull it out.

"What are we going to do, Eric?" Hastey said, sounding scared, his face a mask of blood from the cut on his forehead. "What are we going to do?"

"We need to get out of here," Eric said.

"What?" Darren said.

"We need to get out of here. Now. Right now." Eric paced. Though it was dark, he looked pale and his eyes were black pinpoints.

"We can't just leave her here, Eric," Darren said.

"What are we going to do then, huh, Darren? What are we going to do?"

"We should find a phone and call someone."

"She's dead, Darren. Who are we going to call? The police? What are we going to tell them? That we ran her over?"

"*I* didn't run her over. You did."

"You were in the car. We were all in the car. We all ran her over."

"No," Darren said. "No way, Eric."

"I'm supposed to go in the Army," Archie stammered. "I'm supposed to go in the Army when I graduate."

"Listen to me," Eric said. "They'll go after all of us because we were all in the car. They'll test our blood, and they'll know we were drinking and smoking. We'll all go to jail, and not just for the night or a week. Shit, this is murder. You get the chair for murder. They kill you."

"I can't go to jail," Hastey said. "I can't go to jail."

"We need to leave," Eric said again. "Now."

"We can't just leave her, Eric," Darren said.

"Nobody knows we're out here. Nobody. We have the game tomorrow. Everyone is going to think we were at home, in bed, getting ready. Our parents don't know we snuck out, so they'll say we were home in bed."

"We can't leave her," Darren said again.

"I don't want to, Darren. Goddamn it, I don't want to. But we have to. Don't you understand? We have to."

Darren couldn't stop crying.

"I'll drive you home," Eric said. "I'll drive you home and then I'll use the pay phone at the gas station and call it in anonymous, okay?"

"What about my head?" Hastey said. "What am I going to tell them happened to my head?"

"I got a first-aid kit in the truck. My dad keeps it there for when he goes hunting. We'll clean you up and put a bandage on your head. Tomorrow you wear a ball cap. The cut is high enough that no one will see it. At the game you'll have a helmet on. You can say you cut your head during the game." Eric rubbed his forehead as if fighting a massive headache. Then he wiped away tears. "Nobody will know." He looked at all of them, speaking quickly. "Nobody needs to know, okay? Nothing needs to change. Tomorrow we win a championship and we go on with our lives, just like we planned. We go on with our lives. Archie, you'll go in the Army, and Darren and I will go to UW. And Hastey, you'll go to community college and get your grades up, then you can come join us. We can't help Kimi now. She's dead. It was an accident, but she's dead. If we say anything, then we might as well all be dead too, because then *our* lives will be over."

Darren heard the words, but now they sounded as if they were coming from some far-off place, as if they weren't real, as if none of this were real. White stars continued to flicker in front of his eyes, concussion stars that he'd played through so many times. That's what this was—a concussion. He wasn't thinking straight. He was imagining this. He had to be imagining this. It wasn't real. Couldn't be real.

None of this was real.

Tracy set down the last page of the counselor's report. From the rest of the file, she'd gleaned that Darren had initially gone to the clinic for anxiety, though he didn't know the cause. He'd told his counselor that he'd awake early in the morning, his mind racing, unable to get back to sleep. He said that soon thereafter he became anxious at night, and he'd started having trouble falling asleep. The lack of sleep was making him a zombie at work, so he started taking sleeping pills and washing them down with Scotch. He told his counselor he had nightmares. In them he saw a teenage girl, her body broken and battered. He said the nightmare started when Rebecca turned fifteen, and soon thereafter the girl in his dreams began to haunt him every night, no matter how many pills he took or how much Scotch he drank. She always came.

In his nightmare he stood over her, thinking her dead, but then she'd open her eyes and look up at him from the ground and whisper, "Help me. Please, help me."

The counselor thought the girl was Rebecca, and that Darren was suffering an irrational fear of losing his daughter. It had been a lengthy two-year process before Darren was able to identify the girl and recall what had happened to Kimi Kanasket. In her final report in the file, after Darren had recounted the incident in great detail, the counselor wrote that Darren had "a major breakthrough" and acknowledged that his dream was not a dream—it was recollection. He remembered that night as vividly as if it were yesterday. She wrote that when he left the office that afternoon, Darren had expressed relief and said he felt lighter than he had in years, unburdened.

Then he drove home and shot himself.

Tracy closed the file and stood, but she didn't leave right away. After a long moment, she picked up her pen and her notepad. She hadn't taken a single note.

On the drive back to Tiffany Martin's house, she thought about what she'd say, ultimately deciding she'd keep it simple. She felt anxious as she climbed the porch steps, and her heart raced when she knocked on the front door. Tiffany opened it, Rachel and Rebecca standing behind her, the three looking worn-out.

"Your husband," Tracy said to Tiffany, then looking to Rachel and Rebecca, "and your father, was a very good man. He was just in the wrong place at the wrong time. But he was a very good, decent man."

The three women started to weep, tears streaming from the corners of their eyes, hands covering their sobs. They turned to one another and grasped hold in a fierce embrace.

CHAPTER 31

The image of Tiffany Martin and her two daughters crying tears of sadness and tears of regret, but also tears of joy, was not one Tracy would soon forget. She suspected that even before she had appeared in their lives, the three women had suffered their share of sleepless nights, wondering why their husband and father had taken his life. She knew from experience that when the answer doesn't readily present itself, the mind can come up with terrible things; during the twenty years following Sarah's disappearance, Tracy had imagined all types of horrible scenarios.

Tracy wanted to drive straight to Eric Reynolds's home, to let him know that she knew, definitively, what had happened to Kimi. She wanted to wipe the smug and confident smile off his face, to ask him why he got to enjoy a privileged life when he'd ruined so many others. That was the travesty of a murder. It was never just a single life lost. It destroyed many lives. But Tracy also knew that knowing Reynolds was guilty wasn't the same as proving it in a court of law. Yes, Tracy had the physical evidence from Buzz Almond's photographs. She also had Kaylee Wright's and Kelly Rosa's analyses, but they could only offer opinions, not facts.

Now, on the drive home, her mind was processing the problems with Darren Gallentine's counselor's file. Even if they could get it into evidence, which wasn't necessarily a given, a good defense lawyer would pick it apart. Any number of arguments could be made—the false recollection of a troubled man who was recounting what happened in a manner that he could live with but which was far from the truth. It was also hearsay. What Darren had told his counselor—Tracy might or might not be able to still find her—was an out-of-court statement that would be offered as the truth. The defense would argue it was untrustworthy, not subject to cross-examination, and, therefore, inadmissible.

Tracy began to ask herself if the entire investigation had been one big lesson in futility, and if that was what Buzz Almond had also come to conclude.

Tuesday, November 23, 1976

Buzz Almond drove home but did not immediately get out of the car. He sat staring at the small guesthouse he'd rented for his family. They'd have to move. The house wouldn't be big enough when the baby was born.

He was now certain that Kimi Kanasket had not

committed suicide. He was certain Éric Reynolds, and likely the other three members of the Four Ironmen, had come upon Kimi as she walked home along 141 and that something had happened—what exactly, he did not know, but words were spoken, maybe some high school juvenile exchange, and one thing had led to another horrible thing. They'd struck Kimi with the Bronco, running her over in the clearing. That's why the ground was torn up. Buzz had compared the tread marks in the grass and mud with the tread on the tires on Eric Reynolds's Bronco. From his perception the two matched. That's why there were footprints going in dozens of directions. It had nothing to do with kids partying over the weekend. There had been no kids in town that weekend to party. There had been *no one* in town. They'd all left and gone to the big game. The ground had been torn up Friday night.

Looking at the terrain, he suspected they'd never intended to hurt Kimi, probably just to scare her, but they'd come over the top of that ridge and the Bronco went airborne, and then control of the situation was no longer in their power. It belonged to physics. What went up had to come down, and in this instance it came down fast and powerfully and smashed into Kimi Kanasket—damn near in the exact same spot where the town of Stoneridge had hanged an innocent man a hundred years earlier. Buzz could have forgiven those four boys for running Kimi down; what had happened after that, though, was unforgiveable. What had happened after that had been a deliberate and intentional act. They'd tossed her body in the river like garbage.

Sitting in his car, Buzz also knew the four boys would never be convicted, and it was that knowledge that he was wrestling with, that was causing him to question why he'd become a cop in the first place, that was making him sick to his stomach.

He had gone over Jerry Ostertag's head. He'd taken his information to his lieutenant. He'd sat down and told him everything he had, with earnestness and sincerity, and showed him the photographs. But even as Buzz spoke, he could see from the almost imperceptible grin on the lieutenant's face that he was only being humored.

"How long you been on the force?" were the first words out of the lieutenant's mouth.

Brownie points for you, Buzz Almond, you eager beaver, he must have been thinking, *but you're a newbie, and your inexperience is showing like a virgin on her wedding night.*

His lieutenant wouldn't do a thing, just like Jerry Ostertag wasn't about to do a thing. The coroner said suicide. The circumstantial evidence said suicide. And they were satisfied, lazy, or didn't give a damn. Buzz had reached a dead end. He'd intended to give his lieutenant the file he'd put together, but as he sat in that office he envisioned the file being shoved in some box and shipped off to mothballs in a dusty storage unit, discarded and forgotten, just like Kimi Kanasket. So he decided he'd file it himself, as an active investigation, knowing exactly where he could find it if he ever chose to look at it again.

Jerry Ostertag had not been happy with him. He'd made a point of confronting Buzz when Buzz finished his shift and had come back to the building to clock out. Ostertag didn't mince his words. He'd asked Buzz who the hell he thought he was and what exactly he thought he was doing. He made it clear, in no uncertain terms, that what Buzz had done was not a good way to make friends, that cops watched each other's backs, and that Buzz might want to consider that if he hoped to make a career out of law enforcement, especially in Klickitat County. It was all Buzz could do to not bust Jerry Ostertag in the mouth, but that would have definitely put an end to his career. And this wasn't just about Buzz. This was about Anne and Maria and Sophia, and the baby on the way. This was about giving them a good life. He couldn't sacrifice that for the satisfaction of knocking Jerry Ostertag out.

Buzz got out of his car and walked up the front steps. His feet felt as heavy as if cast in concrete blocks, and his heart felt hardened by the futility of his situation. When he stepped through the front door, Maria and Sophia came running barefoot from the kitchen, still in their matching nightgowns, hair in need of a good brushing, which Buzz would get to after their breakfast.

"Daddy, Daddy, Daddy," they cried, voices sweet enough to melt an angel's heart.

He lifted one in each arm, and they gripped him around the neck, nuzzling and kissing him. It was horrible to even think, but the thought rushing through his mind at that moment was that Kimi Kanasket was dead, and he couldn't do anything more for her. These two little girls in his arms, showering him with unconditional love, and the third baby on the way, had to take priority.

Anne followed the girls into the room. Dressed in her nurse's uniform, she was as beautiful and sexy as the day Buzz first set eyes on her, and just the tonic he needed that morning. *You're a lucky man, Buzz Almond,* he thought, trying to convince himself. *You are so very blessed.*

"Okay, girls," Anne said. "Finish your breakfast before it gets cold."

Buzz lowered their bare feet to the ground, and they padded off on tiptoes. "I made oatmeal," Anne said, starting to gather her keys

395

to get out the door. "With some fresh blueberries."

"Thanks," he said.

She stopped, considering him. "Everything okay?"

"Tough day at work," he said, looking away, though he knew she'd already seen the tears in his eyes.

"Something that can be fixed?"

Buzz thought again of Kimi, and of Earl and Nettie Kanasket. He now knew they would be the hardest part of his job. He'd bring them home with him—and other families like them, families hurting and in pain—long after he punched out of work.

"I don't think so," he said. "Not this time."

Tracy went back to West Seattle and dismantled Buzz Almond's file, spreading it out on her dining room table, twice having to shoo away Roger and finally having to distract him with food.

She'd found with difficult cases that sometimes it helped to see all the evidence in one place. Despite the certainty she now had about what had happened on November 5, 1976, she felt like she still didn't have the complete picture. She was still missing something. It was usually nothing dramatic—not some hidden clue only a Sherlockian mind could unearth. It was usually something much simpler than that, something logic dictated but that her mind had not stopped to consider—the way you don't stop to consider the meaning of a stop sign. You just take your foot off the gas and apply the brake.

She picked up the reports, skimming through them. She moved next to the photos. Was there something staring her in the face that she wasn't seeing? Maybe, but it was unlikely Kaylee Wright would have missed something obvious. She reached the same conclusion with respect to Kelly Rosa and her analysis of the coroner's report. She ruled those out.

Her mind shifted to the evidence she hadn't yet completely fit into the puzzle, and she picked up the receipts for the bodywork and windshield repair at Hastey Devoe Senior's two shops: $68 to Columbia Windshield and Glass, and $659 to Columbia Auto Repair. Buzz had included those in the file because that was where the Bronco had been repaired, for cash. She was surprised a cash receipt even existed, that Eric Reynolds would have asked for one, and even more surprised Buzz had located them. *How* was not the question though. *Why* was the question. Why would Buzz have gone searching for the receipts?

She thought again of Eric Reynolds's statement that Buzz Almond had come to the house to ask if he had been out Friday night. Why would Buzz have suspected Eric? He wouldn't have, not unless he'd first suspected that the tire tracks could have been made by the Bronco's tires. It was more likely that if Buzz had visited, it was not to talk to Eric but to see the car, to determine if the car had any damage. And if the car had still been damaged, Buzz would have never tracked down the receipts because he wouldn't have known it had undergone repairs. The fact that he had the receipts, therefore, had to mean that the Bronco had already been repaired.

That's when what had been gnawing at the back of Tracy's mind—not one thing it turned out, but several, all interrelated—began to become clear.

And Tracy realized she'd been dead wrong.

Kaylee Wright hovered over the table, using a magnifying glass with a bright light on an extension arm to inspect the photographs. Tracy stood beside her, in Wright's home office, trying not to crowd her, or to rush her. She'd called Wright's cell, told her what she suspected, and asked if Wright could go over the photographs again. After nearly ten minutes going over multiple photographs, Wright straightened and moved the magnifying glass out of the way. Tracy felt like she was in court, waiting for a jury's verdict.

Wright looked to her and sighed. "You're right. I missed it."

Tracy felt a huge surge of adrenaline. "How certain can you be?"

"Very certain. I'm sorry. I should have seen this."

"Don't be. You hadn't finished your analysis."

"I should have seen it."

"Water under the bridge, Kaylee."

"The truck that made those impressions entered and exited twice."

Tracy forced herself to ask questions one at a time, not to rush, to be certain they had the evidence to support her hypothesis. "Will you explain to me how can you tell?"

Wright picked through several of the photographs on her desk until settling on the one she wanted. She adjusted the magnifying glass over it. "Take a look," she said, stepping aside.

Tracy looked at the enlarged image as Wright spoke. "This is the best photograph depicting the tire tread. You can clearly see two defined paths in, and two defined paths out. The paths overlap in certain places, but cars, like people, don't move in a perfectly straight line. You can see clearly where the paths deviated."

"Could it have been two separate vehicles, one following the other?" Tracy asked, wanting to eliminate that possibility.

"No. Both sets of tracks were made by the same tires, and within a relatively short period of time."

"How can you tell it was a short period of time? Why couldn't it have been a week or a month apart?" Tracy knew that had not been the scenario because, according to Buzz Almond's report, he'd taken the photographs the Monday after Kimi Kanasket had gone missing.

"Again, you have to look at the impressions. If the second vehicle had come at a time significantly after the first, I would have expected the photographs to depict bits of crumbled dirt. Remember, I said that in my opinion, to get this quality of impressions the ground had to have been wet and then frozen in a relatively short period of time. These impressions in the dirt would have hardened like a plaster-cast mold. If a second vehicle came at a later date, it would have torn up the first set of tracks and obliterated the first vehicle's impressions. We would be seeing large clumps of chewed-up dirt. I don't see anything like that here."

"So the same vehicle had to have come back before the ground had time to freeze."

"I'd say within an hour or two. I'm not certain we can quantify it any better than that. Maybe weather records back that far can tell you the temperatures on that particular night."

Tracy switched mental gears. "Okay, let's go over the boot impressions. They lead from where Kimi's body lay to where the second set of incoming tire tracks stop. Correct?"

Wright nodded. "I'd agree with that, yes. There is a deliberate set of prints between those two points."

"So the person who came back was wearing the boots, and that person carried the body to the vehicle."

"Yes. He walked in a straight line to the body and, after getting balanced, walked back to the vehicle."

Still thinking out loud, Tracy said, "And the fact that the person picked up the body and staggered under the weight, and that there are only the bootprints leading to the vehicle, indicates that he did it on his own, that there was no one else to help him."

"I would agree with that also," Wright said. She looked as if she'd been struck by a thought.

"What is it?" Tracy asked.

"Probably nothing, but remember that I told you those boots were made for soldiers and that the company went out of business?"

"Yeah."

"The company never made boots again . . . which might be helpful to your investigation."

"Tell me how."

"For one, they're rare. You won't find them now, except maybe on some vintage clothing sites and for a lot more money than what they originally cost. People who owned a pair kept them."

"You're saying you think it's possible that the person who owned these could still have them?"

"The boots were highly sought after because they were so durable. A person might wear them maybe twenty-five to fifty days out of the year. Maybe. Someone who owned a pair would have no reason to ever get a new pair. I'm just saying these are not the kind of boots you throw away or give to Goodwill if you don't have to."

Tracy thought about that but didn't say anything.

"Are you going to tell me what you think it all means?" Wright said.

"Remember when you said that what happened in that clearing that night was 'truly frightening'?"

"Yeah."

"I think it goes beyond frightening; I think what happened there was evil."

CHAPTER 32

At just after six that evening, Tracy called Jenny from the car and told her she was coming back to Stoneridge that night to visit Eric Reynolds. Jenny insisted that Tracy have backup, but Tracy declined, and eventually, Jenny conceded. She wasn't being heroic or stupid. She'd thought it through, and she had a good sense of what was about to happen. "He's had forty years to do something," she said.

"He's never *had* to do *anything*," Jenny countered. "Nobody has ever accused him."

"I have my Glock," Tracy said, "and he won't be expecting me. Even if he's armed, I could empty my magazine before he could draw his weapon."

Jenny argued with her, but only briefly. They compromised and agreed that Jenny would wait nearby in a sheriff's vehicle with backup and that Tracy would remain in phone contact.

Tracy had the address in the file from the Accurint check, and when she plugged it into her iPhone, the directions popped up and led her without fault to the large home—very large by Stoneridge standards, though certainly not as ostentatious as some of the mansions people had built in Seattle's wealthier neighborhoods. What the two-story stone-and-wood-siding home lacked in square footage and grandeur, it more than made up for with acreage. After passing between stone pillars, the long drive wound its way through what appeared in the darkness to be a vast expanse of fruit trees and vineyards, as well as a man-made lake. As beautiful as it all was, it also felt isolated and brought to mind the image of a deserted island, uncharted and lonely.

Tracy parked in the circular drive beside a Chevy Silverado truck. The temperature had dropped since she'd left Seattle that afternoon, and a heavy cloud layer obscured the night sky, tempered all sounds, and dampened even the slightest breeze.

She approached a front door of leaded glass and oak and rang the buzzer. She had visions of a butler opening it and greeting her. Inside, dogs barked, followed by Eric Reynolds issuing commands for them to be quiet. They complied.

"Detective Crosswhite?" Reynolds said, opening the door and looking genuinely perplexed. "What are you doing here so late?"

The two dogs looked to be rat terriers. One emitted a low growl.

"Hush, Blue," Reynolds said, and the dog lowered his head, though he kept his eyes on Tracy.

"I have a few more questions. I know it's late, but with all the festivities going on this weekend, I suspected you'd be a hard man to run down."

"I just got home from the banquet," he said. He wore black loafers, slacks, and a button-down beneath a V-neck sweater. Tracy detected a subtle humility to his demeanor not present when they'd spoken at the golf course. Reynolds looked tired and emotionally spent. She wondered if he'd been drinking.

"I won't take up much of your time," she said. "Just a few questions."

Reynolds stepped aside. The dogs retreated. Like the exterior, natural wood and stone dominated the decor, keeping a rustic theme. Tracy didn't note a single family photograph amid the paintings and sculptures as Reynolds led her to a den. Entering, she noted a handgun on a poker table, along with a cleaning kit. She smelled the distinct odor of Hoppe's No. 9 cleaning solvent.

"Doing a little maintenance?" she asked.

Reynolds looked to the table as if he'd forgotten the gun was there. "Actually, I was just starting to watch a movie." He gestured to a very large television across the room. Bradley Cooper, wearing an Army uniform, stood frozen onscreen.

"*American Sniper*," Tracy said. "Late to be starting a movie."

"I'm usually up late."

"You don't sleep well?" she said.

"No. No, I don't. Can I offer you a drink?" he asked, moving again toward the poker table and the gun, the wet bar to his right.

"No, thank you," Tracy said. "You have a lovely home. Is it just you?"

"Just me," he said, offering a wistful smile. "Well, and Blue and Tank here. I'm divorced. Twenty-five years now."

"It must get lonely out here."

"Not with Blue and Tank around. I'm used to being alone."

"No children?"

"No. You?"

"Also divorced. Also many years ago. Also used to living alone."

"No dogs?"

"A very needy cat."

Reynolds offered her a leather chair facing the stone fireplace. Tracy noted a large gun safe in the corner of the room, the heavy door partially open, the stocks of rifles visible. Reynolds took a seat on a matching sofa near one of two table lamps offering soft light. The two dogs hopped onto the couch and curled up beside him, Blue keeping a watchful eye.

When Reynolds crossed his legs, his slacks inched up, revealing tan socks. "So what can I do for you?"

"I'm just returning from Seattle," Tracy said. "I spoke with Tiffany Martin, Darren Gallentine's widow, and his two daughters."

"Oh?" Reynolds scratched Blue behind the ears and about the head.

"The daughters were seventeen and fourteen when their father took his life. They never knew why he did it."

"He didn't leave a note, then."

"No, he didn't."

"A terrible thing," Reynolds said.

"You can't imagine unless you've gone through it," Tracy said. "We like to believe our parents are perfect, but then you realize they're human, with all the same faults and imperfections. I think that's the hardest thing to accept."

"You have personal experience."

"My father shot himself."

"I'm sorry." Reynolds continued to pet his dogs. His right foot bounced rhythmically.

"Darren was in therapy at the time he killed himself." Tracy paused, making sure she had eye contact. "The therapist kept a file. The family had never asked to see it. You can imagine. On the one hand, it could provide answers; on the other, it could reveal faults and imperfections. They'd decided to move on. Only they found that it wasn't so simple to just move on from something that traumatic. Their father certainly couldn't. Neither, apparently, could Archibald Coe. Hastey doesn't appear to have either, and, despite appearances, I don't believe you have."

"I can assure you I don't know what you're talking about, Detective." Reynolds didn't sound defiant. He sounded tired.

"Yes, you do, Mr. Reynolds. Because I have Darren Gallentine's file, and he told his therapist what happened the night Kimi Kanasket died. I'm talking about how the four of you were out drinking beer and getting high. About how you were upset because Cheryl Neal had gone out with Tommy Moore, about how fate, cruel and horrible, put Kimi Kanasket in your path."

His foot continued to bounce. "No," he said. "I was at home."

"Maybe that's what you told Buzz Almond when he came to your house to take pictures of the Bronco, but I know now that was a lie. Darren's account was very detailed. You got angry. You had a temper then, one you've done remarkably well to overcome, it appears, and you chased Kimi into the woods with the Bronco. You didn't mean to run her down. You weren't even thinking straight. You were just angry. You were angry a lot back then. You were just a boy, who had to watch his mother die of cancer and grow up without her, trying to live up to his legendary father's expectations. You were under a lot of pressure and stress. The whole town was expecting a lot of you, in particular. You were the golden boy, the all-American. That's a lot for any eighteen-year-old's shoulders to bear. The other three—Darren and Archie and Hastey—they were part of the Four Ironmen, but they didn't have the same pressures. You were the center of attention.

You were the star. I imagine you were feeling the pressure, particularly that night, on the eve of the biggest game in this little town's history."

"I told you, Detective, I never put much into all that stuff about being the Four Ironmen and all-American. Those were just labels others placed on us, on me."

"Maybe you didn't, but others did. Your father did, and whether you admitted it then or not, you wanted to live up to those expectations. That's why in the photograph of the four of you with the trophy, the others are smiling, but you just look relieved. I imagine you were—relieved to have the season behind you. Relieved to be moving on, away from Stoneridge, away from the memory of what you'd done, away to college, where you could just blend in. You didn't mean to run down Kimi. It wasn't premeditated. It was a horrible thing to have happen. But it happened. And the four of you were scared out of your minds. You didn't know what to do. Your whole life had changed in an instant—if anyone found out, all the accolades and attention and publicity would be forgotten, replaced by one horrible incident that would forever define you. Eric Reynolds, an all-American with a full ride to the University of Washington—a murderer, a felon who threw away his life because he couldn't control his temper."

Reynolds looked like he'd taken a sedative, only partially present in the room, as Tracy continued to recount what transpired that night. Tracy had no doubt the part of him not present had gone back to the clearing, back forty years, to that horrible moment. And she had no doubt that, despite all of his seeming success and wealth, that he'd gone back to that night many times. He just hid it better in public than the others, hid it behind the façade he'd created, behind the big house and the successful business and the gregarious personality, but Eric Reynolds was riddled with guilt. That was the reason he lived alone, unmarried, without children, unable to sleep. That was why the gun was on the poker table, and Tracy bet it had been on that table many other nights.

"Kimi threw herself in the river," he said. "She was upset because Tommy Moore came into the diner that night with Cheryl Neal."

"And I'm sure you want to believe that, Eric. I'm sure that over the years you've done everything you could to try to convince yourself that's what happened. Because the alternative was waking up every morning thinking you'd killed that girl—and that would have been just too horrible to face. That's what our minds do. They protect us. They bury those memories that would cripple us, so that we can live with ourselves." She looked to the still image of Bradley Cooper. "Soldiers understand it. They're asked to do horrible things. They see horrible things. And they wonder if that makes them horrible people. Does doing a horrible thing make you a horrible person?"

"What's the answer, Detective?"

"You didn't mean to kill Kimi Kanasket—not when you ran her over. That was an accident, an accident as a result of a bad decision fueled by testosterone and anger and drugs, but it certainly wasn't intentional. It didn't make you a murderer, Eric. And if you and the others had just owned up to what you did that night, Darren and Archie would likely still be alive, and Hastey wouldn't have spent his life crawling into a beer can every day, and you wouldn't be living out here alone.

"But you didn't do that. You all agreed to never talk about what happened. You left Kimi there, and you drove the others home, but when you got home you realized you couldn't leave her body out there because it left things unfinished. So you changed into your hunting boots because it had started to snow, and you drove back to the clearing. You put Kimi in the back of the Bronco, drove her to the river, and threw her into the water. That, Eric, was a deliberate act. That's what you can't deny. You can't camouflage it behind this façade you've created.

"And when you were finished, you took the Bronco to Lionel Devoe, who was running his father's businesses at that time, and you had it fixed and the windshield replaced, and you thought that was the end of it. But it wasn't. It wasn't the end because Buzz Almond wouldn't let that be the end of it. And it didn't have to be this way, Eric. That's the most ironic and saddest thing of all. It didn't have to be like this."

"It didn't?"

"No," she said. "Because Kimi wasn't dead."

Reynolds stopped petting the dogs. His foot no longer bounced.

"She was still alive, Eric, and if you had just done the right thing, if you had just called for help, Kimi would have lived."

Tracy watched the remaining color drain from Eric Reynolds's face, leaving him as pale and sickly as a corpse.

Reynolds didn't stand when Tracy rose from her chair. The two dogs sat up, watching her. Tracy considered taking the gun, but she had no right to confiscate it, and Eric Reynolds had access to many guns and rifles, and he'd no doubt had those guns out many nights but had never used one. She didn't think he would use it tonight either.

Tracy left him physically sitting in his chair with his two dogs. Mentally, however, she could tell he'd returned to the clearing, a place no doubt he frequented often in his dreams. She wondered if this time Reynolds was staring down at Kimi Kanasket, trying to comprehend what Tracy had just revealed, and wondering what might have been if he'd only done the right thing.

CHAPTER 33

Tracy didn't have to wait outside Reynolds's gate or along the side of the road. If she was right, she knew where he'd go when he mentally returned from the clearing.

And he would go. He'd go because he wouldn't be able to *not* go.

She'd kept her promise to Jenny and remained in phone contact, advising her of her intent. The backup followed.

Tracy parked just up the block, not worried about her truck being seen. Reynolds didn't know her truck, and it blended nicely with the other trucks and older-model vehicles on the block. Then again, she doubted Eric Reynolds would have cared even if he did know. The two sheriff's vehicles were one block over, out of sight.

Snow began to fall through the gaps in the trees, the kind of large, heavy flakes she and Sarah used to catch on their tongues and watch float to the ground from Tracy's bedroom window, as excited as on Christmas Eve. They knew the snow would stick, and that meant a possible snow day from school and playing all day in the backyard with their friends. It was one of the best memories from her childhood, one she clung to and refused to have taken from her.

The sound of the big Silverado's engine preceded the glow of its headlights in her truck's passenger-side mirror as it approached. She imagined the Bronco limping down the same street that night forty years earlier, broken and damaged. Eric Reynolds drove past Tracy without turning his head, continuing to the small one-story home in which he'd grown up, though his gaze still seemed to be forty years in the past.

He parked the Silverado behind the Dodge Durango in the cluttered carport beneath plastic roofing that had yellowed with age and was covered in pine needles. He'd bought the truck for his father the prior Christmas, an extravagant gift, but without his father, Eric Reynolds would have become nothing. That's what he'd thought. That's what he'd been led to believe all these years. He'd been led to believe that without his father, he would have been in prison, a convicted felon, and never would have had all the accolades, the smiles and the waves and the greetings from old acquaintances, which seemed to always begin "Remember when . . ."

He stepped from the truck. The porch light over the side door clicked on, casting a sickly yellow light—such a contrast to the pure-white snow beginning to blanket the ground and flock the trees. The door pulled open, and his father stepped out while putting on his glasses. Despite his age, eighty-two now, he still looked and moved well. People said Ron Reynolds had become an older version of himself, still powerfully built with large forearms and chiseled features, still wearing the crew cut that had survived every decade and every style that had come and gone.

"What are you doing here?" he asked.

"What did you do, Dad?" Eric Reynolds asked. "What did you do?"

⌒

Saturday, November 6, 1976

Ron Reynolds checked his rearview mirror for any sign of approaching headlights. Not seeing any, he turned off the road into the brush and proceeded slowly down the path. The right fender and hood were smashed, but the metal grille along the front bumper had done its job and absorbed most of the impact. Rather amazingly, both headlights still worked, illuminating a light snowfall.

Eric had come home wide-eyed and gibbering almost incoherently about needing to call the police, needing to let someone know. His pupils were as small as pinheads and as black as night. It took a strong slap across the face just to get him to calm down and to stop talking. He'd started to cry, great gasps and sobs, almost wailing. Then he started gibbering again, about Kimi Kanasket, about how he'd killed her.

Ron Reynolds had been angry when he'd learned that his son had snuck out of the house the night before the biggest game of their lives. He had been waiting for Eric to return, thinking about how or if he could discipline him, but when he heard those last words, his blood had run cold and his legs had gone weak.

"What are you talking about?" he'd asked.

Eric sat on the couch sobbing, shaking his head.

"Tell me, Goddamn it!"

And Eric told him. He told him about how he'd snuck out to drink beer with Hastey and Archie and Darren. He told him about Cheryl Neal going out with Tommy Moore. He told him about how, while they were driving home, they came upon Kimi walking along the side of the road.

"I didn't mean to hit her, Dad. I swear to God, I didn't mean to hit her."

"What are you talking about? What do you mean you hit her? Did you punch her?"

He told his father how they'd exchanged words, about how he had lost his temper and chased her into the woods in his car. "I just wanted to scare her," he'd said. "But then we went over a hill and . . . and I couldn't control it. The front end, it just came down. She must have fallen, Dad. She must have fallen, and the car, it just . . . We have to call somebody, Dad. We have to call someone."

Ron had rushed outside, disbelieving until he saw the damage to the car. Then the gravity and magnitude of the situation hit home. It was the damage that made him realize that everything . . . everything they had worked for had potentially been lost.

When he went back inside, Eric had gotten up from the couch and held the telephone.

Ron ripped the cord from the wall and yanked the phone from his son's grasp. "What the hell do you think you're doing?"

"We have to call the police, Dad! I wasn't going to, but we have to. We can't just leave her there."

"Call them and tell them what? Huh? What are we going to tell them? That it was an accident?"

"It *was* an accident."

"Do you think they're going to believe that? Four white boys chasing an Indian girl in their truck. To what end? Huh? To what end, Eric?"

"Just to scare her."

Ron grabbed Eric by the hair. "Scare her? Or rape her?"

"No, Dad. No."

"Drunk. Smoking weed. They'll never believe your bullshit. I don't believe your bullshit."

"We wouldn't do that, Dad."

"They'll prosecute you. They'll prosecute all

of you. And they'll convict you. And everything, everything we have worked for since you were born will have been for nothing."

"We can tell them, Dad. We can explain what happened."

"And do you think that girl's parents, all those Indians, are going to understand? Huh? What do you think they're going to do? Just accept what you're telling them? You think they're going to say, 'Okay, well, it was just an accident. Thanks for letting us know'? And what about tomorrow, huh? What about the game? Do you know how many college recruiters are going to be at that game? Do you have any idea the trouble I've gone to for you? It will be over. It will all be over—the scholarship, college, the NFL. You can kiss it all good-bye, Eric. Is that what you want?"

Eric dropped onto the weathered couch, breathing heavily, tears streaming down his face.

"What did you tell the others?" Ron said. "What are they going to say happened?"

Eric looked up at him. "Nothing. They're not going to say anything. Their parents don't know they snuck out. They're going to say they were in bed, getting ready for the game."

Ron pointed a finger at him. "And that's what you're going to say. Do you understand?"

"Dad, I can't—"

"You're going to say you were home in bed

getting ready for the game. And I'm going to say I was here with you. Do you understand? I'm going to *lie* for you, boy. I'm going to put my ass on the line and lie for you. Do you know what that means? It means that from this point forward, we're joined at the hip. You go to prison, and I go to prison with you. You understand? I'm not going to prison. So you're going to say you were home in bed. You got that?"

Eric nodded.

"I want to hear you say it. Say it, damn it!"

"I was home in bed."

"And where was I?"

"You were home too. You were home with me."

"Where is she? Where did you leave her?"

"The clearing. She's in the clearing."

"Give me the keys."

"What? What are you going to do?"

"I'm going to clean up your mess. I'm going to make this right," he said. "Now get your ass in bed. And don't you get up. You understand me? Don't you get up, and don't you even think about talking to anyone about this."

Ron crested the top of the hill and drove slowly down the slope. The snow continued to fall. A light dusting now covered the field and began to accumulate on the windshield. The car's headlights inched across the ground to where the slope flattened, until illuminating an irregularity, what looked like a log, the top covered in snow.

Ron stopped the Bronco and slowly got out.

She lay on her side, not moving. The snow had begun to cover her, turning her black hair white. The cold was biting now. Ron heard a noise, what sounded like a man moaning. He looked back up the slope. The trees began to shake and sway, and the snow went airborne as if from a sudden explosion. The moaning increased, and a strong breeze carried the snow in a gust down the slope, hitting him flush in the face and rushing past him. He turned and watched the wind continue on, the flakes swirling clockwise along the edge of the clearing, the branches shimmering. Then, just as suddenly as the wind had started, it died, the snowflakes settling gently onto the ground.

Ron stepped closer to the body. Kimi Kanasket. The girl looked broken, though there wasn't much blood, probably because of the cold and the snow. The ground had been chewed up by the truck's tires. *Good,* he thought. It would look as though someone had gone four-wheeling.

He bent to a knee. Moisture seeped through his sweatpants. Uncertain how to carry her, he reached beneath her, one hand at her hip, the other at her shoulder, and rolled her toward him. He tried to stand, but he stumbled. He tried a second time and managed to get to his feet, though he was off balance. He worked to reposition the weight, nearly falling backward, nearly dropping her.

When he'd regained his balance, he carried her to the back of the Bronco. The spare tire hung off the tailgate, and he couldn't lower the gate with his arms full. He moved to the side and rolled her out of his arms into the bed, where he'd placed an open sleeping bag. She landed with a dull thud, arms and legs flopping. Ron was breathing heavily, white gasps that the wind quickly dissolved. His heart raced, and he was perspiring, despite the cold snow melting atop his uncovered head and dripping down his face.

He covered her body with the sleeping bag and quickly got back in the cab, rubbing his hands in the blast of heat from the vents. When he could flex his fingers without feeling pain, he put the car in reverse, looked back over the seat, and saw something at the edge of the clearing in the muted glow of the backup lights.

A man?

Reynolds's heart skipped a beat, and his breath caught in his chest. He jumped out of the car into the snow, but when he looked back he saw nothing now but swirling snow.

He got back in and quickly drove from the clearing, avoiding the hill and driving back along the path leading to 141. He'd thought about where to take her. The rafting boats put in up by Husum, near the bridge. He could get the Bronco close to the river there. People would assume she'd jumped off the bridge.

He checked the mirrors. No cars followed. He looked over the seat into the bed of the truck. The sleeping bag had started to slip down, and he could see the top of her head.

He made a right on Husum Street and shut off the Bronco's lights as he drove across the concrete bridge. Just off the bridge, he turned right into a dirt lot and drove forward, parking amid the scrub oak, careful not to get too close to the edge that dropped to the river, but hoping to camouflage the car in the trees.

He shut off the engine and took another moment to gather himself. He checked the rearview and side mirrors, took a deep breath, and pushed out of the car. With his hands free, he was able to lower the spare tire and open the tailgate. He gripped the sleeping bag and slid her body toward him. When he got her to the gate, he lifted her again. The snow had melted, and her body didn't feel as cold. It was easier to carry her this time, not having to stand from a crouch. He was better balanced and could more evenly distribute the weight. He heard the river—not a roar, but a hushing sound like the din of traffic on a freeway. It grew louder as he stepped closer to the edge.

She moved.

He nearly dropped her.

She moved again, twitching.

Then she opened her eyes.

Reynolds's breath caught in his throat.

She lifted her head and looked up at him. Her lips parted, emitting a long, shallow gasp, like air escaping a tire. With the rush came a whisper. "Help me."

Ron Reynolds stood paralyzed, not breathing, his legs unable to move.

"Help me," she said again, her words soft but more distinct. "Please. Help me."

His breathing came in quick gasps. He took a deep breath and found his voice. "I can't," he said. "I can't."

And he stepped to the edge and rolled her out of his arms.

Her body struck the water with a splash, submerged for a moment, then bobbed to the surface, her arms flailing before the current pushed Kimi Kanasket quickly downstream.

⌒

Eric Reynolds stood in the driveway of his boyhood home. Snow had begun to stick to his hair and clothing, melting and trickling down his face. His father didn't ask him what he was talking about. He didn't ask him to come inside. He must have envisioned this moment, though after four decades, maybe his father had come to believe he would never have to experience it.

"I did what I had to do," he said, unapologetic.

"She was still alive?"

His father did not answer.

"And you knew it. You knew she was still alive."

"Whether she was or wasn't is not relevant."

"Not relevant?" Eric said, disbelieving. "You've let me believe all these years that I killed her. You let us all believe we killed her."

"You did kill her. She would have died."

"No, Dad. She wouldn't have died. I just spoke to the police detective. She would have lived."

"There's no guarantee."

"If you had let me call, she could have lived."

"And then what, Eric?" his father said, still calm. "Then what were you going to tell everyone? That bullshit story about it being an accident?"

"It was an accident. It was a Goddamn accident. We were just kids."

"You were eighteen. They would have prosecuted you as an adult."

"You know something? I wish they had. I wish they had because I've been punishing myself for the past forty years, and nothing could have been worse than what I've been through, what I know Darren and Archie went through, what Hastey continues to go through."

"Seems to me you've done pretty well for yourself."

"Really? Have I, Dad? Have you even noticed? Do you know why I'm divorced, Dad? You don't, because you never bothered to ask. I'm divorced, Dad, because I wouldn't have kids. I had a vasectomy before we were married without telling her, and I let her believe she was the problem. And do you want to know why I did it? I did it so I could be certain I would never have children. Because I was afraid that I'd have a daughter, Dad, a little girl who would grow up to be a teenager someday, and that I wouldn't be able to look at her without seeing Kimi. And every day she would be a reminder of what I did. What I *thought* I did. You allowed us to live our lives thinking we killed her, and it killed Darren and it killed Archie and it's killing Hastey. That's what you did, Dad. You let us all kill ourselves."

"I did what I did to protect my son. To protect everything we worked so hard to accomplish. You would have lost everything—your scholarship, college."

"You traded her life for my scholarship?"

"You would have gone to prison."

"I wish I had. You have no idea how often I just wish I had. Because then, at least, I could have said that I got what I deserved, and maybe I could have moved on with my life instead of living like this, like a coward."

"You don't have children. You don't know. You would have done the same thing."

"No," Eric said. "I wouldn't have. I would have called if you had let me. I would have called,

Dad. I wanted to call. But you wouldn't let me, because this was never about me. It was always about you, about preserving your legacy. That's what this stadium is all about. That's why you let me believe I killed her—because you could keep control over me, let me believe if it wasn't for you, I would have nothing. That's why you did what you did. It had nothing to do with me."

"When I lost your mother, I swore I would never lose anything ever again. I did what I had to do to preserve what was left of this family."

"She would have been ashamed of me. And she would have been more ashamed of you."

Ron Reynolds did not immediately respond. They stood in the blanketing silence, the snow falling heavier now. "What's done is done," Ron said, sounding resigned. "You can't change the past. Tomorrow they'll dedicate the stadium, and our names will be forever etched in history."

And with that, Ron Reynolds took a step back and slowly shut the door. A moment later the yellow light went out, leaving Eric standing in the dark, the snow cascading around him. He started for his truck, then stopped, wondering. His dad was always so organized, so detailed, and so practical. It's what had made him such a good football coach. He looked behind him, to the carport. Then he turned and walked alongside the car. It was dark, but he used the flashlight on his cell phone to scan a lifetime of accumulated sporting equipment. Fishing waders hung from nails in studs beside camouflage hunting pants and jackets, a crossbow, tennis rackets, golf clubs in golf bags, baseball bats in a bin, a backpack. Below them he found the blue plastic storage bins marked with a black marker, the words faded but still decipherable.

Eric moved the bins around until he found the one that said "Hunting Equipment." He snapped off the top and directed the light inside. His father's hunting boots stood neatly inside, newspaper stuffed into each leg to keep the boots straight.

CHAPTER 34

Tracy watched Eric Reynolds exit the carport. She stood in the road just beside her truck. Reynolds didn't startle at the sight of her, as if he'd been expecting her to be there. Maybe he'd come to his father's house just to get the boots, but then his father had opened the door. Tracy could tell from the two men's body language that they were having a conversation they should have had forty years earlier. There were no hugs, no handshakes, no displays of affection or warmth of any kind. They kept their distance. Physically, it was just a few feet, but clearly it was a much greater divide. The conversation had been short, which meant there had been no denials, no arguing, no attempts to explain. Each man had done what he'd done and had lived with the consequences of his decision.

Though Eric Reynolds didn't wear a jacket, he did not look cold. He held up the hunting boots.

"Photographs revealed two sets of tire tracks in and out," Tracy said. "Someone came back, alone, and moved her. I couldn't reconcile that being any of the four of you. You would have done it together. And even if it had been you, there was no reason for you to change your shoes, no reason to go home and put on boots and come back. It was snowing, but you wouldn't have considered that, not under the circumstances. Then there were the two cash receipts. Seven hundred dollars would have been more than a high school student playing football would have had readily available, even if all four of you had pooled your resources. Nor did I see any of you having the foresight to ask for a cash receipt. Lionel did your father a favor, but he wasn't about to do it for free, and I'm guessing your father wanted the receipt in case Lionel ever got squirrely—to remind Lionel that he, too, was now involved."

"He thought that way," Eric said. "Details. Never a loose end. He thought that it had come back to bite him in the ass when Lionel called to tell him the deputy had come and gotten the two invoices. Lionel's mother was the bookkeeper. She had no idea. She just made him copies. My father determined that the deputy had also been the man who'd come out to look at the car, acting like he wanted to buy it. We waited for the other shoe to drop, but then nothing more came of it. Later, when Lionel became chief, my dad asked him to look into it, whether there was an open investigation. Lionel found the file, and I thought he'd destroyed it, but I guess I was wrong." He glanced back at the house. "What will happen now?"

"The sheriff will turn everything over to the county prosecutor. He'll decide what charges to file."

"What happened wasn't Hastey's fault—or Darren's or Archie's. It was mine. Hastey has suffered enough."

"That will all get sorted out," she said. "The gun on the table at your house . . ."

Eric Reynolds nodded. "I take it out just about every night, and just about every night I've thought about it, but I can never do it. I clean it and put it back in the safe. I'm a coward," he said. "Maybe I knew all along this day would come. Maybe I was hoping it would. I want people to know the truth. As strange as it sounds, it's a relief."

"I'm going to need to take that gun, Eric. And any others you own."

"I understand. I'm worried about my dogs."

"We can go back to your house so you can get your things in order—send out e-mails or make phone calls. I'll call the sheriff; she's a friend of mine. I'll tell her that you've agreed to come in voluntarily. After we go back to your house, I'll take you to the sheriff's office and get a statement. We'll keep this all very civilized. You'll be taken into custody, and the process will play itself out."

"And my father?"

"He'll be taken into custody also." Tracy paused and looked at the house.

"Don't worry, Detective. He's not going to kill himself either. Ron Reynolds's ego would never allow him to admit that he's finally lost."

CHAPTER 35

Tracy debated placing Eric Reynolds in hand-cuffs but decided against it. She followed him back to his house, calling Jenny on the way. She told her she was escorting Eric Reynolds to his house so he could arrange care for his pets and get his affairs in order. Jenny and the other unit would arrest Ron Reynolds and meet them at the West End office, where both men would be booked and Eric would provide a full statement. They doubted Ron Reynolds would say anything.

Tracy and Eric entered his house together, the dogs jumping up to greet him, Blue barking at her. Tears pooled in the man's eyes. The dogs must have been the only family he'd had for many years.

They crossed the living area and entered the den. The flat-screen television was black. The .45 was no longer on the poker table.

"I must have put it away," Eric said.

As Eric started for the large gun safe in the corner of the room, the two dogs, who never strayed far from his side, suddenly did a one-eighty and started barking. At nearly the same moment, as Tracy's mind processed the situation, a voice came from the doorway on the other side of the den, which led out to the backyard.

"Is this what you're looking for?"

Lionel Devoe stepped in holding Eric's .45, the barrel leveled at Tracy.

Tracy reached for her Glock, but even she wasn't that fast.

"I wouldn't," Devoe said.

Tracy froze, one hand on the butt of her gun, her mind working quickly to assess the gravity of the situation.

The two dogs circled Devoe as he stepped farther into the room. Blue growled and snarled. Tank kept barking.

Tracy considered everything in the room she might be able to use for cover, as well as the exit. Could she get there? Not likely.

"What are you doing, Lionel?" Eric said.

"Slowly remove your hand, Detective." Devoe was dressed in full uniform and appeared calm and calculating; he'd thought this through.

Tracy removed her hand from the butt of her gun. She kept her focus on Devoe, looking for any opening, a moment when he became distracted and shifted his gaze. All she needed was a second or two to draw and fire. Silently, she urged the dogs to do something heroic—bite his leg, lunge at him, anything.

"Lionel," Eric said, more forcefully. "What the hell do you think you're doing?"

Devoe kept his gaze on Tracy. "Shut up, Eric. And shut up those dogs, or I swear to God I'll shoot them both. Raise both your hands very slowly, Detective."

"This is crazy, Lionel," Eric said.

"I said, 'Shut up.'"

Tracy lifted her hands to shoulder height. Devoe had done her a favor. In shooting competitions she'd always been faster using her opposite hand, earning her the nickname Crossdraw. Now with both hands raised, it would take one quick motion.

Eric continued to talk. "It's over, Lionel. Put down the damn gun."

Devoe walked cautiously to where Tracy stood, gun still leveled at her chest. The dogs followed at a safe distance, still barking. "Turn around."

"Lionel, put the damn gun down. The sheriff already knows."

"I know," Devoe said. "I monitored their frequency. The sheriff had backup ready. But she isn't here. They're arresting your father." Devoe spoke to Tracy. "I said, 'Turn around.'"

Tracy turned. Devoe stepped behind her. Cautiously, he reached out and removed her Glock, then quickly retreated. Tracy had just lost her best chance. She needed to reassess. Find a different option.

"Lionel, this is crazy," Eric said.

Devoe glanced briefly at Reynolds, looking more confident now that Tracy was unarmed. "Is it? Is it really, Eric?"

"Put the gun down, Lionel. I've already told her everything. She knows everything. So does the sheriff."

"You shouldn't have done that, Eric. You shouldn't have said anything. We had a deal. Everyone remains silent." Devoe stepped back and set the Glock on the poker table. "Can you shut the damn dogs up?"

"It's what dogs do," Eric said. "It's instinct."

"You shouldn't have broken the deal, not without talking to me and to Hastey."

"She knew, Lionel. She already knew."

"Maybe, but she had no way of proving any of it. You should have kept quiet. You should have kept your mouth shut. Goddamn it, shut those dogs up."

"It's been forty years, Lionel. What good has keeping quiet done any of us?"

"It doesn't matter. You should have checked with us. You should have checked with Hastey. That was the deal. But I guess we both knew it was going to come down to a situation like this, didn't we?"

"A situation like what?"

"Either you or Hastey deciding to do something stupid like this. And me having to stop you."

"She's a homicide detective, Lionel. Are you going to kill a homicide detective? How long do you think it would be before they hunted you down?"

Devoe smiled. "*I'm* not going to kill anyone, Eric."

"He has your gun," Tracy said to Eric, continuing to watch Devoe, waiting for any opportunity, assessing the distance between her and the poker table and how quickly she could get to the gun. *Not quick enough.* "He shoots me with your gun, and shoots you with mine. Makes it look like we had it out."

Devoe smiled. "See, Eric, that's why she's a detective. But that isn't quite accurate. I don't see you both getting a shot off. I see Eric surprising you. The way I see it, the detective here brought you back to your house after exposing you and your father. She was giving you the chance to take care of things before she brought you in. But you had other plans. You had your gun out. You always had your gun out at night. I can testify to that. So will Hastey. You lured her back here, and you surprised her. You weren't going to prison, not a guy like you. So you shot her. Then you shot yourself." Devoe shrugged. "Since we are technically within the Stoneridge city limits, I'll have jurisdiction over the investigation. And when I close the case, you can be damn sure I'll destroy that file."

"You don't need to do this, Lionel," Reynolds said. "I've already taken the blame. I've told her Hastey didn't have anything to do with it and neither did you."

"That's very generous of you, Eric, and I wish we could turn the clock back forty years and make it true, but that wasn't the case then, and it isn't the case now. I fixed the car for your dad. If she has Buzz Almond's file, she knows that. She also knows I removed the report with the photographs Buzz took of your car. I'm not going to prison for you or for your father, and I'm not letting Hastey go to prison for you either." Devoe looked to Tracy. "I told you, Detective, you should have left this one alone. What was done was done. Nobody meant for it to happen. It was an accident. You should have just let it be."

"Tell that to Earl Kanasket," Tracy said.

"It isn't going to bring his daughter back, is it? So what was this all for? What's it going to get him?"

"Closure, Lionel," Eric said. "It's going bring closure for him and for all of us. It's the right thing to do. We should have done it forty years ago. We should have done it then."

"Yeah, well." Devoe took aim at Tracy. "I guess we all find closure in our own ways."

The dogs' barking became more violent.

"Don't," Eric said.

"Shut up, Eric. For once in your life, just shut up."

"Lionel!" Reynolds charged.

Devoe diverted his attention and his aim for a split second. That was all Tracy needed. She dove to her right, hitting the edge of the poker table and upending it. Poker chips went scattering and clattering on the hardwood. The .45 roared, the sound reverberating up to the vaulted ceiling and echoing off it like a cannon blast. Tracy half expected the table to explode, but it didn't. She grabbed her Glock from amid the colorful chips and rose up from behind the table.

Devoe remained in the center of the room, already swinging the barrel of the .45 in her direction, his eyes searching.

Too slow.

She squeezed off two rounds, center-mass shots that drove Devoe backward, like a drunk falling off balance. When he landed, his head hit the ground with a dull crack.

For a moment, time froze. The smell of gunpowder permeated the air, and Tracy's ears rang from the percussion of the shots. The dogs were still barking, but now their barking sounded hollow. Across the room Eric Reynolds sat slumped against the side of the couch, a bloody hand pressed just below his right shoulder, blood seeping between his fingers.

Tracy stood and moved first to Devoe. She kicked away the .45, then bent to a knee and put two fingers to his neck. No pulse. Devoe had not been wearing his vest. She moved to Eric Reynolds. His two dogs, anxious and unnerved, pranced and whined.

"It's okay," Eric said, voice weak, free hand reaching out, trying to soothe his dogs. He was pale, pupils dilated, quickly slipping into shock, if not already there.

"Stay with me," Tracy said, already on her cell phone. "Stay with me, Eric."

An hour later, Tracy stood on the covered front porch of Eric Reynolds's house, protected from the falling snow, watching as the ambulance carrying him drove off, lights swirling. A half-dozen Klickitat County sheriff's deputies milled about the front yard, awaiting the Crime Scene Response Team Jenny had requested from the Washington State Patrol's Vancouver office. As the ambulance departed, Jenny approached.

"How is he?" Tracy asked.

"He's stable," Jenny said. "They're transporting him to the county hospital in Goldendale. They'll assess him there and see if he needs to be airlifted to Harborview. They don't think so."

Reynolds had been fortunate to take the bullet in his right shoulder, and lucky that Devoe hadn't shot him in the head when he'd lowered himself to charge.

"You picked up Ron Reynolds?"

Jenny nodded. "He's not saying anything. Asked for an attorney. Didn't even ask about his son. Only seemed concerned with himself."

Jenny looked about at the beautiful grounds,

flocked in snow. "This really is a tragedy, isn't it?"

"On so many levels," Tracy said.

"Can you imagine a parent doing that to his own child, letting him believe he killed someone all those years? Letting him take the blame? That's horrific."

It made Tracy think of Angela Collins, and the A Team's inability to fully reconcile her or her son's confession with the crime scene evidence, and Tracy realized they'd been looking at that case all wrong.

"Tracy?"

"Yeah?"

"You okay?"

"Yeah," she said. "Just thinking of another case."

CHAPTER 36

L ate Friday afternoon, Kins hung up the phone and turned his chair to face Faz. "Hold on to your ass, Faz. This case just got a whole lot stranger."

"Let me guess," Faz said. "Tim Collins rose from the dead and confessed that he shot himself."

"Close. That was Cerrabone. Atticus Berkshire just withdrew as counsel of record for Angela Collins."

That got Faz out of his chair and crossing the bull pen. "No shit? He quit on his daughter?"

"Cerrabone said the notice just came across his e-mail. No reason given, just withdrawing."

"Did it provide notice of new counsel?"

"Nope. Just a withdrawal. No substitution."

Faz considered the information for a moment. "Maybe she doesn't think she needs onc. She hasn't been charged."

"That's not a reason for Berkshire to withdraw," Kins said.

"He thinks he's too close to it, too emotionally invested?" Faz said. "You know that old saying about an attorney representing himself having a fool for a client."

"If that were the case, wouldn't you have

expected him to have secured new counsel for his daughter before withdrawing?"

"Maybe that will come Monday," Faz said.

"Maybe," Kins said. "I guess we'll find out." Faz had his jacket on. "You on your way home?"

"Not for a while. Husky game tonight. Traffic in the U District will be a killer until seven. I was going to take a walk up to Palomino and watch the first half there."

"You mind making it a working night?" Kins asked. "I'd like to talk some things through." A flat-screen TV hung over the adjacent B Team's bull pen.

"You're staying?"

"Might as well," Kins said. "Shannah's got book club, and the boys are with friends. I agreed to pick them up on my way home."

"I'll call the Palomino and have it delivered," Faz said.

An hour and a half later, Faz and Kins sat in the A Team's bull pen talking through the potential various scenarios. Empty boxes of takeout littered the center table—not a spare piece of pasta, bread, or even a shred of lettuce to be found. In the background, they could hear announcers giving the play-by-play of the Husky football game, and from the bits and pieces Kins had caught, it didn't sound pretty. Stanford was up 21–0 nearing the end of the first half.

"Okay, so the father comes storming in, ranting and raving," Faz said. "He picks up the crystal sculpture and starts beating on her. The kid intervenes, and he smacks the kid."

"So then why does he go to the back bedroom?"

"That's where the wife has gone."

"When?"

"When he beats on the kid."

"Why does he drop the sculpture? Why doesn't he take it with him?"

"He's done with it," Faz said. "He's already dropped it before he kicks her a few times in the ribs."

"Tell me how she gets to the bedroom if he's whaling on her."

"Connor said he stepped in to stop him, and his father hit him," Faz said. "That gives Angela enough time to get down the hall. The husband goes after her, Connor grabs his leg, trying to stop him, and that's how the fingerprint ends up on the father's shoe. He kicks Connor off of him and goes down the hall. Connor gets up and goes for the gun."

Kins thought it through a minute. "Okay, and if Angela shot him?"

"Then it's like she said; the husband is whaling on her, and Connor is cowering in the back bedroom. When the husband gets finished, he drops the sculpture and goes to the back room to get Connor, except Connor is upset and doesn't want to go with him, so the father smacks him. Meanwhile, Angela has gotten the gun, comes down the hall and shoots him."

Kins mulled over that scenario. "So then what is she doing for twenty-one minutes?"

"That's where I think the evidence points to Connor as the shooter," Faz said, sitting up and leaning forward. "She's trying to clean up his mess. She trying to protect the kid, so she's taking the time to get their stories straight. She tells him that she'll confess, that she'll tell the police she shot him. She's grown up the daughter of a criminal defense attorney, right? It's like Tracy said, they probably had sit-down dinners where Berkshire regaled them with all his war stories. She probably grew up thinking about things like Miranda rights and self-defense. She uses the time to calm the kid and get him on board, and makes him rehearse his story until she's satisfied he's got it straight."

"So why does she wipe down the sculpture? If she's thinking about fingerprints, Tim Collins's prints on it would help prove he used it to hit her."

"That, my friend, is the sixty-four-thousand-dollar question," Faz said.

"That and why would Connor come in and confess if his mother agreed to take the fall?"

"Two thoughts. Either he feels guilty and doesn't want anything to happen to his mom for something he did, or it was all part of her plan to get them both off."

"And Berkshire withdraws why?" Kins asked.

"Don't know," Faz said, sounding and looking tired.

Kins tossed an empty can into the wastebasket. Faz stretched his neck and checked his watch. They'd reached the same dead end again.

"Getting late," Faz said. "I think we both could use a good night's sleep. We can get a fresh start Monday morning. Come on. Let's head out."

"You go," Kins said. "Kids asked to stay an hour later at their friends'."

Faz got up from his chair and grabbed his sport coat from the hanger dangling over the corner of his cubicle. "Don't stay too late."

"I won't." Kins sat back, frustrated. They were doing something wrong. He knew it. He knew he was missing something, something that would help make sense of the evidence. In his mind, Angela had shot Tim. Not only did she have the financial incentive, but the evidence indicated that she was cashing out, trying to milk as much money out of her husband to dump into a home she knew she was going to sell. If Tim wasn't in the picture, she stood to take 100 percent of the proceeds and control over the entire estate—all because Tim hadn't finalized his new will yet. And Kins just didn't see Connor having the guts to pull the trigger—at least not without something more.

Kins opened the case binder and thought of Tracy's trick of laying out the evidence in one place. He grabbed the file and the Bekins box and carried it into the conference room. There he dismantled the file and began laying out the witness statements, the photographs, the reports, the sculpture, and the other evidence in plastic evidence bags.

He started through it again, scanning his and Tracy's typewritten reports, the witness statements, and forensic reports from the crime lab. Nothing new jumped out at him. He considered the crime-scene photographs. In his mind, he saw Connor sitting beside his mother on the couch in the living room, neither of them talking, both of them barefoot. A thought came to him.

"Why are you barefoot?" he said out loud. Connor was supposed to be going with his father. His father had sent a text message he was picking him up, and Connor had responded, *K*. It was winter. Why didn't the kid have on shoes, or at least socks?

Another thought. Kins went through the photographs and found the ones of the room where Tim Collins had been shot.

No suitcase or duffel bag or backpack. There hadn't been one in the front room either.

"Why aren't you packed? If you're leaving for the weekend, why didn't you pack?"

Maybe he kept clothes at his father's apartment. "Or maybe he wasn't going with his father," Kins said, talking it out. "Maybe he had no intention of going with his father."

Another thought came to him, something he'd read in the ME's report and dismissed but that now seemed relevant. He went back through the report, finding the paragraph on the condition of the body when first found. Tim Collins wore black lace-up shoes, but the shoelaces of one of those shoes were untied.

Kins went back to the coroner's photographs taken at the scene and focused on Tim Collins's shoes. One was indeed untied.

He knew how Connor's print got on his father's shoe.

CHAPTER 37

The celebration to rename the renovated athletic complex Ron Reynolds Stadium was postponed indefinitely, although the game was played that Saturday night.

Stoneridge lost.

Monday morning, Tracy and Kins walked to the King County Courthouse to meet Cerrabone to discuss what they wanted to do about the Angela Collins case. Cerrabone was trying another case but said he could speak to them during the morning recess.

They stepped into a marble conference room full of yellowed oak furniture that looked as old as the building. Kins explained why he thought Berkshire's withdrawal confirmed his theory that they were going about the case wrong, and Tracy proposed her idea on how they might move the case from its current state of limbo. Cerrabone expressed skepticism, but he agreed that there wasn't anything unethical about her proposal and that they had nothing to lose by giving it a try.

"Angela's no longer represented by counsel," Kins said. "If she agrees to talk to us, Berkshire can't prevent it. All he'll have to do is watch and listen, and I think he will. I think he wanted her to go on record about what happened. I think he wanted her to lock herself in."

"It definitely was out of character; I'll give you that," Cerrabone said. "Maybe you're right." He checked his watch. His break was coming to an end. "I'll make some calls this afternoon and let you know."

Angela Collins voluntarily agreed to come to the Justice Center when Kins called and told her he had a few more questions about her son's statement that he wanted to go over with her.

She had expressed reluctance, but it seemed halfhearted.

She came in alone, without counsel, as Tracy had also predicted.

Kins placed her in the hard interrogation room with the one-way mirror. In the adjacent viewing room, Tracy and Cerrabone stood watching. Moments later, Faz brought in Connor Collins and Atticus Berkshire.

"What's my mother doing here?" Connor asked.

"She's being asked a few questions also," Tracy said.

She flipped a switch, and Kins's voice came through the speaker. "We've had an interesting development, Angela."

"Have you?" Angela Collins looked and sounded calm. Her bruising was only slightly visible beneath her makeup. She looked to have recently had her hair styled and her nails done. Far from the grieving widow, she looked like she was dressed for a date, wearing straight-leg jeans, ankle boots, and a soft red sweater.

"Am I correct that you are no longer represented by counsel?"

"That's right."

"Your father no longer represents you?"

"We had a mutual parting."

"And you haven't hired another lawyer?"

"As there are no pending charges against me, Detective, I hardly see the reason to spend four hundred dollars an hour on a defense attorney."

Kins tapped the table. Then he said, "You're obviously aware Connor has confessed?"

She nodded, solemn. "Yes."

"So that means one of you isn't telling the truth."

She shrugged.

"You told us that you called 911 within minutes of the shooting."

"That's right. I called my father. Then I called 911."

"Except we have a neighbor who heard the gunshot just as the bus pulled up outside her window at 5:18. You called your father at 5:39, and called 911 at 5:40. We have twenty-one minutes unaccounted for, Angela."

If the information came as a surprise, Angela didn't display any. "I was emotionally distraught, Detective. I don't recall how much time passed."

"It was twenty-one minutes."

"I'll take your word for it."

"You also said that your husband hit you with the crystal sculpture."

"Would you like to see the stitches?"

"No. I've seen the photographs," Kins said.

"Then what's your point?"

"My point is, if your husband hit you with the sculpture, why aren't his fingerprints on it?"

This time, Angela was clearly caught off guard. "Excuse me?"

"There are no fingerprints on the sculpture. Not his, not yours, not Connor's."

"I . . . I don't know."

"Did you wipe the sculpture down, Angela?"

"Why would I do that?"

"Because you were protecting Connor."

"That's ridiculous."

"Connor saw your husband hitting you and tried to stop him, didn't he? He grabbed the sculpture, and they scuffled. Your husband knocked Connor to the ground, and you used that time to try and escape to the back bedroom. Connor was on the ground and reached out and grabbed your husband's foot, trying to stop him. He even yanked the shoe off. That's why Connor's fingerprints are on your husband's shoe."

Angela Collins had begun to shake, as if about to cry. She crossed her arms and looked to a corner of the room. Tracy alternately watched her and Atticus Berkshire's and Connor's reactions.

Kins said, "Why don't you tell us the truth, Angela?"

Tears rolled down Angela's cheeks. "Connor was just trying to protect me," she said. "He was just trying to protect me. I don't think he meant to shoot Tim. He didn't mean to do it."

"What?" Connor said softly, and Tracy knew her hunch had been accurate. The one consistent thing about psychopaths was their ego. They never imagined getting caught because they believed they were smarter than everyone.

Atticus Berkshire placed a hand gently on the boy's shoulder. Not like a lawyer. He was acting like a grandfather.

Connor looked up at his grandfather. "Why is she saying that?"

In the other room, Angela wiped her tears with Kleencx. "After Connor shot Tim, I panicked. I didn't know what to do. I told Connor to drop the gun on the bed and go in the other room. I picked it up so that my fingerprints would also be on it. Then I just started wiping things down. I wasn't thinking clearly. I just remember my father saying once that the police can use any evidence against you, so I just started wiping everything. When I went back to the living room, Connor had taken the sculpture off the floor and was replacing it on the mantel. I shouted at him to put it back. That's when I realized his fingerprints would be all over it, so I wiped it down also."

"She's lying," Connor said, looking up at his grandfather, eyes wide and starting to breathe heavily.

"He's just a boy, Detective," Angela said, "trying to protect his mother."

"She's lying," Connor said again, louder, starting to cry. "Why is she lying?"

"Why did she shoot your father, Connor?" Tracy asked.

Berkshire remained silent.

"She told me that she had to do it. She said my dad was going to take everything from us, that she was going to get nothing in the divorce. She said he didn't want anything to do with us, that he had a girlfriend, that he was selling the house and we were going to have to move, that we would have no place to go."

"How did your mother get her injuries?"

Connor was weeping, shoulders shuddering. Berkshire wrapped an arm around him. "Tell us what happened," Berkshire said.

"She had me hit her with the sculpture. She told me to hit her in the back of the head so I didn't leave a scar. I didn't want to do it, but she told me that I had to, that if I didn't we'd both go to jail, that they'd say I was an accomplice, that I'd lured my dad into the house under false pretenses."

"What about the injuries to her ribs? How did your mother get those?"

"She told me to kick her, but I couldn't because I wasn't wearing any shoes. She said to put on one of my dad's shoes, that they could tell from the bruising the type of shoe I was wearing."

"That's why your fingerprints are on the shoe?"

"I guess."

"And that's why your father's right shoe was untied. When you put it back on his foot, you forgot to tie it."

"I don't know," he said. "I don't remember."

Tracy looked to Atticus Berkshire. He had an arm around his grandson's shoulder but was staring through the glass at his daughter. He looked as though someone had stabbed him in the heart.

"Why is she doing this?" Connor said, wiping his nose on the sleeve of his jacket.

"She has a mental illness, Connor," Berkshire said. "Your mother is sick."

"Can you help her?" Connor asked.

Berkshire shook his head, solemn.

Tracy and Kins had suspected Berkshire knew, or strongly suspected, not only that his daughter had shot her husband, but that she was at least a sociopath, and likely had a borderline personality disorder. It was a terrible thing for a parent to have to admit about his child, and

Berkshire probably would have rigorously defended Angela right up until the moment he'd realized that Angela was willing to sacrifice everyone to save herself, even her own son. Berkshire likely hadn't agreed to let Angela give a statement. He'd likely had no choice in the matter. After all, he was in a position to know that Angela had always done what Angela wanted to do and got what Angela wanted, or there would be hell to pay. Berkshire was too experienced and competent a defense attorney not to have known that his daughter's statement was potentially a huge mistake and likely wouldn't match the evidence.

"Can anyone help her?" Connor asked.

"They'll try," Berkshire said. "But some mental illnesses can't be helped. At the moment, your mother is a danger to you."

"Did your mother tell you to confess?" Tracy asked.

"She told me what to say. She said they couldn't convict both of us of the same crime." He looked at Berkshire. "She said you would get us both off. She said we had nothing to worry about, that we could get all the money, and she'd have control and we could stay in our house. She said all I had to do was exactly what she said, and everything would be fine. She said if I didn't, we'd both go to prison." Connor Collins began to sob again. "I didn't want anything bad to happen to him. I didn't know she was going to shoot him."

Atticus Berkshire turned his grandson away from the window. "It's okay," he said. "It's going to be okay. But now you have to tell the truth. You have to tell the truth about what happened."

"Will you do that, Connor?" Tracy asked.

"What will happen to her?" Connor said.

"She'll go to trial for killing your father, Connor, but not because of you. None of this is your fault."

Connor looked again through the window, to the woman sitting in the chair. Tracy sensed that although he saw his mother and heard her voice, Connor was anything but certain he knew the person in that room. Then, as if stricken, he looked to Tracy. Gone was the look of sadness, replaced by a more sobering emotion. Fear.

"Will she go to prison?"

"Yes," Tracy said. "She will."

"Will she ever get out?" he asked.

"No, Connor," Tracy said. "She never will."

After Angela Collins had been booked and processed at the King County Jail, Tracy and Kins returned to the A Team's cubicle. It was late, and they were both emotionally spent. Del and Faz had gone home, and Tracy was about to do the same. Dan was flying back from Los Angeles, and this time they were going to spend a few days in Cedar Grove.

"I'm going to head home," she said. "It's been a long week."

Kins rotated his chair. "How did you know it would work?"

She thought of Eric Reynolds. "It's a terrible thing when a child is stripped of his perception that his parents are perfect. Kids want to believe their parents will always be there to take care of them. One of the hardest things about getting older is losing that naïveté that allows us all to believe in myths and fantasies, having it replaced by harsh reality. We don't want to believe our parents aren't perfect, some far from it."

Kins sat rocking in his chair. "Something else I wanted to talk to you about," he said.

"Amanda Santos?"

Kins shut his eyes and blew out a breath. "Nothing happened, Tracy. It was just a couple of lunches."

"Thanks for telling me," she said, glad that Kins had come clean.

"Things haven't been great at home for a while. You know that. When I met Amanda on the Cowboy investigation, I felt something I haven't felt for a long time."

"Everybody wants to feel like that, Kins."

"I know. I never thought I'd act on it, but I

found an excuse to call her and talk. Then I found another excuse to ask her to lunch."

"She's a beautiful woman."

Kins nodded. "But I realize now this isn't just about Shannah and me, is it?"

"I don't have kids," Tracy said. "I'm not about to preach on a subject I don't know much about."

He smiled. "I'm betting you know a lot more than you're admitting."

"Maybe from those years teaching high school, seeing what divorce did to kids."

"I'm not perfect," Kins said. "Far from it. But I'm not ready for them to know that."

"None of us is perfect, Kins."

"No, but you're right—I'm as close to perfect in their eyes as I'm ever going to be, and I'm not going to throw that away without giving my marriage a better effort."

"I hope it works."

"I do too. Total honesty, right?"

Tracy smiled. "That was the deal."

CHAPTER 38

A week later, Tracy took the exit just after the water tower and drove past the murals decorating the buildings in downtown Toppenish. She turned onto Chestnut Street and drove past a series of modest but well-maintained homes. She pulled up to the curb of the last home on the right. The older-model Chevy truck and the Toyota remained in the carport. Parked in the street was Tommy Moore's white commercial landscaping truck.

This time Tracy didn't hesitate at the gate, though she did notice that the yard looked to have been freshly mowed and tidied. The ramp for the wheelchair to the porch had been disassembled, and someone had fixed and replaced the screen door. She pulled it open and knocked. No dog barked.

Élan Kanasket opened the door with a look of satisfied resignation. He gave her a sheepish smile. "I guess you proved me wrong," he said.

"Actually, Élan, I proved you right."

His smile widened, and he stuck out his hand. "Thanks," he said. "I owe you an apology."

"Don't worry about it. Where is he?"

"Come in. I'll take you."

Élan closed the door behind her. The interior

458

had also been cleaned and straightened. The walls had been prepped to be painted, spotted with patches of spackling, blue painter's tape along the trim.

"You're fixing up the house," she said.

"It was time," he said. "After my father passes, I'm moving to Arizona to take a job down there." He smiled. "A friend has a sister."

"I hope it works out for you." She followed Élan up the stairs.

"It's just a matter of time, now that he's asked to come home," Élan said. "Hospice is here in the mornings, but I stay with him in the afternoon."

"I'm very sorry," she said.

Élan stopped at the landing and faced her. "Don't be. My father is at peace for the first time that I can remember. He's ready to go, thanks to you."

"What about the dog?"

"He died," Élan said. "When my father went to the hospital, the dog went to his chair, laid down, and went to sleep. He never woke up."

He led Tracy to a room just to the right of the stairs. The door was open, the hospital bed placed so that Earl Kanasket could look out the window at the expansive green field that seemed to stretch to the horizon. "I wanted him to have the best view in the house," Élan said.

Tommy Moore, seated in a chair at the side of the bed, stood as they entered. He shook Tracy's hand. "Thank you, Detective. You've lifted a huge burden from our shoulders."

Tracy looked down at Earl. He'd been thin when she'd come to see him initially, but now he was just a skeleton of that man. "Is he coherent?"

"Not this afternoon, I'm afraid," Élan said. "But he wanted you to have something."

"Something for me?"

Élan left the room and returned a moment later carrying the feathered dream-catcher earring Tracy recognized from Kimi's senior photo. "This was Kimi's," Élan said. "He kept this hanging in his bedroom window. He wanted you to have it for bringing Kimi home to him."

"I don't know what to say," Tracy said. "Thank you."

"Don't thank me. Thank him. The nurses say that he senses our presence. Talk to him. He'll hear you."

Tracy walked to the side of the bed. Earl Kanasket's hair was no longer in a braid. She reached out and touched his hand, which was cold and nearly translucent.

"Mr. Kanasket," she started.

"He would want you to call him Earl," Élan said, smiling.

Tracy looked to Élan, then back to Earl. "Earl? It's Tracy Crosswhite, the detective from Seattle. I came to tell you that you can put Kimi to rest."

She felt Earl's hand twitch, an almost imperceptible flutter.

"We found the men responsible for Kimi's death," she said.

Earl slowly opened his eyes. Élan and Tommy stepped closer, to the opposite side of the bed.

Tracy squeezed Earl's hand. "Buzz Almond and I found them. Kimi did *not* take her own life, Earl. The men responsible are being brought to justice."

Earl's expression didn't change, but Tracy thought she might have detected just the faintest indication of understanding in his eyes. Then she noticed them pooling, and a lone tear trickled down his pronounced cheekbones. Tracy reached out and gently brushed it away with the tip of her finger.

"Tears of joy," Élan said.

When Tracy looked back, Earl's eyes remained open, but he was no longer looking at her. He was staring out the windows, beyond the field, to the distant horizon.

Gone.

EPILOGUE

Tracy waited until spring, when Jenny invited her and Dan back to Stoneridge for the ceremony dedicating the headstone that would mark Buzz Almond's grave.

On the drive down, she and Dan stopped at the Central Point Nursery, where Archibald Coe had cared so diligently for his plants. Tracy had never been much of a gardener, so she told the woman at the nursery she wanted something hardy, some-thing that could grow anywhere, maybe with a flower that would bloom.

She left with four plants.

From the nursery they drove to the turnout just past the dilapidated log building that had once been the Columbia Diner. Dan carried the box containing the plants and followed her into the brush and along the path Kimi had run during the final moments of her life. The muscles of Tracy's legs strained when she came to the incline, and she heard Dan's breathing as he carried the heavy box of plants up the hill.

"Be careful," she said when she reached the top. "The grass can be slick."

Halfway down the other side, she stopped, uncertain of what she saw.

"What is it?" Dan asked.

Tracy walked to where Archibald Coe had planted his single bush. She'd expected to find it dead, but the plant looked instead to be flourishing, the leaves no longer brown, the branches longer and fuller, and even sprouting small buds.

Dan set down the box, and Tracy smiled. She'd bought four plants, but she'd only need three— one for Earl Kanasket, and one each for Darren Gallentine and Archibald Coe. She'd been skeptical that the plants would survive.

She was much more optimistic now that they, too, would live.

Tracy and Dan arrived at the cemetery at just past one in the afternoon and ascended the slope together, hand in hand, stepping between the tombstones to where Jenny's family waited patiently at the top.

Tracy had stayed in close contact with Jenny and the Klickitat County prosecutor, but her involvement had otherwise been limited, and it likely would remain that way. Eric Reynolds had pled guilty to vehicular homicide, for which no statute of limitations existed. His lawyer could have argued that Eric was not the proximate cause of Kimi Kanasket's death, that his father had been an intervening cause, but Eric wasn't interested in legal arguments. He knew he'd have to go to prison, and he wasn't fighting it. The prosecutor was recommending four years and a fine of $50,000. With good behavior, Eric Reynolds would be out in two years.

No charges were filed against Hastey Devoe. He'd served thirty days in jail for his latest DUI conviction and upon release was placed on seven years' probation. A requirement of his release was that he regularly attend Alcoholics Anonymous meetings. Instead, Eric Reynolds had paid $60,000 for Hastey to enter a six-month inpatient addiction center in Oregon that would treat not only his alcohol addiction but also his weight and self-esteem issues.

Ron Reynolds had refused to plea. He was being held without bail at the Klickitat County jail. The prosecutor was pursuing a second-degree murder charge.

The ceremony to name the stadium for Ron Reynolds had been permanently canceled, and Eric had withdrawn his father's name from consideration. Instead, at Eric's request, the stadium would be renamed Kimi Kanasket Memorial Stadium. The ceremony was to take place at a football game the following fall. Élan Kanasket had called and invited Tracy to attend, and told her that several thousand Native Americans intended to caravan from the Yakama Reservation to Stoneridge for the ceremony.

Jenny stepped from the gathering and greeted Tracy. The two women hugged. "Thanks for coming," she said.

"Wouldn't have missed it," Tracy said. Buzz Almond's final resting place afforded views of the Columbia River Gorge and both Mount Adams and Mount Hood. "It's a beautiful spot."

"My father bought it when they made him sheriff," Jenny said. "I guess he figured he'd die in office, one way or another. He was always big on putting down roots."

Tracy greeted the rest of the family. Anne Almond looked thinner but still stately in a soft blue dress, and the kids were again in their Sunday best, fidgeting like racehorses in the starting gate.

The same priest who had presided over Buzz Almond's funeral performed the ceremony, blessing the blue-tinted marble headstone and sprinkling it with holy water.

Theodore Michael "Buzz" Almond Jr.
Klickitat County Sheriff
March 3, 1949–Oct. 25, 2016

After the blessing, members of the family stepped forward to place items at the grave, as Jenny had informed Tracy when she'd invited her. Tracy didn't know the significance of each gift, but clearly they meant something to each family member. One of the grandsons left a model airplane; a granddaughter left a small stuffed elephant. Sarah and her brother, Trey, walked hand in hand with Jenny and Neil. Trey left a baseball. Sarah left a tiny plastic pony. When the family had finished, Tracy reached into her purse and retrieved the slip of paper she'd brought with her. She walked to the tombstone, bent to a knee, and placed the final closing papers on the Kimi Kanasket investigation against the blue stone.

"Rest in peace, Buzz Almond," she said.

At the conclusion of the ceremony, Jenny said, "We're going to have lunch back at the house. Very informal. Can you come?"

"Thanks," Tracy said, squeezing Dan's hand, "but we're going to get started for Sunriver."

Jenny gave them each a hug. "Thanks for everything you did," she said to Tracy. "It meant so much to me and to my family."

"It wasn't me," Tracy said. "It was your father. He did all the legwork. This was his investigation."

"You'll come back soon and visit?" Jenny asked.

"Count on it," Tracy said. "And when you come to Seattle, you call. You tell Sarah and Trey that Auntie Tracy will take them anytime the two of you want a night on the town."

Jenny looked to Dan. "You on board for that, Dan?"

"If I can handle Rex and Sherlock, I think I can handle a couple of kids."

Tracy laughed. "You have no idea," she said.

Inside the Tahoe, Dan buckled his seat belt but

didn't start the engine. "If you'd like to go to the reception, I don't mind."

Tracy shook her head. "Thanks, but I want this to be our time together."

Dan looked suddenly serious. "Speaking of time together, I have something to talk to you about."

"Okay," she said, uncertain from his solemn tone what might be coming next.

"I'm going to be moving."

"What?"

"I've come to realize that at this point in my life, Cedar Grove is just too isolated, and it isn't healthy being alone that much."

Tracy felt as though she'd been kicked in the gut. "Where are you thinking of going? Back to Boston?"

"Boston? No. Why would I go back to Boston?"

"I don't know. I just thought—"

"Boston is in the past," Dan said, still looking serious. "And you know I don't like cities. Do you *want* me to move back to Boston?"

"No. I just . . . I'm confused. Start over. Where are you moving to?"

Dan smiled, and Tracy realized he'd been playing with her. "I found a little five-acre farm in Redmond that's got a small fixer-upper on it to keep me busy, and a stream, and plenty of pasture for Rex and Sherlock."

Tracy punched Dan in the arm. Redmond was just half an hour from downtown Seattle.

"Ow. I thought you'd be happy," he said.

Tracy tried to be upset, but she could feel her entire face flush and couldn't keep from smiling. "I'm not sure about this," she said, playing coy. "What about your law practice?"

"Well, seeing as how most of my work is down here now, it seems to make sense."

"So this is a business decision," she said.

"I wouldn't call it business. I'd call it very personal." He leaned across the car and kissed her.

When their lips parted, Tracy said, "But you love Cedar Grove, Dan."

"I do," he said, reaching out, touching her chin, and drawing her closer. "But I love you more."

They kissed again, and this time when they parted, Dan sat back. "Besides, I'm not selling the house. I thought it would be a great place for the two of us to get away on the weekends to do some fishing and hiking. Maybe play a little golf."

Tracy cleared her throat. "You know I don't golf."

"No, but I can teach you."

She laughed. "I'm not sure that's such a good idea. The last time you gave me a lesson, we ended up in bed together."

"Oh, I remember," he said. "And as your golf instructor, I'm recommending frequent lessons."

"Then I'm hoping my second lesson will be tonight," Tracy said.

ACKNOWLEDGMENTS

Thanks to all the readers who send me e-mails expressing how much they enjoy my acknowledgments. After eleven books, I've found this to be a place to not only say thank you, but to express how blessed and grateful I am for everyone in my life.

First and foremost, while I always get a kick out of reader e-mails and reviews telling me the towns in my books don't exist—such as Cedar Grove in the North Cascades (*My Sister's Grave*), let me say this up front. Stoneridge is a *fictional* town I created in Klickitat County. Yes, some readers may find some of the details of the town resemble White Salmon, a place I thoroughly enjoyed exploring for two days, but Stoneridge is *not* White Salmon. Why do I do this? Because it is never my intent to embarrass anyone or the town in which they live, and often readers write to ask me if the events in my novels are true— which is a good thing. Again, I write fiction. The events, like the towns and the characters that populate my novels, are fictional. The details pertaining to the White Salmon River, however, as discussed below, are true.

That being said, thank you to Maria Foley, executive director of the Mt. Adams Chamber of

Commerce. When I arrived in White Salmon, I didn't know where to start. Maria provided me with materials on the area, including its history, directed me to the local newspaper office and diner, and provided me with the names of several people who could help.

One of those people was Mark Zoller, of Zoller's Outdoor Odysseys, which runs guided white-water rafting trips. I stopped by the Zollers' office during my visit to the area, but, it being winter, the office was closed. I subsequently reached Mark by phone and quickly realized he was indeed the man I needed. Mark grew up on rivers and was guiding rafting trips for his father's business before he could drive. He possesses a wealth of information and provided me with all the cool details on river flow, temperatures, and the specifics of the White Salmon River, including where someone might dump a body and the path the body would take. Timing did not allow me to actually raft the river before my deadline, but I walked a good portion of it, and next summer I'm hoping to take my family.

Thanks also to my friend Jim Russi, a Rotarian in Yakima, for taking an afternoon to give me a tour of the Yakama Reservation and show me some of the beautiful towns there. We'd discussed a barbecue at the end of the day but had a beer instead, and time ran short and we each had to ask for a rain check. Shortly after my trip, Jim lost his beloved wife, Kris, unexpectedly to cancer. I was deeply saddened to hear this news. I will continue to honor Kris by using her inflatable boogie board, which Jim shipped to me. I'll think of her every time I'm riding a wave. Note to self: make time for the next barbecue.

As always, the people acknowledged below are experts in their fields. I am not. Any mistakes or errors are mine, and mine alone.

I am grateful to Kathy Decker, former Search and Rescue coordinator for the King County Sheriff's Office and well-known sign-cutter, otherwise known as a "man-tracker." Detective Decker first helped me when I wrote *Murder One*, and I was overwhelmed at the response from readers interested in her skills. She again was gracious enough to offer her assistance to explain how a tracker can follow signs that most of us would never see. This time I made her task even more difficult, asking her how she would proceed to analyze a forty-year-old homicide, but she was up to the task. It is a fascinating science, and I hope I did it justice.

Thank you to Kathy Taylor, forensic anthropologist at the King County Medical Examiner's Office. Kathy's talents are in such demand that her schedule is hectic and we couldn't coordinate a meeting this time, but I used a lot of her expertise from past interviews to help with the forensic aspects of a body pulled from a river.

Thank you to Adrienne McCoy, King County senior deputy prosecutor, who helped me with the nuances of probable cause hearings, charging papers, and how her office would likely proceed given the unusual murder scenario I present in this novel. I am grateful for her patience and expertise.

I've also been fortunate to meet many wonderful people in the police community who are always generous with their time and their knowledge. I have tremendous respect for people who choose law enforcement as a profession. It is often a thankless job under trying circumstances.

I flat out could not write these books without the assistance of Detective Jennifer Southworth, of the Seattle Police Department. Jennifer first helped me with *Murder One* when she was working for the CSI Unit. With her promotion to the Homicide Unit, she became the inspiration for Tracy Crosswhite in *My Sister's Grave*. She helped with that novel, with *Her Final Breath*, and again with this novel. I am so very grateful.

I also could not write these novels without Detective Scott Tompkins, King County Sheriff's Office, Major Crimes Unit. Scott's willingness to always help me by sharing his knowledge, or by putting me in touch with others who could provide information, has been invaluable. For this novel I literally sat down with Scott, gave him a scenario, and said, "Walk me through it." He did, providing me cool details and suggestions along the way. Talk about patience. Scott and Jennifer are active helping the families of victims of crime through Victim Support Services, a worthy cause to which I donate signed novels. Consider it: http://victimsupportservices.org.

Thanks also to Kelly Rosa, legal services supervisor for the Most Dangerous Offender Project and the Violent Crimes Unit for the King County Prosecuting Attorney's Office. Oh, and also a lifelong friend. Kelly has helped me in just about every novel I've written, and she promotes them like crazy. I thought it time she take a new step in her career, so I made her a forensic anthropologist in *My Sister's Grave*. I suspect she'll be making more cameos in these books. Thanks, Kelly. You continue to be an incredible support.

Thank you to super-agent Meg Ruley and her team at the Jane Rotrosen Agency, including Rebecca Scherer, who offers terrific suggestions for my manuscripts and is an absolute wiz on everything to do with e-books. You want to know how wonderful the people who work at JRA are? When I traveled to New York and had a business dinner, Rebecca took my daughter out for a night in Manhattan, which Catherine is still talking about. Then the agency secured orchestra tickets to *The Lion King*. Made me look like the world's greatest dad! To top it off, Meg and her husband delayed a trip to London to be at the International Thriller Writers awards dinner when *My Sister's Grave* was nominated as one of the best thrillers of the year. Great agency, better people. These past two years have been phenomenal on so many levels, and the culmination of ten years of terrific guidance and insight into the business. I am so very grateful.

Thanks to Thomas & Mercer for believing in Tracy Crosswhite. This is the third book in the series, and I look forward to writing more. Special thanks to Charlotte Herscher, developmental editor. She's edited all the Tracy Crosswhite novels and made every one infinitely better. Thanks also to Elizabeth Johnson, copyeditor. I asked for the best—grammar and punctuation
not being my strength—and they immediately recommended Elizabeth. She pushes me on just about every sentence and word choice, and the books are infinitely more accurate.

Thanks to Jacque Ben-Zekry in marketing, who is a true force of nature and does an incredible job promoting my novels. Your efforts pushed me to number one in the past, and I hope we will do it again. Thanks to Tiffany Pokorny in author relations for always going the extra step to make me feel appreciated. My family has become a big fan of Thomas &

Mercer for all the terrific gifts and little acknowledgments you send. You are the best. Thanks to my publicist, Gracie Doyle. She works tirelessly promoting my books and always has a creative idea and a bit of good news to go with her relentlessly upbeat demeanor. Thanks to Kjersti Egerdahl, acquisitions editor, and Sean Baker, production manager. Thanks to publisher Mikyla Bruder, associate publisher Hai-Yen Mura, and Jeff Belle, vice president of Amazon Publishing. These people all walk the walk when it comes to their authors and their authors' work, and each has helped me to quickly feel at home.

Special thanks to Thomas & Mercer's editorial director, Alan Turkus, for his guidance, spot-on editorial advice, and friendship. I sincerely hope we get to light the "#1" sign again and keep it lit many weeks and months. You have been a true guiding force.

Thanks to Tami Taylor, who runs my website, creates my foreign-language book covers, creates my newsletter, and otherwise does a fantastic job. Thanks to Sean McVeigh at 425 Media for his help with all my social-media needs. You're both a lot smarter than I am, and I'm glad to have you on my team. Thanks to Pam Binder and the Pacific Northwest Writers Association for their tremendous support of my work.

Thank you also to the loyal readers who write

to tell me how much they enjoy my books and await the next. You are the reason I keep looking for the next great story.

By the time this book is published, my son, Joe, will be finishing his first year of college. Today, however, as I write this, he is still at home, and I am reminiscing on just about everything over the last eighteen years. I remembered with sadness the morning I awoke to make Joe his final school lunch. After twelve years, my wife and I calculated that we had probably made him close to two thousand lunches. I'd already experienced his last high school football game, and there was his last prom, his last class, his last assembly, and his graduation dinner and ceremony. I'm not looking forward to his last night at home before we take him off to college. I'll keep a stiff upper lip, but I'm Italian, and inside I'll be crying like a baby—just like that final-school-lunch morning when I smeared mayonnaise on his turkey-and-cheese sandwich; and as I stood in the stands and watched the clock tick to 0:00; and when I tried to tell him at that graduation dinner how proud I am of him; and as I sat in the audience and wiped tears as he walked across the stage in his cap and gown with a big smile on his face. You get the point. The thing is, I'm not just sending a son off to college. I'm losing my late-night TV partner, the best sandwich maker in Seattle, my workout buddy, and the audience for all my *Seinfeld* references and corny jokes. I know this is not an ending but a beginning, and I'm excited for Joe as he starts what will be a great next stage in his life. I'm proud of you, son. Time to fly.

While my daughter, Catherine, is not celebrating such a milestone, she did turn sixteen and passed her driving test. She also got to spend four days in Manhattan with me on a father-daughter trip that only confirmed that I am truly blessed. What a great kid. Poised, polite, respectful, and as fun and funny as ever. That is a memory I'll cherish forever. And she took several hundred photographs to document it!

Saving the best for last, to the love of my life, Cristina, who continues to stand beside me with each step of life's journey. Thanks for always being there. Time for us to fly as well. After all, we do have forever . . . and a day.

ABOUT THE AUTHOR

Robert Dugoni is the critically acclaimed bestselling author of nine thrillers. *My Sister's Grave*, the first book in the Tracy Crosswhite series, became a #1 Amazon bestseller and a *New York Times* and *Wall Street Journal* bestseller. The popular series includes *Her Final Breath* and the short stories *The Academy* and *Third Watch*. Dugoni's first novel, *The Jury Master*, made the *New York Times* bestseller list and launched the popular David Sloane series, which includes *Wrongful Death*, *Bodily Harm*, *Murder One*, and *The Conviction*. Dugoni's books have been likened to those of Scott Turow and Nelson DeMille, and he has been hailed as "the undisputed king of the legal thriller" and the "heir to Grisham's literary throne."

Visit his website at www.robertdugoni.com and follow him on Twitter @robertdugoni and on Facebook at www.facebook.com/AuthorRobert Dugoni.

Center Point Large Print
600 Brooks Road / PO Box 1
Thorndike, ME 04986-0001 USA

(207) 568-3717

US & Canada:
1 800 929-9108
www.centerpointlargeprint.com